MW01631235

岳 敏 君 YUE MINJUN

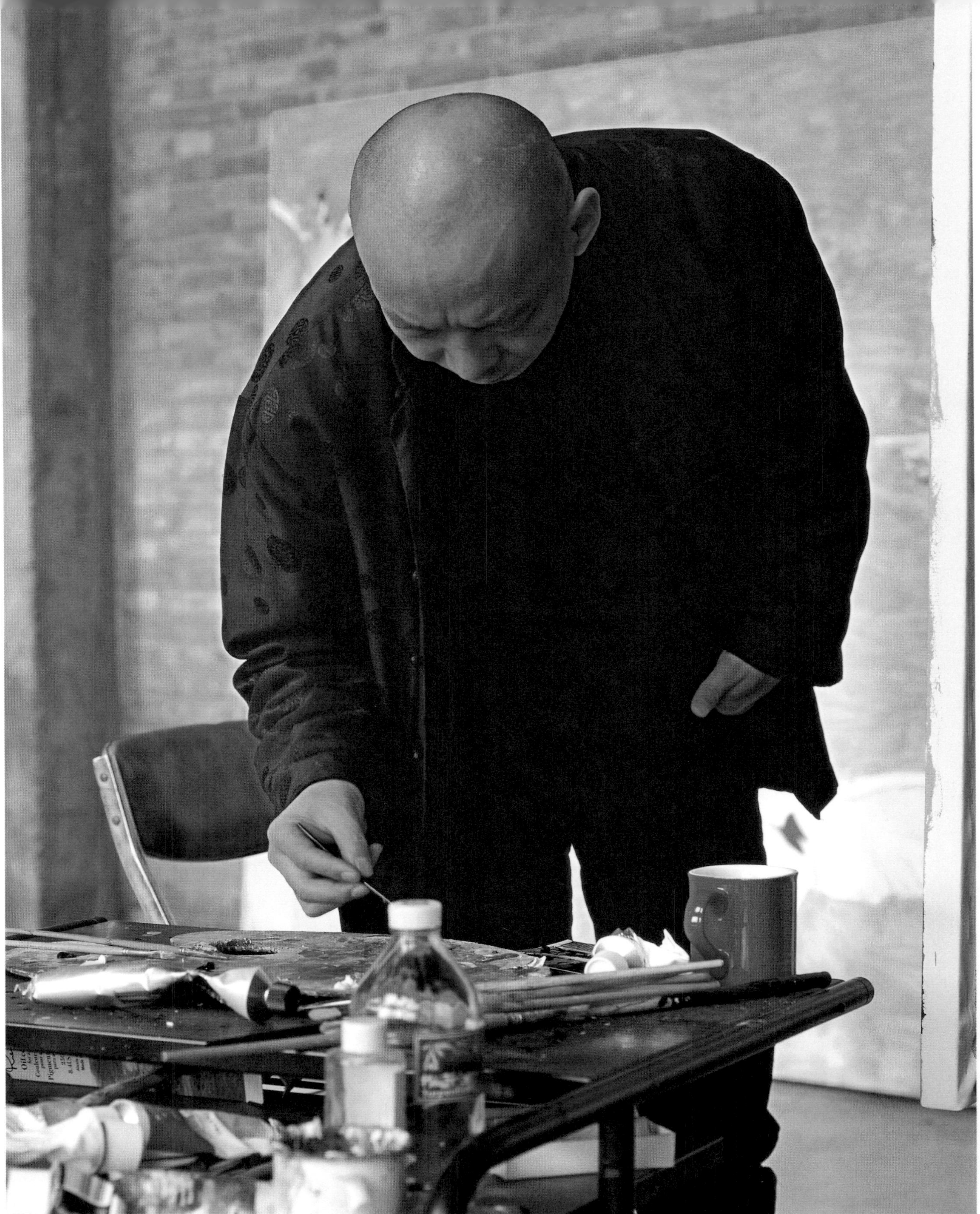

Reproduction Icons: Yue Minjun Works, 2004-2006

復制的偶像：岳敏君作品 2004-2006

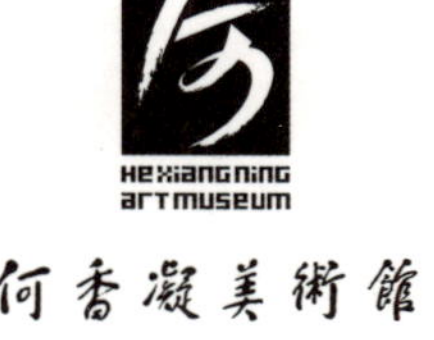

Reproduction Icons: Yue Minjun Works, 2004-2006

Is published on the occasion of Yue Minjun's solo exhibition exhibited at
He Xiangning Art Museum, Shenzhen

Executive Director: Ren Kelei
Director: Chen Jian / Le Zhengwei

Curator: Feng Boyi
Coordinating Curator: Karen Smith

Published by: Museum Collection Services Co.
Email: museumcollectionservices@yahoo.com

ISBN: 0-9785764-0-3

Editorial Direction: Karen Smith
Design: He Hao

Printed in China 2006
FIRST EDITION

Cover detail: *Untitled (detail)*, 2005, oil on canvas

CONTENTS 目録

To Be Is Just Absurd: The Art of Yue Minjun

By Feng Boyi

存在便是一種荒誕 — 關于岳敏君的藝術

馮博一

It was the autumn of 1992 when I first got to know Yue Minjun. Xu Bing–who had just returned to Beijing from the United States–and I were visiting the artists' village near Yuanmingyuan (the site of the original Summer Palace that was destroyed by Allied Forces in 1860) in the western suburb of Beijing. Yue Minjun wore his hair long, which gave him the look of a maverick avant-garde artist, or perhaps jokingly, that of a troublemaker (*wanzhu*). By contrast, the painter Yang Shaobin, who was also there, seemed a more gentle character, for Yue Minjun's gaze was distinctly cynical. I was impressed by the scale of Yue Minjun's large paintings, which occupied the whole wall of the farmhouse he rented as his studio. One of the paintings pictured rows of people: a giggling crowd standing in front of the Tiananmen Tower. The image was absurd, but regular, coherent and intuitive, with a force that reminded me of the National Day parades that took place every year on October First, or of Chairman Mao inspecting Red Guards during the Cultural Revolution. Yue Minjun had recently decided to settle in the artists' village. This decision rather went against convention, but it was here that his personal style begun to take shape.

In the early 1990s a number of important artists emerged, such as Fang Lijun, Liu Wei and Yang Shaobin. Their survival was conditioned by the especial historic climate in China from the end of the 1980s to the early 1990s. In the 1980s, across the board, Chinese society embarked upon a transformation to a market economy. This permitted some liberation of the self in the realm of culture. Passionate expressions–largely based on the promoting of Enlightenment philosophies, the power of reason, and humanist concerns–and the '85 New Art Movement, which was primarily a campaign of experiment in the language of painting, became the central theme of avant-garde art in China. It was the harbinger of a new age.

The notion of a "new age" in art came as a reaction to the preceding era in which art was subjugated to politics: a demand which had been imposed even before the Cultural Revolution (1966-1976). In essence, this new era saw a metamorphosis of the art of the Cultural Revolution, which is why we define the art of this period as post-Cultural Revolution art. The "China/Avant Garde" (sic) exhibition, held at the China National Gallery in early 1989, can be regarded as a retrospective survey of avant-garde artworks that had been produced in China in the 1980s. After the June Fourth Incident in 1989, Chinese art and culture entered a period of stillness and reflection, signalling the end of the '85 New Art Movement. The stillness and introspection also brought a conclusion to the '85 New Art Movement. By the end of 1990, artists like Fang Lijun, Yue Minjun, Yang Shaobin, Xu Yihui, and Xu Ruotao–described as "vagabonds" in the media–had begun to settle near Yuanmingyuan. In the early 1990s, Yuanmingyuan became a primary dwelling place for China's avant-garde artists: the first artists' village.

The appearance of a community of artists on the border between the urban and rural areas near the capital, and the general behaviour of these new residents can be explained as a yearning for a professional identity, which was of abiding necessity for Chinese artists when they graduated from any art academy. They further sought to eschew the limitations of a socio-political system in which all occupational identity *was required to be transparent*, whereby individuals were obliged to 'be governed by registering their household' across China.

Their yearning to live freely as professional artists engendered certain common features in their works, namely a strong desire for self-expression. For avant-garde artists, the ideal of 'independent and free' expression pivoted upon highly abstract and ideological notions of

— 第一次見到岳敏君，大概是1992年的秋季，我和剛從美國回京的徐冰去北京西郊的圓明園畫家村。那時，他的頭發長長的，一看就像是個另類的、前衛的藝術家扮相，或者調侃一點兒描述，更像是一位京城的“頑主”。相比較而言，當時在場的楊少斌倒顯得文質彬彬，而岳敏君的目光所及已透出一種玩世不恭的神態。印象較深的是他的畫兒，很大，占滿了他租用農民房做畫室的整個墻面，畫的是一排排的人在天安門前傻笑。雖然荒誕，但整齊、一致、直觀，有股純粹的力量感，很容易讓人想起新中國每逢十一國慶節的閱兵式和毛主席在文革時期檢閱紅衛兵的場景。在那時，岳敏君就選擇了圓明園畫家村作爲栖居地，其行爲狀態具有些放蕩不羈的反叛，其作品的風格樣式也已初見端倪。

現在看來，之所以在90年代初期産生如方力均、岳敏君、楊少斌等這樣一批藝術家以及他們的生存狀態，是由80年代末和90年代初期中國特殊的歷史處境所決定的。80年代的中國，一方面是全社會向市場經濟轉型的改革開放，另一方面是文化領域的自我解放。以啓蒙、理性的人文關懷爲基本文化情勢的激情表現和以繪畫語言方式實驗爲主體的“85美術新潮”，成爲中國前衛藝術的主旨,也標識着一個新時期的到臨。這個“新時期”的概念是相對于中國的“文革”時期“藝術爲政治服務”而提出的，如果用“文革後藝術”來界定的話， 那麽這個新時期實際上是從“文革”蜕變而來的。1989年初在北京中國美術館舉辦的的“中國現代藝術大展”可以説是中國80年代前衛藝術的一個帶有總結性的回顧展。“六四風波”以後，中國的文化藝術處在沉寂和反思階段，也意味“85美術思潮”的終結。而這種沉寂和反思從某種角度來説恰恰是告别“85美術思潮”的前提和條件。1990年底一些被社會媒體稱之“流浪”的藝術家，如方力鈞、岳敏君、楊少斌、徐一暉、徐若濤等在生存方式上開始自尋地入住北京城郊的圓明園，成爲90年代中國前衛藝術家的主要栖息地——畫家村的雛形。這一圍繞着北京都市城鄉結合部的邊緣藝術家群落的出現和他們的行爲方式，集中説明了他們在各大美術學院畢業後的以往中國人所必需的職業身份的轉化，擺脱了中國傳統的“編户齊民”式的體制身份的限制，而成爲職業藝術家的一種對個體生存狀態自由的尋求、向往，其作品的共同特徵也表現爲一種强烈的自我表達的願望。對于前衛藝術家來説，其“獨立、自由”的表述與其説指認着脱離體制的行爲，不如説成爲構置一種高度抽象化和意識形態化的“自由、獨立”的文化想象。 他們的生存方式在90年代中國社會和文化中一直扮演着特殊的角色。 這類人物就像是王朔小説中的那種典型——京城的“頑主”。他們在社會轉型期，從計劃經濟的體制中游離了出來，最早感受到自由的風氣，對于傳統的秩序有一種玩世不恭的叛逆性，他們并不按照當時的價值行事，而是在邊緣處以一種强調自我、快樂和嘲諷的調子展示自己的存在。 如果説王朔的小説是在文學上表現這一類人物的最有力的文本，那麽在視覺藝術領域裏，他們就是與這一文化現象相伴而生的并將其予以視覺化呈現的代表性畫家。在中國市場化和全球化發展的前期，這類人物是傳統秩序否定的對象，却有着難以抗拒的吸引力，他們看似在社會的邊緣“躲避崇高”，其實却异常引人注目。

River Bank
海邊
120 x 80cm
1991
oil on canvas
布上油畫

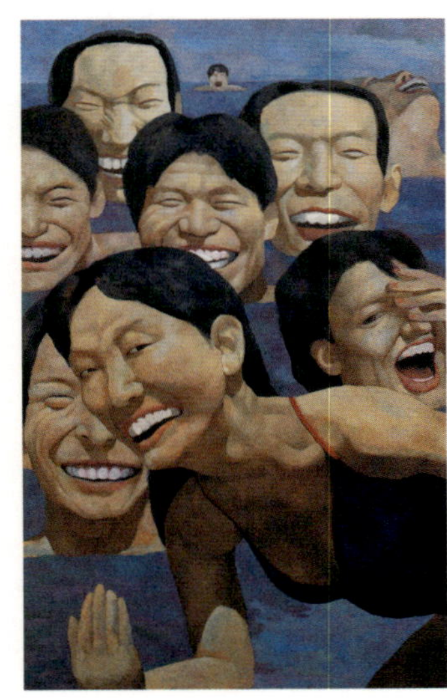

'independence and freedom' rather than a desire to get rid of the system. Thus, these individuals appeared rather like characters from the novels of Beijing-based author Wang Shuo: meaning that in the eyes of ordinary people artists were made to appear troublemakers. In this period of social transformation, the artists had dissociated themselves from the system of planned economy, for they felt the fresh air of new freedom earlier than other people, and rebelled against traditional social order in a cynical way. They remained on the fringe of society, determinedly independent, proud of their stance for individual choice, the pursuit of personal enjoyment, all the while jeering (at society). If Wang Shuo's novels are the best texts to portray such characters in literature, in visual art the same mission was carried on by leading painters who co-existed with the socio-cultural circumstances, whilst presenting them in their works. In the early phase of China's market economy, these individuals were denied by the strictures of traditional social order, but these artists managed to maintain overwhelming appeal: intent to maintain a distance from conventional society, they still commanded attention.

Yue Minjun is a representative painter of this period. His artistic creation has pretentious narrative manners: uninhibited imagination, self indulgence, cynical tones towards existence, which put in bold relief the nature of existence. It makes his works showy yet intelligent, fantastic yet realistic, and disordered yet well composed. We get no overall delight from viewing the works, but when we immerse ourselves in every scene that seems to be absurd, and ruminate over every conversations that sneer, brag, satire and tease, we are impressed by the unreasonable human nature, absurdness of survival: the artist's oppugning radiates from their expressions.

I think that what is most characteristic of Yue Minjun's creative ideas and his language is the way in which his works manage to demonstrate the spirit of the age. Yue Minjun's works have always presented a multiple arrangement of characters: each invariably the same, with a bald head, exaggerated limbs, a laughing mouth, and a dense row of tiny white teeth. These images have become a symbolic feature of his work. The context for his ideas derives from a characteristic element of so-called modern industrial civilization with its emphasis upon standardization, repetition and reproduction. For example, production lines in modern industry, skyscrapers, commodities and popular media are all outcomes of standardization and pluralism. The way we dress and make-up is an essential feature of contemporary social life that distinguishes modern sensibilities from classical ones. Social order has also been standardised. The neatly formatted role one plays in society is largely imposed upon them. In Yue Minjun's art works, the restrictions imposed by standardization and pluralism are transmuted, distorted or interfered with. This leads our thoughts to stray from established order and conventional rules to daringly unconventional ones.

Yue Minjun's artworks appropriate China's socialist propaganda posters as well as the language of consumer advertising. Many of his earlier works contained specific symbols, such as Tiananmen Square, red flags, the sun, slogans, red lanterns, red air-balloons and army caps. These referred to the vestige of didactic functions advocated by official mainstream art: to present a beautiful life, to be an active participator in life, and to spur people towards progress. At the same time, Yue Minjun purposefully invokes the visual character of materialism that emerged with the market economy from the early 1990s. The profusion of advertisement is an earmark of contemporary culture, littered with advertisements that overwhelm the senses. Life is an open and extending arena, across which advertisements are diffused and spread. Yue Minjun combines the basic elements of past propaganda posters with those of modern advertisements: simple, flashy, superficial, and visually direct images and dazzling colours feed

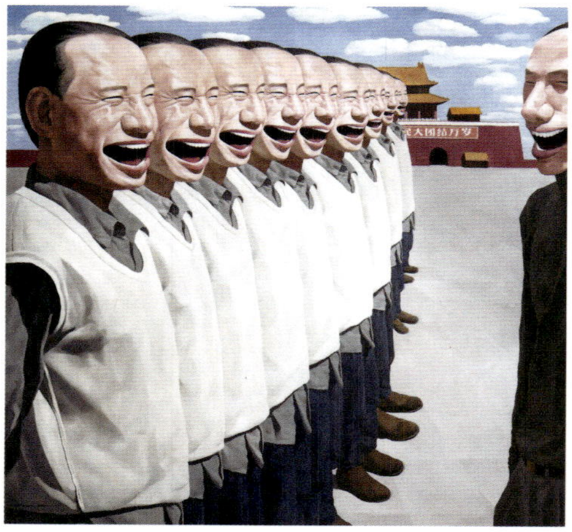

岳敏君是那一時期典型的代表畫家之一。 他的藝術創作有着一種張揚的叙事理想：放縱想象，沉醉自我，以嘲諷的語調質疑現實的生存，以荒謬的形式凸現存在的本質。這使得作品既虛泛又靈動，既荒誕不經又直指現實，既凌亂無序又布局嚴謹。它使我們的觀看不可能獲得整體上的輕鬆和愉悦，但是，當我們沉浸于每一個看似荒謬的畫面場景，沉浸于每一幅類似于冷嘲、誇張、反諷、戲謔的對話之中，我們又可以非常鮮活地感受到某種人性的乖張，生存的悖謬，以及話語中洋溢出來的創作主體的質疑心態。

我以爲在岳敏君創作觀念和語言方式上最具特色的是他作品的當代性體現問題。

一方面，他作品中總是以光鮮的頭形，誇張的肢體，嘻哈的大嘴及細密的小白牙等人物形象的復數性排列來呈現的，這些造像構成和貫穿了岳敏君藝術的符號化特徵。其觀念的背景支撑則來自于所謂的現代化工業文明的特徵之一，即强調標準化、重復性、復制性。比如，現代化工業的流水綫作業、現代的高層建築、商品、大衆宣傳媒介等等都是標準化、復數性的産物。非個性化的臉譜和面具是現代社會生活的本質特徵，而這種特徵是區分出古典情感和現代情感的界限。另外，我們的現實生活秩序，也是被不斷地整齊規劃了的，每一個生命的存在，都是一種機械的重復，猶如套在他們身上的社會角色，被濃縮在某種格式化之中。這種標準化、復數性的限制在岳敏君的作品中得到了轉化，甚至造成歪曲與幹擾，使我們的思維跳出正常的秩序與約定俗成的法則，從而誘發各種荒誕的想象。

另一方面是他作品中利用了中國社會主義宣傳畫和消費主義時代廣告性的話語方式。他早期的許多畫面背景都是圍繞着天安門、紅旗、太陽、標語、紅燈籠、紅氣球、軍帽等符號，它象徵着官方主流藝術所倡導的美化生活、積極向上、鼓舞人心的宣諭教化功能的時代痕迹。但同時他又有意地將 90 年代以來中國市場經濟的消費欲望在視覺上的特徵與其結合，即廣告文化的急速衍生成爲當代文化的特徵之一，廣告無所不在地存在于人的感官可以觸及的任何地方，生活世界成爲一個傳播廣告的開放的、無限延伸的廣場。岳敏君將以往政治宣傳畫與當代的廣告畫有機地結合或置換起來，廣告的單純、亮麗、表面、直觀的形象和眩目的顔色成爲岳敏君作品突出的風格樣式和話語方式。隨着中國二十多年來的改革開放，當今中國正在發展出一種最没有意識形態的現實生活。文化傳統處在中空狀態，政治熱度和敏感早已降温，中國人現實生活的經驗已經相當西化，在精神上却缺乏皈依與寄托，追求物質化和娱樂化占據着日常生活的所有空間。所以如果中國的當代藝術拿出的依舊是政治戲謔的符號化游戲的老把式，那無非是在用一代和幾代人的藝術生命去維持一個虛假的中國想象。所以他 90 年代末期到近幾年的一些作品的畫面背景出現了風景、園林、花鳥、動物，甚至天空、宇宙等等“閑雲野鶴”式的唯美圖式。既有個人成長的經驗記憶，又有時代審美趣味的變遷，構成了中國社會轉型的生活烙印。從這一角度考察，岳敏君的作品

Great Solidarity
大團結
190 x 200cm
1992
oil on canvas
布上油畫

Manipulation-10
處理 -10
210 x 200cm
2003
oil on canvas
布上油畫

Actions of Chinese Characters-1
漢字動作 -1
200 x 210cm
1999
oil on canvas
布上油畫

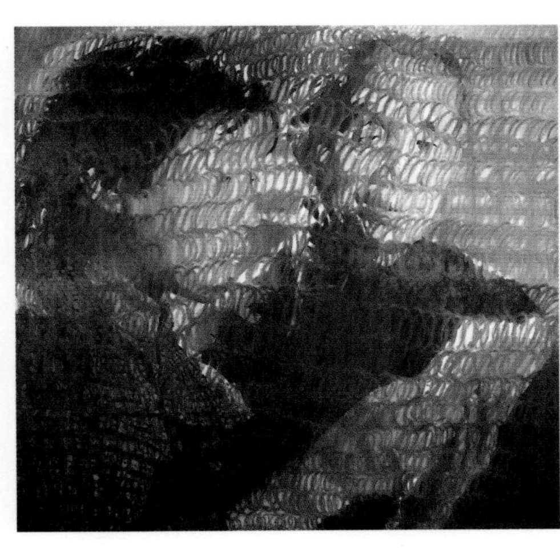

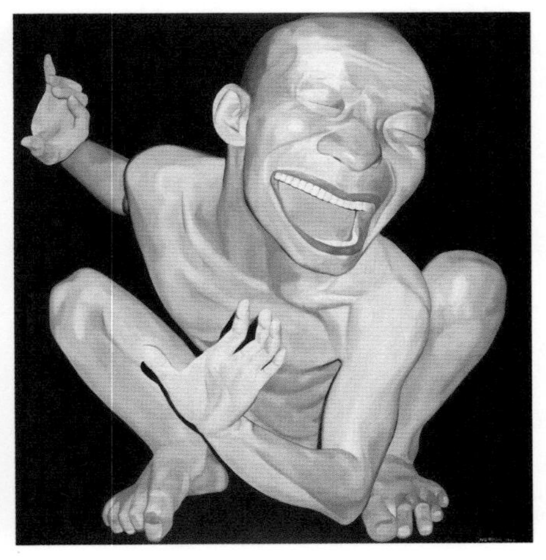

the language and style of his art. Through more than twenty years of opening and reform, China has reached a period in which daily life is least influenced by ideology. Cultural traditions have become hollow, and political zeal and sensitivity has already begun to diminish. The direct experience of most ordinary Chinese people is largely westernised, and spiritually people have little to embrace or believe in. The pursuit of materialism and amusement dominates daily life. Therefore, those contemporary artists who continue to invoke political symbols are but sustaining an illusion of China at the expense of artistic achievement.

Since the end of the 1990s, aesthetic images from Nature, such as landscape, gardens, flowers and birds, beasts, even sky and outer space, have appeared in Yue Minjun's works. He also uses memories born of his personal experience, as well as an exploration of the shifts in aesthetics that mirror the times. The works track reality through a period of social transformation in China. Viewed from this perspective, Yue Minjun's works correspond with the nature of a Chinese society desperate to modernize; in other words, his works exhibit the changing reality during a period of social transformation in China.

Yue Minjun also uses his own image as a subject is his works. In fact, his efforts to exalt the culture of our time start with the image of himself. To be in 'vogue' today is to be a face of our time, and there is no better expression than his own face. He comically depicts the affected poses and attitudes, which are omnipresent within commercial culture. His style pays homage to pop art, and outlines a realistic but absurd picture of physical and spiritual quirks of today. The jocular language belies the his deep and earnest reflection upon contemporary life.

In an era of electronic technology, our thinking has altered from the linear thinking characteristic of eras of mechanism and printing; a new way of looking at things and aesthetical frame of mind have been formed. In practical appreciation activities of art works, new ways manifest themselves. The viewer does not look at and enjoy artworks with a leisurely mentality, but instead, glances over them, understanding them intuitively instead of brooding over them as might have been done in times passed. The aesthetics this engenders reflects the changing rhythm of contemporary life, as well as an ideology of life reflected in art. Yue Minjun has done more than eradicating any sense of the personal from his works, or accentuating the mechanical apathy of modern life. He presents himself in his paintings in a quite superficial fashion, to highlight the anxiety and disappointment people bring upon themselves in the pursuit of enduring or profound expression. Anxiety and disappointment are metamorphosed into a flat plane without any depth, such that refutes any anxiety or concern. It seems that it is unnecessary to choose and to define anything; the value and significance of life have been dissolved in games and mechanical operations. Perhaps new art comes from such uncertain states, and is accomplished by those artists who feel modernity most keenly: perhaps artistic transformation is achieved by artists who conform to the tide of time, not as observers of cultural phenomenon, but as participants who help it to extend culture's potential.

Alongside industrialisation, popular culture has begun to sprout in China; this culture aims at comic, superficial and directly perceptible forms. A new aesthetic, derived from the contemporary cultural context, discards traditional grandiose epic narration and heavy-hearted introspection in favour of close-up and direct personal experience, and merely sensational perceptions. Following the trend of the 1990s as the political Utopia in China began to disintegrate, as a

恰恰適應或對應了現代化社會和中國急于現代化發展的本質特徵，換句話來說，他的作品從某種角度在測度或凸現着中國社會轉型期的現實變化。

第三，這些年來他所創作的系列作品基本上是以自己的形象爲模特的，或者説他對我們時代文化的敏感及提升是以爲“自己”造像爲切入點的。“時尚”正在成爲我們這個時代的標志和面孔，而“自己”恰如是這一標志性面孔的表情，將在商業文化影響下流行的矯揉造作的姿態和曖昧矯飾心理狀態滑稽而誇張地表現出來，試圖把當代中國正在興起的消費社會中的時尚化、虛擬化生活加以典型化波普化地處理，勾勒出這個時代物質與精神崇拜的生動且荒誕的情境，而戲謔的語言背後隱含的是他對當下生活的深刻關注以及嚴肅認真的反思。

第四，在電子媒介時代，我們的思維已不同于機械時代和印刷時代那種綫性的思維方式，形成了新的觀看方式和審美心境。在審美的具體活動中表現爲在轉瞬即逝的圖像面前，不在是以一種悠然自得的心境來觀看、欣賞藝術，而是由瀏覽取代古典審美的静觀，直覺取代沉思，在審美理想上追求視覺的衝擊力，對心靈的震撼力。這種審美是現代人生活節奏、生活方式與觀念在藝術領域變化的顯現。當藝術從意識形態、從文化特權中釋放出來之後，它的平面化的出現是理所當然的。但岳敏君不是單純地抽離或剔除了個人性的痕迹，或簡單地强化現代化的機械性冷漠，而是將自身的形象反復地、平面化地呈現在畫面中，意味着人們對永恒、深度模式的追尋所形成的焦慮和失望被幻化成消解式的無深度的膚淺平面。仿佛一切無需選擇、無需確定，生命的價值和意義消泯于游戲與操作之中。新的藝術或許就在這種不確定的形態中産生，它是通過敏感到當代性和順應時代潮流的藝術家以藝術的轉化方式來完成的，他們不僅是對某一文化景觀的觀察者，更成爲幫助擴展其可能性的參與者。

第五，作爲工業文明産生以來才出現的文化形態之一的大衆文化在中國也已開始萌芽，大衆文化的旨趣是喜劇性、膚淺、感性的，因此代替宏大叙事的深度模式和沉重的精神反思是當代文化景觀中衍生出一種消解傳統審美觀的近距離、强調對過程的直接沉浸和體驗的、止于感官的審美方式。岳敏君順應着 90 年代中國政治烏托邦神話的破滅和商品經濟盛行以及文化市場化的衝擊，將對時代的思考設定爲大衆文化的原則，銜接并植入到當代文化的神經，他不是簡單地回到啓蒙傳統的老路上去展開質疑與批判，而是使用了後現代主義的方式進行戲謔和反諷。對當代文化境遇的思考和敏鋭，將導致對舊有藝術形式在方法論上的改造，而藝術家需要的就是用一種規定爲“藝術”的方法來體現這種思想和觀念。

岳敏君的作品話語基調無疑是荒誕式的，這種荒誕方式主要是源于他對冷嘲、反諷、誇張手法的高度迷

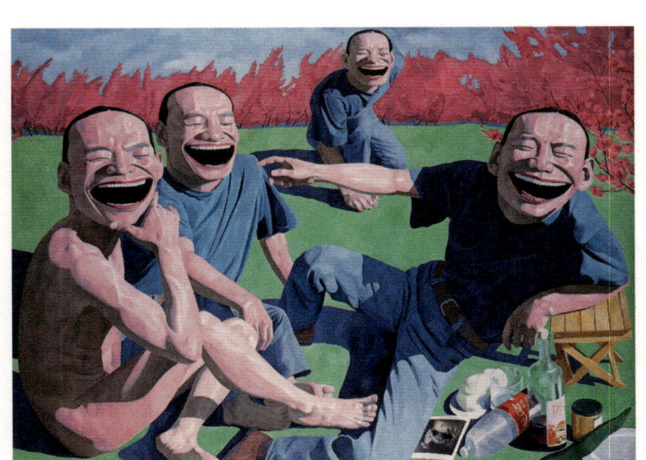

Luncheon on the Grass
草地上的午餐
182 x 250cm
1995
oil on canvas
布上油畫

consumer economy became prevalent, the cultural market posed a new challenge to the established order. Yue Minjun reflects upon time as a guiding force of popular culture, and presents this as the kernel of contemporary culture. He does not simply go back to the old path of Enlightenment ideas to question and criticise established conventions, instead he ridicules and satirizes in a post-modernist manner. His sensitivity to contemporary cultural circumstances encourages a methodical remoulding of an old art form, while what artists need is a method prescribed as an 'artistic one' with which to present such a thought and concept.

Undoubtedly, the keynote of Yue Minjun's expression is a sense of the absurd/fantastic, which comes primarily from his obsessive leaning towards sarcasm, irony and exaggeration. The context of his works is set in a dramatic structure, which possesses a strong flavour of irony, and presents a playful and unreal existence in a rapidly changing China. At the same time, it provides an ideological background where 'to be is just absurd'. More importantly, Yue Minjun presents these ideas through a series of giggly and bald-headed people, depicted with flashy colours, and awkward anatomies. He seems to emphasize mannerist elements in his visual images which transform any showy and vulgar image about himself into a mere expression manner, and give full rein to the form until it looks both dazzling and dreadful. These typical, unreal images are processed with some exaggeration, but reveal the vivid and absurd circumstances of 'his' existence. China's prevailing consumerism is refracted through this prism. His figures float in air, apparently starting from nowhere and never reaching anywhere either. This is also true of their lives. They just open their eyes wide, laugh and joke open-mouthed, dazed and bewildered. The contrasts between raffish, slick facial features and deformed limbs present not only the conflict between desires and their catharsis, which are rooted in the human heart, and also between the dreams of humankind that are dissimilated ceaselessly during their existence.

Of course, judging by his mode of expression, Yue Minjun's works satirise the intellectuals' attitude towards their own existence, as well as the pride and vanity inherent in human nature. These ironies add not only some aesthetic reason to his narration but also reflect his suspicion about all kinds of existing order and value. We can see that Yue Minjun intends to play the key images and depicted behaviours in his paintings to the full. The result has a complex symbolic effect, and illustrates the on-going expansion of material consumption in today's society. This is achieved through a series of images of grotesque figures, pagodas and Taihu Lake stones, which symbolize tradition, and even by cannibalising the structure of Chinese characters and images processed with computer programmes. In this way his images transcend their fantastic realm and enter the real world, revealing his concerns for present-day society. In this time of morass and absurdity his works focus on the fashions of post-modern consumer culture. Therefore, The theme of his works contains an imprecation against the cause of such social phenomena, rather than merely presenting his own facial expression.

Where this self-image appears in Yue Minjun's pictures, his passions, ideals and intentions are presented fully; without exception 'he' is made to look like a fool. I think this is the purpose of Yue Minjun's irony: to deride absurdity in reality, especially the roots of absurdity. Through an exaggerated allegory of histories heroes and politics, Yue Minjun lays bare the absurdity of the creators of such absurd phenomena. He does an especially good job of criticising social problems. What makes his works attractive is the monotonous and repeated focus of his subject: absurdity juxtaposed with freedom, which invokes a longing for freedom and liberation that is felt in the

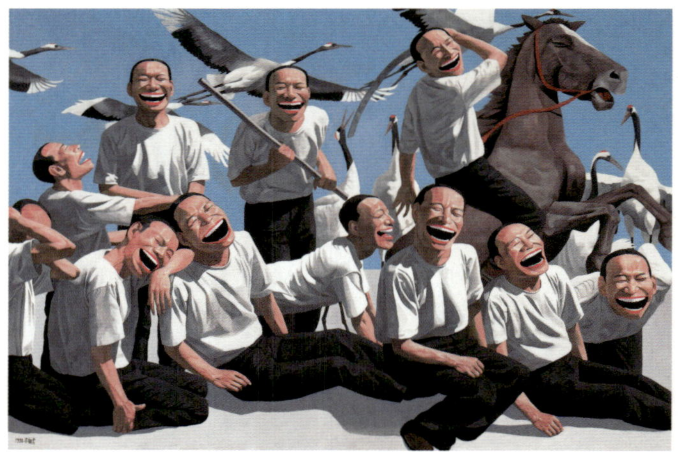

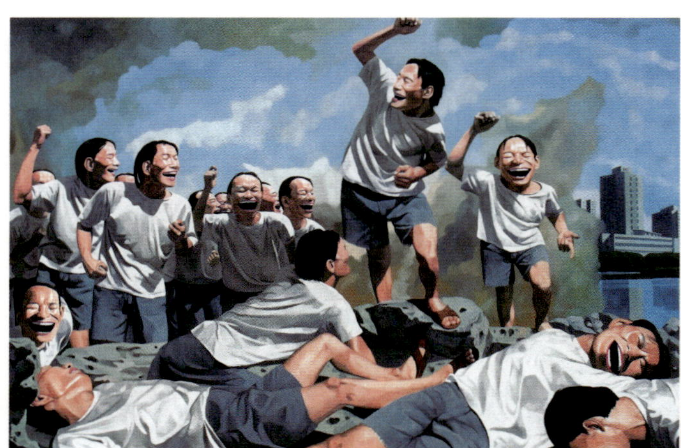

戀。他以戲劇化的結構形態設置了作品語境，這種戲劇化結構本身就帶着强烈的反諷意味，表達了中國現實急劇變化的游戲性、虛擬性生存景象，同時又隱喻着“存在便是一種荒誕”的思想背景。但更重要的是岳敏君的作品是以一系列傻笑的光頭而呈現的。色調的艷麗、形態的怪誕，甚至還有些血腥氣。似乎他在强調視覺圖像中的形式主義趣味，即把艷俗的自我形象變成純粹的形式感，并將這種形式感發輝到令人眩目、驚怵的程度。雖然這些形象帶有誇張的虛擬化典型化處理，却恰恰地凸顯出“他”生動和荒誕的生存處境。而這種處境集中折射出了中國目前時尚的消費文化的一個側面狀態。他們在漂浮中行走，沒有起點也沒有終點。他們的現實化生活也同樣如此，他們衹有睁大眼睛，張開嘴地嘻哈，似乎錯愕而困惑地在尋覓着什麽。在艷俗而光滑的五官與變形肢體的對比中，既表現出根植于人内心的欲望與宣泄這一矛盾的心理情結，又演繹了在生存過程中不斷被异化的人生夢想。當然，從話語表面上看，作品還處處體現了對知識分子生存心態的反諷，對人性中某些自信與虛妄本能的反諷。這些反諷，不僅使叙事增加了某些審美的智性成分，還使作品在内蘊上折射出對各種現實生存秩序和價值觀念的懷疑。可以看出岳敏君的用意是把畫面中的一個關鍵性的行爲形象同時賦予了内容和形式方面的最大效果，這種效果具有復雜的象徵意義，把我們現今社會日益膨脹的物質消費的情景，通過系列“我”的怪异形象和象徵傳統的寶塔、太湖石等景致符號化和現實化了，甚至挪用了漢字結構和網絡的photoshop，强行拼貼、處理後現代與前現代文明的兩種不同的話語，從而凸現出當代中國巨大的文明落差，正是這種文明的巨大落差構成了他反思中國時尚消費文化的一個參照系。于是視覺的圖像從非現實的層面進入到一個現實的層面，以此來表達他對當下現實社會的深刻關注。作品要表現的主題思想也集中于反思後現代主義式的消費時尚文化在這個時代的困境和荒誕性上。所以，與其説這是復制了他自己的統一表情，毋寧説是他對産生這種社會現象的一種憂患、揭露與批判。

我很注意岳敏君作品中的“自我”都處理成“傻笑”的模樣。其實，現實中人們的瘋和傻，都是來自于那些企圖讓人們變得瘋和傻的人的自我認定。這裏，當他們以此身份出現在岳敏君的畫面裏時，他們的激情、理想和意圖都會變得不留餘地和不加掩飾，并無一例外地變成了瘋子和傻瓜。我想，這正是岳敏君的反諷目的。反諷是試圖以這種現實的荒誕現象特别是對荒誕的各種造因的針砭和嘲弄。對于岳敏君來説，就是通過英雄、政治的歷史進行寓言式虛構和誇張，揭示荒誕制造者和承受者雙方的荒謬。由此，他實實在在地履行了自己作爲藝術家應該履行的社會批判的使命。作品的精彩之處，也正是他的重復單調之處，對某種政治模式、社會秩序、機制系統、思維慣性的反復描繪地嘲弄，使他的筆觸停留在一個始終不變的思想領域。荒誕與自由并立，從荒誕中釋放出來的是來自人的靈魂深處的另一種人性自由與解放的要求，在荒誕的背後透出了岳敏君對不合理現實存在的反抗和對一種新的、更高的理想追求。

The Massacre at Chios
希阿島的屠殺
250 x 360cm
1994
oil on canvas
布上油畫

Freedom Leading the People
自由引導人民
250 x 360cm
1995 -1996
oil on canvas
布上油畫

岳敏君同時還是一位具有不斷實驗性精神的藝術家，盡管他一直是利用架上繪畫的方式，除了做一些雕塑

depth of human soul. It reveals Yue Minjun's resistance to irrational elements of reality.

Yue Minjun never stops experimenting. With the exception of some prints and sculptures, he focuses mainly on easel painting. Yue Minjun's conceptual paintings epitomise his understanding of painting *per se*. As early as 1994, he began to simulate and imitate classical paintings by western masters, such as *Dejeuner sur l'Herbe, Massacre at Si'a Island* and *Liberty Leading her People*. Such prankish imitation actually carries on his sense of absurdity in artistic creation, and enhances the absurdity through deliberate mockery, transforming the paintings of revered western masters into comical parodies. He re-writes classical art using this painting language and symbolism, modifies and updates traditional styles, simultaneously distorting them. This excludes a single interpretation of (the history of) classical works, subjecting classical themes to contemporary zeitgeist, and fabricating many absurd japes. Since people have become accustomed to a stereotyped aesthetic understanding of these works, Yue Minjun's experiments estrange these well-known modes, keep the audience in suspense, whilst providing them with pleasure derived from new approaches and perspectives, and a sense of freedom that comes from casting off classical rules demonstrated in works like *Celebration of National Day*, Manet's *Olympia*, David's *Death of Marat*, Vermeer's *Maid Reading before Window*, *Chairman Mao on the Road to Anyuan* by Liu Chunhua and *Tunnel Warfare* by Luo Gongliu. Central to the reinvention of these paintings is that Yue Minjun removes all the central characters from each composition, obviously intending to rid them of their mythical colour. In this way he challenges the authority of stereotyped interpretation of established works by revealing limitation of widely accepted versions, and makes the standards set by these well-known works ephemeral and unreliable. It appears to Yue Minjun that artists need to change their perspective constantly, so as to create new styles and stave off stagnation. Simultaneously, Yue Minjun unleashes dormant memories of past events, which have been stifled by traditional narration.

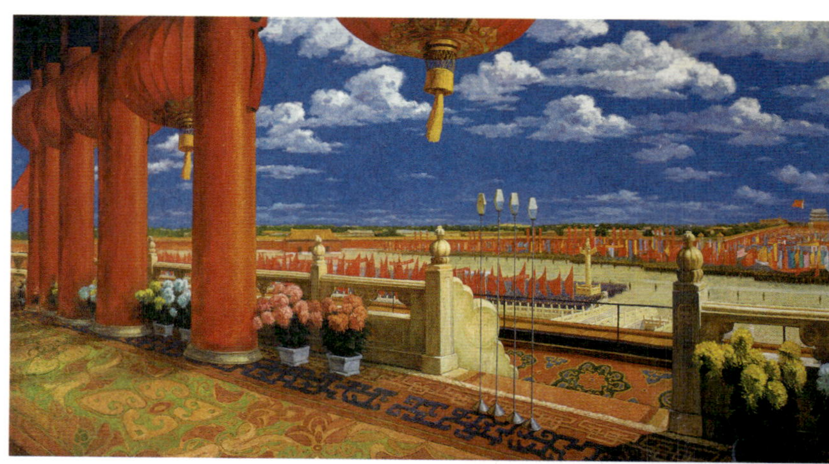

In the 21st century, China is employing new criteria to achieve a new order: a new ideology is taking shape. This ideology, and order, is based on a market economy, one of the results of globalisation. Yue Minjun's art has always been closely related to his time: he knows that avoiding taboos and abiding by rules are always conflicting goals both tantalising and irreconcilable. However, in spite of the pitfalls, the only real choice is to experiment courageously. There are beautiful confusions everywhere in China today; it is a source of creativity that, for a true avant-garde artist, is unlikely to dry-up. I think that Yue Minjun's spirited experiments always lead the field. The troublemaker Yue Minjun seems never to grow old.

(Translated by David Mao and Wen Jingen)

和版畫之外，他没有過多地在其它材料和媒介上進行嘗試。代表岳敏君的觀念性繪畫是他對繪畫本身的認識。早在1994年，他就開始對一些西方的經典名畫進行戲擬、戲仿，如《草地上的午餐》、《西阿島的屠殺》、《自由引導人們》等作品。這種戲仿其實還是在延續他創作上的荒誕意識，或者説是以刻意地模仿來强化他的荒誕性，將我們曾經膜拜的西方大師的經典畫作轉化爲戲謔的喜劇感。他用他的繪畫語言和符號改寫經典，修復和更新傳統的樣式和風格，使它們變形，取消了經典直綫發展的可能，從而使古典題材既有主題上的時代性，又用各種荒誕的手法制造了許多笑料。這種改畫一方面是發掘未被充分利用的資源，另一方面是爲了表現經典的虚構性，向單一叙述提出質疑。因爲人們對它們的審美已基本定型，岳敏君的實驗使這些熟悉的模式陌生化，以控制觀者的期待，讓觀者體味新模式和新視角所産生的驚喜，以及擺脱經典規則後的自由。而後，從1998年開始，其實驗則是臨摹、拷貝了這些經典名畫，創作了如《開國大典》、《奥林匹亞》、《馬拉之死》、《窗前讀信的少女》、《毛主席去安源》《地道戰》等近二十幅作品。但關鍵之處是他抽離了畫面中心人物的形象角色，在借鑒經典作品的同時又具有消除其神話色彩的明顯意圖。在經典内部處理經典，用殘留在經典中的能量破壞它們的控制力，改變他們力量的作用方向。通過揭示已被接受的版本的局限性，而對單一叙述的權威性提出了挑戰，使這些耳熟能詳的作品所提供的標準變得短暫而不可靠，從而在忍俊不止的幽默中更耐人尋味。他還探討了經典模式生成的潛能，表達了將藝術教條化會産生的危險。也許在他看來，我們爲錯綜復雜的人類經驗創造適當模式的能力是極其微弱的，所以人類需要不斷地變换視角，探索新隱喻，創作新樣式，以便不斷地抵制静止或者混亂，使衆多長期被傳統叙述壓抑的其它叙述和記憶得到了某種解放。

在21世紀今天的中國已經有了新的規範和秩序，開始生成新的意識形態。這種意識、規範、秩序乃是建立在市場化的基礎之上，也是全球化的後果之一。隨着文化情境和語境的變化，雖然有些“頑主”們老了，開始從時代的焦點中銷聲匿迹，退隱江湖。但考察岳敏君的藝術綫索，他却始終與時代保持着密切的關系，這對于在當今早已是功成名就的藝術家來説，能够始終保持探索的姿態是非常難能可貴的。不言而喻，逾越禁忌和恪守規範在藝術中始終是一對不容易調和而又令人神往的矛盾。在這裏，坦途和陷阱的概率幾乎相等。但是除了勇于實驗，我們還有更合適的選擇嗎？而中國當下的現實到處都在勃發出美麗的混亂，這或許是一位真正前衛藝術家取之不盡的創作源泉。我以爲他的創作觀念仍在被新的社會結構所接納，他的實驗性精神仍會引領着藝術的潮流。岳敏君，“頑主”不老矣。

Tian An Men Remains
開國大典
400 x 220cm
2002
oil on canvas
布上油畫

The Death of Marat
馬拉之死
220 x 292cm
2002
oil on canvas
布上油畫

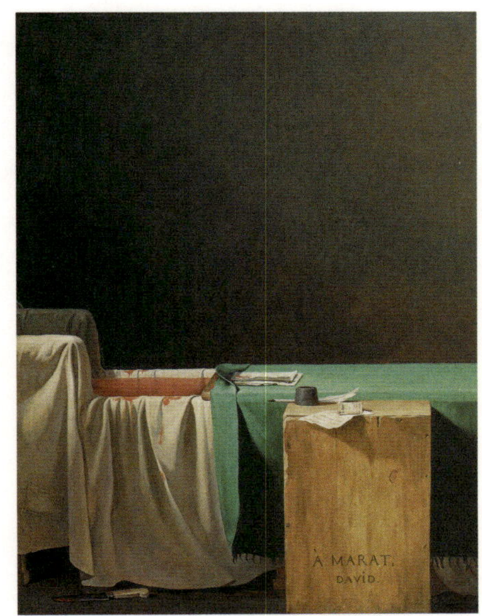

Yue Minjun produced the first laughing face at the beginning of the 1990s. Although a number of the familiar characteristics were already taking shape–the pink hue of the skin, the smart rows of toothpaste white teeth, framed by a smooth, neat crop of black hair–at first, the features were not his own, but those of friends: artists within his immediate community, each of whom was grappling with a brave new world of independence in a society that viewed individualism with grave suspicion. Early on, Yue Minjun revealed himself to be a very distinctive character. It was therefore natural that as he work evolved, his own features should transcend that of others in his paintings. This face, his face, and that incorrigible laugh, has since become one of the foremost icons of contemporary Chinese art and, in many ways, a symbol of the shifting sensibilities of an entire generation. These sensibilities germinated in tandem with a sense of freedom that was spreading across all society in the 1990s, but in particular that was permeating Yue Minjun's generation, as economic change began to exert an irrevocable force upon the lives of, and the opportunities afforded, the Chinese people. Whilst the socio-economic change had its roots in the 1980s, it gained greater velocity from the beginning of the 1990s, as people became used to the idea of reform, less apprehensive of change and, as a result, more ready to embrace the opportunities it proffered.

Yue Minjun is a central character in the new wave of creatively attuned self-styled individuals to emerge in the early 1990s, and who were ultimately responsible for driving contemporary art practice in China into its important secondary phase. Today, he is widely acclaimed as a leading painter of his generation and the era, counted amongst the handful of contemporary Chinese giants that include Wang Guangyi, Fang Lijun, Zhang Xiaogang and Yang Shaobin. Here, he describes how, against the odds, his style found form, through to the significance of works created for this, his first solo exhibition in China.

* * *

The first laughing face had complex origins. You can find it in the early paintings I created as far back as 1990. Just prior to that time, a huge exhibition of new art[1] took place in Beijing–"The Big Chinese Art Exhibition" as it was titled[2]. I didn't see it myself, but there were articles about it in all the art magazines of the day, together with numerous reproductions of the works that were exhibited in the show. One painting in particular made a great impression on me. That was Geng Jianyi's four-panel painting *The Second State*. This is a series of four heads that each fill the canvas with a face creased in laughter. It made me think of the Maitreya Buddha, the Buddha of the Future, which takes the form of a sculpture of a smiling, pot-bellied Buddha[3]. These can be seen at the entrance to every Buddhist temple in China. His smile is meant to remind people of the need to hold dear the truths of Buddhist teachings in all the goals we set ourselves in life; to remind us that even in the face of stress and adversity, we should not lose control, nor give into negative feelings. Geng Jianyi's painting invited comparison with this image of the Maitreya Buddha, yet at the same time resonated a mood of bitter frustration that was a common emotion amongst our generation. It further alluded to the Daoist belief that a smile was the best means of mediating life's awkward situations, especially potentially confrontational ones, because to laugh is a more effective–if not more productive–course of action than the unleashing of anger, or of internalizing a problem, which saps energy and allows negative thoughts to breed. The idea of finding a means to navigate the obstacle that life throws in your path, of not taking things to heart, is central to Daoist philosophy. We laugh even when tragedy strikes, not because we are without sympathy, or empathy, but because we are profoundly conscious of human frailty and helplessness where confronted with adverse situations. How else to protect the soul from pain and suffering?

By the time I saw Geng Jianyi's painting in 1989, the necessity of this approach had acquired particular prescience. Following the events of 1989, our generation was subsumed in a period of chaos, wracked by contradictions and complex emotions. We each instinctively felt that despite being availed of an opportunity to assert our independent, as long as we were marginalized by our choice of lifestyle, our desire to explore individual creative impulses, our existence could never be entirely happy. In this context, up against a society that had been taught to frown upon those who deviated

— 岳敏君在20世紀90年代初開始創作第一張大笑面孔的作品。盡管一些熟悉的特徵在此之前早已出現——粉紅的膚色，整排牙膏一樣潔白的牙齒，光滑齊整的黑發——然而，最初的時候，畫中的人物形象并不衹是他自己，也包括身邊的朋友——在疑忌個人主義的社會中，勇敢奮爭獨立自主的藝術家伙伴們。由于他的自我形象在早期就非常突出，後期發展中超越了他人的形象而存在也是很自然的事情。這張面孔，這張岳敏君自己的面孔，這張狂笑的面孔，自此成爲中國當代藝術最重要的符號之一。就很多方面而言，這面孔也標志着整整一代人的意識變遷。這些意識是伴隨着90年代席卷全社會，深深影響了岳敏君那一代人的自由思潮而產生的。當時經濟變革伊始，中國人民的生活受到了不可抗拒的外力的改變和各種機遇的衝擊。社會經濟變革在80年代開始，在90年代初期加速，人們開始習慣于改革的思想，對變化的疑慮減少，從而做好了抓住各種機遇的準備。

岳敏君是90年代初期新藝術浪潮的代表人物之一，他們創造性的調和了以自我爲風格的個體形象，懷着極高的責任感，將中國當代藝術推進到重要的第二階段。今天，他已成爲公認的當代最重要的藝術家之一，其他中國當代藝術巨匠還有王廣義，方力均，張曉剛和楊少斌。在此，通過介紹國內首次個展作品的特點，他描述了其藝術風格是如何超越偶然，找到其表現形式的歷程。

* * *

— 大笑面孔出現的原因很復雜。你可以在我1990年的早期作品中看到它。90年之前，北京有一個很大的新藝術展覽[1]，叫做《中國現代藝術大展》[2]。我没有去看那個展覽，但在雜志上看到了相關報道文章和參展作品圖片。其中一張油畫給我的印象特别深。那是耿建翌的一件四聯張的油畫作品《第二狀態》。它是4張頭像的組合，每張都是一個充滿整個畫面的，皺成一團的笑臉。讓我想到中國佛教寺廟中極爲常見的一種佛像——大腹便便，眉開眼的彌勒佛[3]。彌勒的笑容是要提醒人們謹遵佛法教誨；一切苦難皆不可移心性，亂分寸。耿建翌的作品形象是與彌勒形象的一種對比，同時也表現了我們這代人常常感到的那種痛苦的挫折感。他的作品更隱含着道家思想，笑是反省人生困境的最好方法，尤其是内心的矛盾掙扎，因爲笑是比釋放憤怒或壓抑問題更爲有效——如果不是更有建設性——的行爲方式，後者衹能耗費精力，助長負面情緒。尋找方法跨越生活擺在你面前的障礙，做到心無挂礙，這是道家哲學的核心思想。就算悲劇發生，我們依然要笑着面對，這并非是冷酷，没有同情心，也不是冷漠，没有感情，而是因爲我們深深明了人類面對逆境時的脆弱和無助。爲了讓靈魂遠離苦痛磨難，我們還能怎麽做呢？

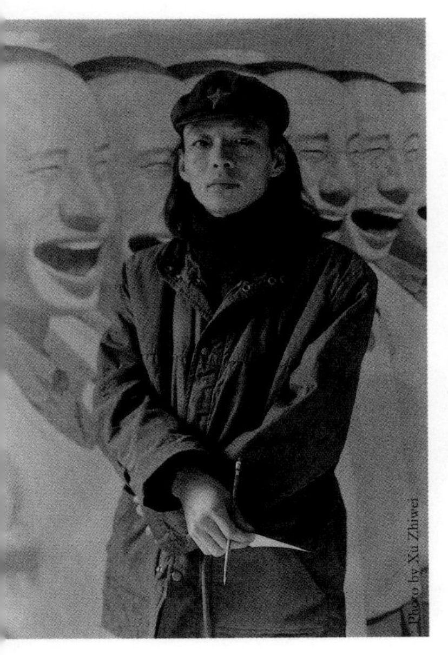
Photo by Xu Zhiwei

我在1989年看到耿建翌的作品的時候，這種行爲方式的必要性已經由特别事件的得到預證。89事件之後，我們這代人經歷了一段混亂的時期，經受着錯綜復雜的矛盾和情感的衝擊。我們都深深感覺到，盡管有機會實現獨立的生活，但我們對生活方式的選擇，我們對探索個人創造靈感的需要，使得我們被歸置于社會的邊緣，在這樣的前提下，我們的存在永遠都不會是完全快樂的。在這種一貫不歡迎離經叛道者的社會中，大笑的形象對我而言是一種保證，保證一切都會變好，就像佛教所承諾的來生完滿。但現實并非如此，混亂而怪誕，很難讓人有這樣的信心。我決定用這個大笑的形象來提醒我圈子裏的人，明天會

from the norm, the image of a laughing face was to me an assurance that things would get better: that a future life could be as rewarding and meaningful as the Buddha promised. But against the reality of the times, which was so entirely chaotic and strange, it was hard to hold onto that faith. I decided that my laughing faces would serve as a reminder of a better tomorrow within my circle just as the Maitreya Buddha in the temples do, and would resonate with those individuals who had learned to laugh because they understood that almost any other response was futile.

The main circle of friends in my life at that time were the artists living in the same community as I was at artists' village at Yuanmingyuan. Before coming to the village, in 1991, I was employed as a teacher in a State oil enterprise–Huabei Shiyou in Hebei province. All my life I had lived in a State-run *danwei* [4], first with my parents as a child in the oil fields in Daqing in the Northeast of China, then in Hubei province when they were transferred in 1969, and finally in Beijing in 1972. After school, in 1980 I was sent to work at the Haiyang State Oil Company in Tianjin, and was transferred to the oil refinery in Hebei in 1983. It was there that I persuaded my director to send me to university to study art. When I graduated, I returned to my *danwei* in Hebei to work in its affiliated teaching training college. I lasted just over a year as a teacher before deciding to move to Beijing. The problem for me was that these enterprises were uniformly operated within an extremely narrow structure that was largely inflexible, and incapable of making any concession to individuals within its employ, because all people were all supposed to be equal and the same. Of course they weren't all equal: everything depended upon maintaining good relations within a complex web of inter-personal connections. This meant that the pressure of existing in a potential minefield, where everyone had to appear to do the right thing, to conform, consumed the working life of many individuals. Everybody in China lived their life this way at that time, which is why the act of smiling, laughing to mask feelings of helplessness has such significance for my generation. Until the 1990s, the possibility of an alternative was almost inconceivable: people were encouraged to believe it was impossible to exist outside of the system. There was no place for individual ambition within the socialist machine. For this reason, most people could not conceive of stepping outside the confines of the State structure; less still to move to Yuanmingyuan with the aim of becoming an independent artist. Yet for some reason that is exactly what I felt compelled to do.

I guess you are wondering what made me different? I can only conclude that I was born that way! My parents are fond of saying that even as a young child, I was totally capable of taking care of and amusing myself without getting into any trouble. I would trundle off to kindergarten with my two younger brothers, prepare meals for us, and do chores around the house. It all came naturally for neither of my parents told me that these were things I ought to do. My independence proved a great asset, and gave me all the experience I needed to be able to live on my own. Thus although it must have seemed alarmingly radical to challenge convention and go it alone, to me the idea of setting up home at the artists' village was the most natural thing in the world. I certainly didn't see what to others were the obvious obstacles involved. I guess I did have some kind of a desire to rebel, although I don't think it could be described as a conscious awareness of self; of myself as being entirely different from others...or of having a wish to stand out from others. A quiet confidence perhaps, but I was primarily concerned about my future, about the possibilities that might be open to me if I was open to them. I didn't want to become resigned to life as a worker in the way my parents had had to be. I remember thinking clearly that if our society could not change, or accept change as part of modernization and advance, then there would be no point in striving for anything at all: life would just carry on the way it was; the dull eternity of an entirely meaningless existence.

But society was already altered by the effects of economic reform that had been implemented through the 1980s, and by issues that the

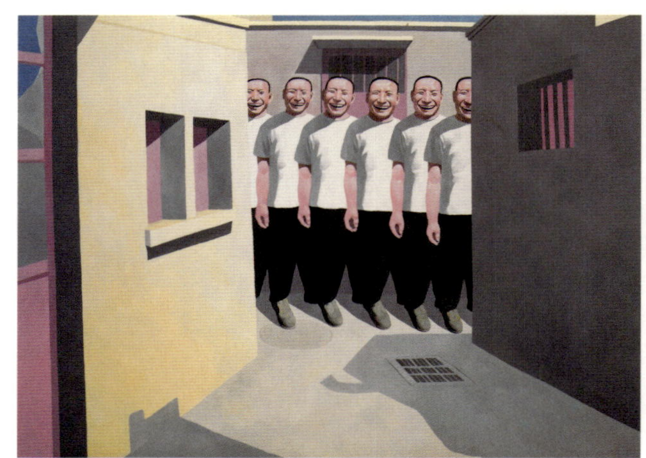

更加美好，就像廟中的彌勒所作的那樣。同時，這個形象也會同那些已經學會笑面人生的個人産生共鳴，因爲他們已經明白，其他任何反應都是没有用的。

在圓明園畫家村的時候，我主要的朋友圈子都是住在一起的藝術家。去村裏之前，91年我在河北省的一個國營單位[4] ——華北石油作老師。之前我的生活一直都在國營單位中度過，小的時候跟着父母在東北的大慶油田，69年父母工作調動，跟着他們到了河北，最後在72年到了北京。高中畢業後，80年到天津海洋國家石油公司工作，83年轉到河北煉油廠。在河北的時候，我説服領導送我到大學學習藝術。大學畢業後，我回到河北的單位，在附屬學院作教學工作。一年後，决意離開，來到北京。原因是這些國營單位的統一管理框架極爲狹隘，僵化，没有個人的空間，每個人都要保持一致和平等。事實上他們并不平等，一切都取决于人際關系的好壞，非常復雜。在這樣的環境中生活，如入雷區，必須小心翼翼，壓力非常大，每個人都得表現出行爲端正，協調一致，個人的工作生活幾乎成爲一種消耗。那時每個中國人過的都是這樣的生活，這正是爲什麼用笑來掩飾無助的行爲在我們這代人中間如此突出。直到20世紀90年代，改變都是幾乎不可能的事情。人們都認爲，離開現在的系統根本没有辦法生存。在社會主義機器内，没有個人野心的地位。因此，絶大多數人都無法想象走出國營框架，更不用説到圓明園去做一個獨立的藝術家了。然而，出于某些原因，這正是我覺得必須要做的事情。

我猜你一定很好奇，是什麼讓我與衆不同？我衹能説是天生如此！我的父母總喜歡説我小的時候就能自己照料自己，自己找東西玩，什麼麻煩都没有。我能推着小車送兩個弟弟去幼兒園，做飯給我們三個吃，照料家裏家外的雜務。這些事情都是我主動去做的，而不是父母讓我去做的。這種獨立精神是非常重要的資本，使我擁有了獨立生活所需的經驗。所以盡管打破常規，孤軍奮鬥的想法顯得驚世駭俗，特立獨行，對我而言，自己在圓明園畫家村生活却是最爲順利成章，天經地義的事情。其他人覺得是障礙的東西對我而言根本不存在。我覺得自己肯定有一種叛逆心理，盡管不能説那是對自我，對與他人完全不同的自我......或是希望遠離他人的自我的清醒認知。或許是一種自信從容，但我首先考慮的是我的未來，考慮的是可能出現在我面前的機會。我不想像我父母一樣，到最後成爲退休工人。我記得當時想得很清楚，要是我們的社會不改變，或者不接受現代化和社會進步所帶來的改變，那麼就根本没有必要去爲了任何事情而奮鬥：生活會永遠一成不變，成爲枯燥且完全無意義的永恒存在。

但是，80年代實行的經濟改革和89學潮早已改變了這個社會。我感覺這樣的變化是無法從整體記憶中抹除的，自由的體驗也是無法抹煞的。因此，在河北教藝術的我感到非常的空虚和迷茫。之後，很偶然的，我發現了圓明園的藝術家群落，而這正是我一直在等待的機會。

Sunshine
正午陽光
182 x 250cm
1993
oil on canvas
布上油畫

畫家村對我而言也是一個非常熟悉和舒適的環境。72年我們全家到北京之後，就住在北京石油學院，和圓明園非常近。盡管圓明園已經殘敗，但風景還是非常美的，和當時很多學生一樣，我年輕的時候經常騎着自行車去圓明園寫生。我對這個區域的熟悉了解使得遷居圓明園更加自然。

students raised in 1989. I felt that such change could not be entirely erased from the collective memory, nor that taste of freedom eradicated.

So there I was, teaching art in Hebei, feeling entirely unfulfilled and wondering what to do. And then completely by chance I stumbled upon the artists' community at Yuanmingyuan and I knew that this was the opportunity I had been waiting for.

The village was both a familiar and comfortable environment for me. When my family came to Beijing in 1972, we lived at the Oil and Petroleum University, which is close to Yuanmingyuan. All the original palace building and gardens had long since been destroyed, but the natural landscape remained very beautiful. Like many students of that time, in my youth I used to go there to make drawings and paint from nature. This familiarity with the area made the move even more natural.

I came to Beijing in 1991 to visit a friend who was living in a rented room in a small yard in the village. I immediately noticed the artists who were living in the neighborhood. Yang Shaobin was renting a studio in the same yard, which doubled as his home. It was exactly as I had imagined the life of an artist to be, and it all seemed so great that I decided to make the move from Hebei. Compared with life at the *danwei*, it didn't seem so very hard to be an independent artist. The rent was low, and the environment was everything the *danwei* wasn't. Most important was that there, I was free to decide how I spent my days, and of especial delight at the time, how long I grew my hair!

*

In the beginning I experimented with the styles of other artists I knew living in the village. These artists also became the subjects of my paintings. Initially, it was difficult to determine my own preferences, or to see where my sensibilities would lead me. That changed when I began painting myself. Even then, this was less about me than achieving a form that could express my ideas, but the smile was definitely there. It was an impulsive first step but I realized it was something I could work with.

A major turning point occurred in a painting that featured a row of figures: the type of line-up so common our communal experience of life. The appearance of conformity and abeyance, yet so often enacted without conviction of purpose. Here, I chose to depict the same figure, similar stance, and same features, to highlight the inanity of such parades. To use one figure in such a manner lent them the appearance of cartoon caricatures: satirizing humanity to tell a particular story. It occurred to me that such stories about social reality outweighed that of referencing specific individuals who would never be identifiable to an audience. A caricature could express so much more humanity, and having decided that this would be my ultimate subject, why not create a caricature of myself to convey the stories I wanted to relate. This is how the figure emerged as the motif that has become the recognizable feature of my work. It subsequently dictated how all aspects of my art evolved.

As with many cartoon characters, the expression changes very little. The power and the charm of what cartoon characters are able to express is the essence human nature. Where these characters are evoked in simple, stylized forms, the ways in which their creators makes them interact with the world becomes paramount. The situations in which they are placed, and the nature of the stories they act out, have to reinforce the attitude we understand them to encapsulate. Thus I approach each series of works like writing a play, or mapping out a storyboard. Much of the inspiration comes from my

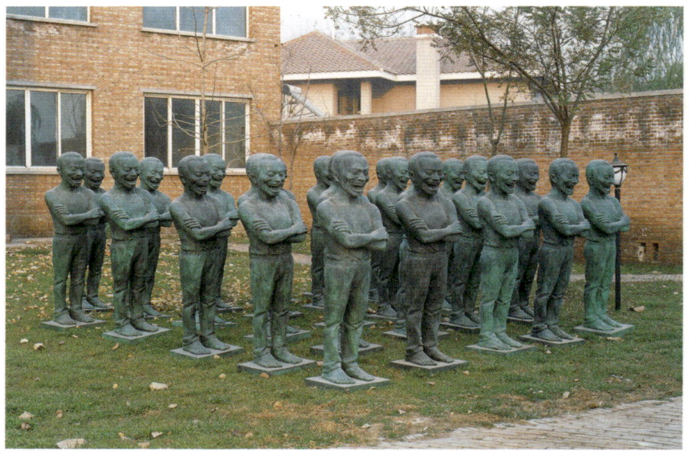

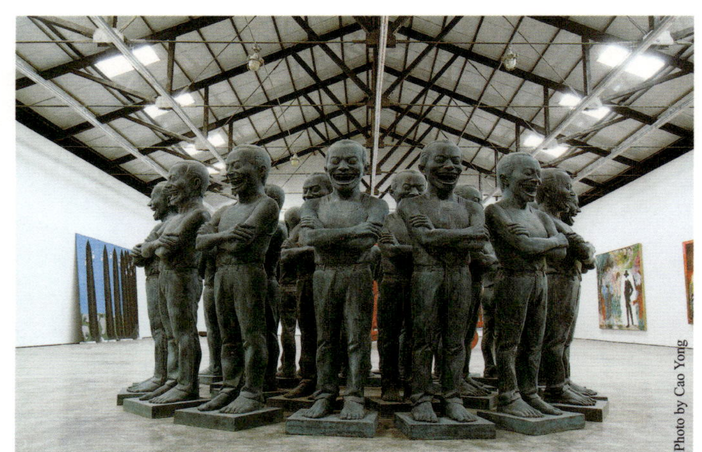

Photo by Cao Yong

1991年，我到北京看一個朋友，他住在圓明園附近一個合租的小院裏面。在那裏我很快就注意到了周邊的藝術家們，像楊少斌，他在我朋友的院子裏租了一間畫室，是他住的房間的一倍大。這正是我所想象的一個獨立藝術家的生活，一切看起來都那麽棒，所以我决定從河北搬過來。同我在單位的工作而言，做一個獨立藝術家看起來也没那麽難。租金很低，環境比單位好多了。最重要的是，我一下子就可以自己决定自己的生活，决定每天的日子怎麽過，甚至頭發留多長！

*

開始的時候，我嘗試了一些村裏其他藝術家的風格。這些藝術家也成爲了我作品中的主題。起初很難决定自己的風格，找到自己的感覺方向。直到我開始畫自己的時候，這種情况才開始改變。即使在那時，作品更多的是一種表達自己思想的形式，而不是關于我自己，但是笑容已經有了。那衹是在瞬間感情衝動之下邁出的第一步，但我感覺到這是我能繼續做下去的東西。

重要的轉折點是我的一張畫了一排人物的作品：排隊的形式在我們的社會生活中極爲常見。表現得遵規守據，然而通常缺乏確信的目標。就這樣，我選擇描繪同樣的人物，同樣的姿勢和特徵，來强調這種行列的愚蠢。以這樣的方式來運用同一形象使得他們具有卡通人物的觀感：嘲諷人性以講述一個特别的故事。我發現這種關于社會現實的故事要比具體人物的經歷更有力量，後者對于觀衆而言是無法識别的。由于卡通形象能够表達如此多的人性，而我也决定要用這種形象作爲主要内容，那麽爲什麽不創造一個我自己的卡通形象來演繹我想要講述的故事呢？就這樣，這個形象成爲了我作品的主題形象和標志，并隨之决定了我藝術的各個方面的發展。

同許多卡通形象一樣，這個形象的表情變化非常少。他所能够表達的東西的力量和魅力是人性的本質。由于這些形象的表現形式簡單而程式化，創作者令他們與這個世界互動的方式變得極爲重要。他們所處的環境，所演繹的故事的性質，必將强化我們對他們的理解態度，從而得到一個總體的概括。因而，每個系列作品的創作對我而言都像是寫一出劇本，或勾畫一個故事輪廓。靈感大多來自我自己的思維框架，情緒，或我所經歷的事件，還有我所觀察到的身邊的景象。所有這些事情都能够引發一系列的作品。此次展覽的很多作品都是關于帽子的主題。我對帽子所具意義的興趣來自雅典奥運會期間，贏得獎牌的運動員都會帶上橄欖頭冠。從而令我思考帽子對于身份，社會地位，以及國籍，種族的表述。對于個人而言，帽子要比其他任何東西更能表達人的個性：帽子的選擇從來都不是件可以馬虎的事情。帽子是我們對個人形象，風格的表達，提升有形物質部分在整體中的比例。因而，如果選擇帽子的過程决不是漫不經心的，那麽在我作品中，人物所佩戴的各種帽子的作用就是表述和强化他們各自不同的社會身份，以及圍繞帽子而衍生的支配社會政治規則的概念的荒誕。

Chinese Contemporary Warriors - 6
現代兵馬俑 -6
55 x 182 x 55cm x 25 pcs
2005
bronze
青銅

近來在西方頗受關注的功夫電影激發了此次展覽中另外一個系列作品的創作。我的女友告訴我，中國語言中關于功夫最早的名稱意思是“古典體操”。傳統上，功夫與戰鬥没什麽關系，而是一種體育舞蹈，優

own frame of mind, from moods, or incidents I have experienced. Then there are also scenes that I have observed unfolding around me. All of these things can inspire a series of paintings. Many of the works in this exhibition are about hats. My interest in the nature of hats was piqued at the time of the Olympics in Athens, where the ranking of medal winners was defined by a hat shaped like an olive. It made me think about how hats denote status, a social position, as well as those that signify nationality, or an ethnic group. For individuals, hats, more than any other accessory, are extensions of the wearer's personality: people never choose a hat lightly. A hat becomes an expression of what we perceive to be our look, our style, and that enhances our physical proportions. So if the process of choosing a hat is never casual, or random, the placing of various hats on the figures in my paintings points to their role in asserting and reinforcing social differentials, and the absurdity of the ideas that govern the socio-political protocol surrounding hats.

The flood of kungfu films that have recently received so much attention in the West inspired a second group of paintings in the exhibition. It was my girlfriend who pointed out that the original Chinese name for kungfu means 'classical gymnastic ballet'. Traditionally, this is less about fighting than about engaging in an athletic dance in which grace and agility determine the superior master, not the ability to demonstrate physical prowess and damage one's opponent. Many of the original moves were derived from observations of the motion and gestures of animals and birds, for whom such skills were applied to self-preservation, not conscious aggression. Through time this dance was reconfigured as a fighting art, primarily for reasons of self-preservation and survival, because it represented to the Chinese people a source of national strength and power. Today, against the pre-eminent power of the glamour of action films and on-screen violence, the essence of kungfu has been distorted. I decided to make a parody of the animal and bird postures that originally inspired the 'dance'. The contortions to which I subject the figures highlights how far the art has come from the innocence of its roots.

There are numerous other symbols and references in my work. One example is the painting titled *Within and Without the Great Wall*. During the Cultural Revolution, the title was given to many propaganda paintings. The message was that within and beyond the wall China was a vast and mighty land, which was a very political statement in terms of the national ideology. Yet at the same time, within China, the people's spirit of positivism and enthusiasm for the cause was subconsciously tinged with a sense of anxiety and stress. I am constantly drawn to explore polemic sensations like these.

To date I have painted so many laughing faces, but increasingly this feature is only as important as the story it tells. It is essential that an artist knows how to move forward with their work or how else does one makes progress? You paint a few paintings like this...a few like that...but then what do you do?

My style has definitely matured, yet the challenges remain: how to keep developing the motif, and keep up the supply of fresh stories for my figure to act out. In the early stage of his development, the element of political satire was definitely more pronounced in the paintings. Through time this has given way to broader responses to the social situations and conundrums of today: to my attitude towards society, and the culture of the times. In the 1990s, society was not so open. Today we are overwhelmed with information. We can't hold on to the simple perceptions we started out with. Today the onus is on exploring new ground, with new ideas and new philosophies that push each generation into new territory. But what is most rewarding is that through the process of that search, new stories are always just around the corner.

(Translated and edited by Karen Smith)

1. New art was the name given to the thrust of the avant-garde movement, where "new" contrasted the "old" that had been erected by Mao Zedong in the form of Socialist Realism.
2. "China / Avant Garde" is the more commonly used translation in English.
3. Maitreya, the Buddha of the Future, who will appear at a time when the Buddhist teachings have been lost, in order to reestablish the Dharma. There is another legend in Buddhism concerning a bonze sculpture from the Five Dynasties period known as Hip-Pocket Bonze (bu dai he shang), but who called himself Chang Dingzi. He always carried a hip pocket to beg alms, so he was believed to carry the riches of the world in his pocket. He is said to be the reincarnation of the Maitreya Buddha.
4. A Chinese-styled Communist-inspired work unit
5. Shiyou Xueyuan

雅和敏捷是決定舞蹈者技藝高低的因素，而不是迸發力量和摧毀對手的能力。最初很多步法的編排來自對鳥獸的動作和姿勢的觀察和模仿，而鳥獸的這些動作姿勢都是用于自衛，而不是進攻。隨着時間的變化，舞蹈演變成了打鬥的藝術，首先是出于自衛和生存的原因，因爲它是中華民族的力量源泉之一。今天，功夫的本質已經被功夫片和影視暴力所扭曲。我決定模仿激發最早的功夫舞蹈的鳥獸姿勢創作一系列作品，人物的扭曲强調着這種藝術背離其單純的起源已經有多麼遥遠。

我的作品中還有很多其他的符號和象徵，援引一例，比如這張《長城内外》。文革期間，很多宣傳畫的主題都是“長城内外”。意思是長城内外，都是我中華無垠疆土，這是國家理想主義的極爲政治性的表述。同時，在中國内部，人民的樂觀主義精神和愛國主義激情帶着一種潛在的焦慮和壓力。我經常會表現這一類的争論性主題。

回頭看看，我已經畫了這麼多的大笑面孔，而漸漸的，這個形象已經和其所叙述的故事一樣重要。一個藝術家應該知道如何繼續發展他的作品，或者如何通過其他途徑取得發展，這是非常重要的。你畫些這個...再畫些那個...然後該做什麼呢？

我認爲，我的風格現在已經成熟，然而挑戰依然存在：如何繼續發展這一主題，如何爲我的主題形象提供新鮮的故事來表現。在他早期的發展過程中，政治諷刺的元素是畫中的重點。隨着時間的推移，讓位給更廣義的，對當今社會狀況和問題的反饋，即我對社會，對當前文化的態度。90年代，社會還不太開放，今天，我們被信息淹没。因此，我們不能再固步自封，停留在最初的簡單認知之上。今天的任務是要用推動了每一代人進入新領域的新思想和新哲學，探索開發新的領域空間。而最有價值的事情是，在這種探索的道路上，新的故事永遠都會在拐彎處出現。

---

1. 新藝術是對前衛運動的稱呼，與新相對的舊是指毛澤東時代的社會主義現實主義。
2. “中國前衛藝術展”是最爲普遍的英文翻譯。
3. 彌勒，即未來佛，出現在佛教衰落的時代，旨在重建達摩。五代時期有一尊布袋和尚（自號長定子）的銅佛像，相傳他總是背着一個布袋到處化緣，世間財富皆在袋中。這個布袋和尚據説就是彌勒轉世。
4. 單位，是中國式的，共産主義精神管理下的工作環境。

PLATES * 圖版

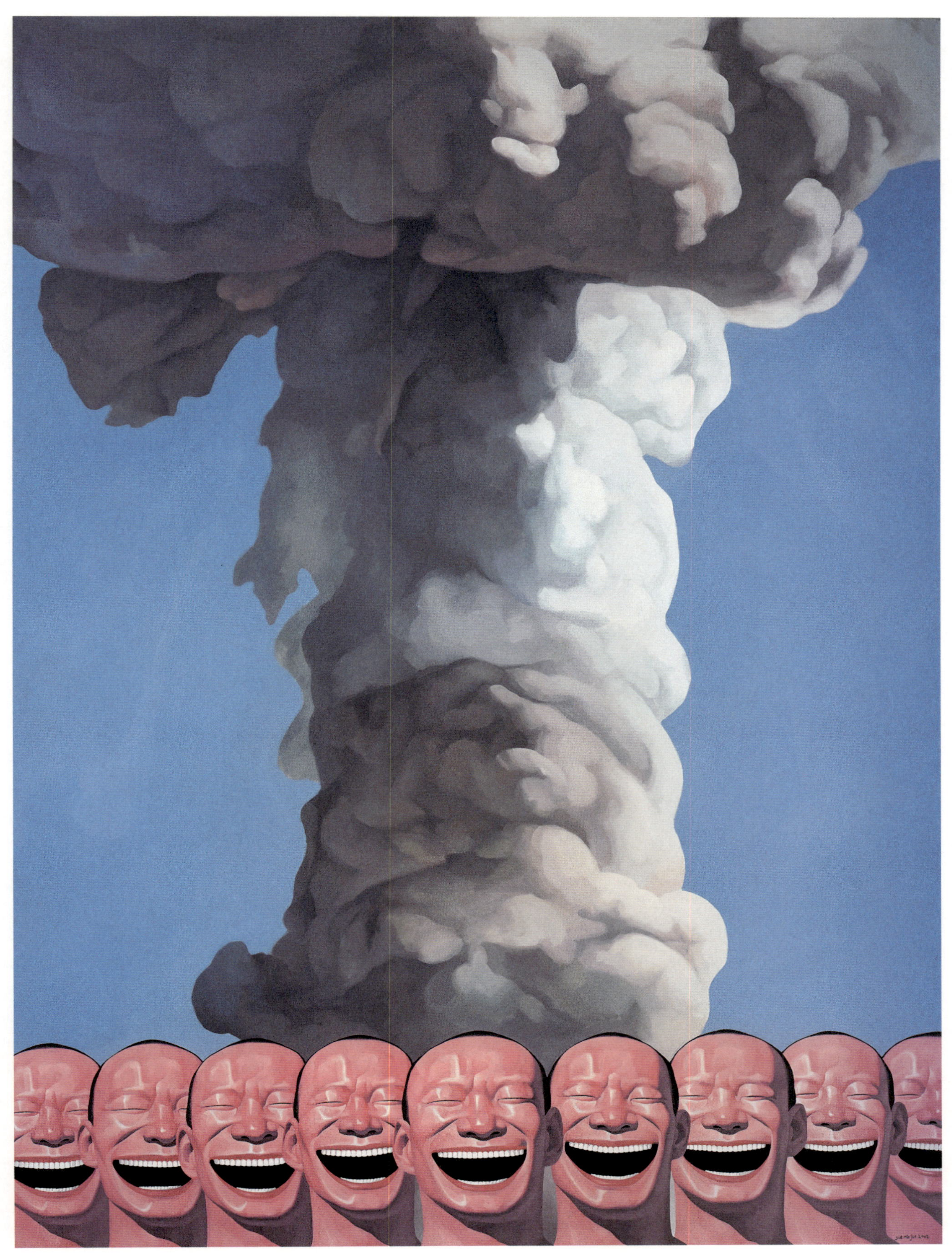

Mushroom Cloud * 蘑菇雲 * 300 x 220cm * 2002 * acrylic on canvas * 畫布丙烯

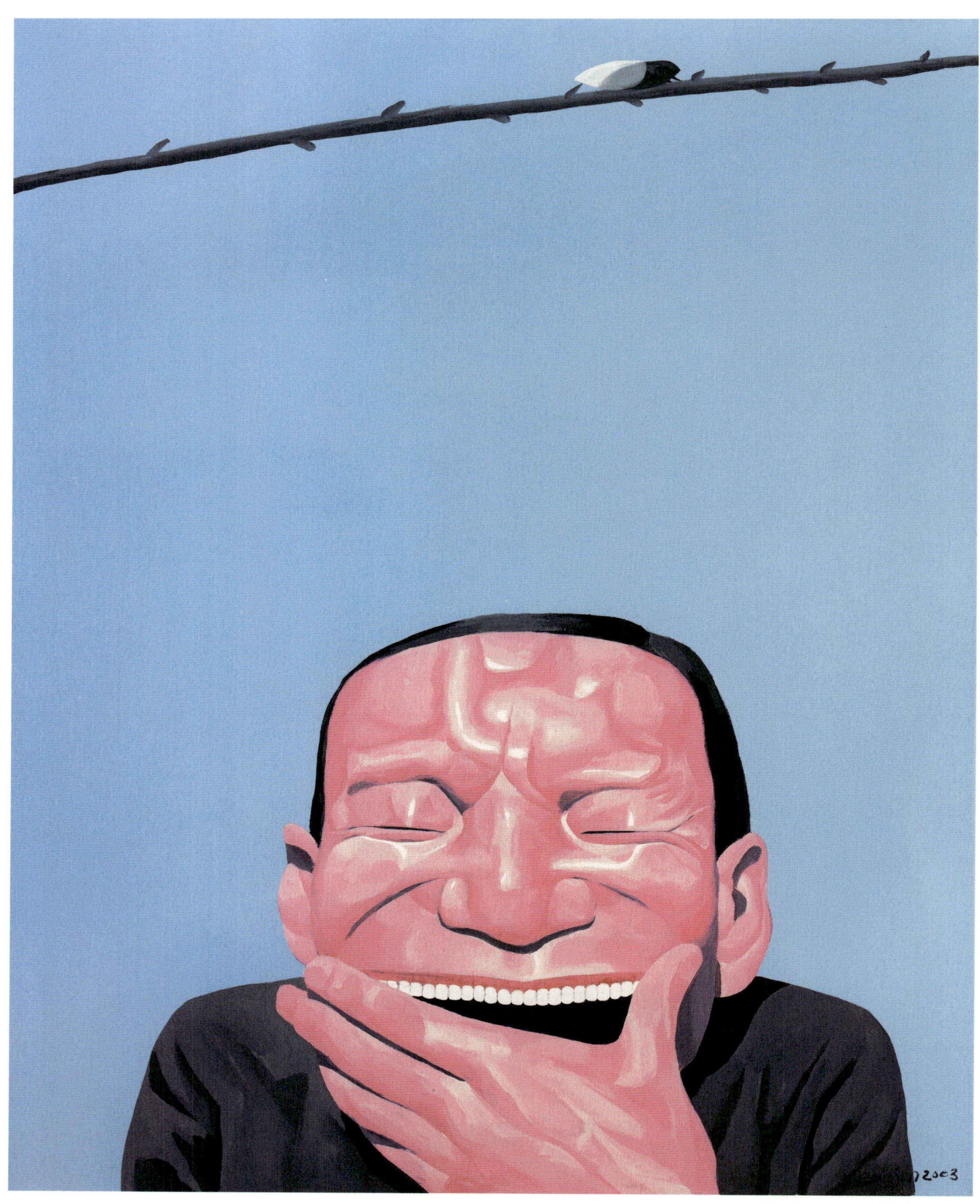

Musician * 音樂家 * 100 x 80cm * 2003 * oil on canvas * 布上油畫

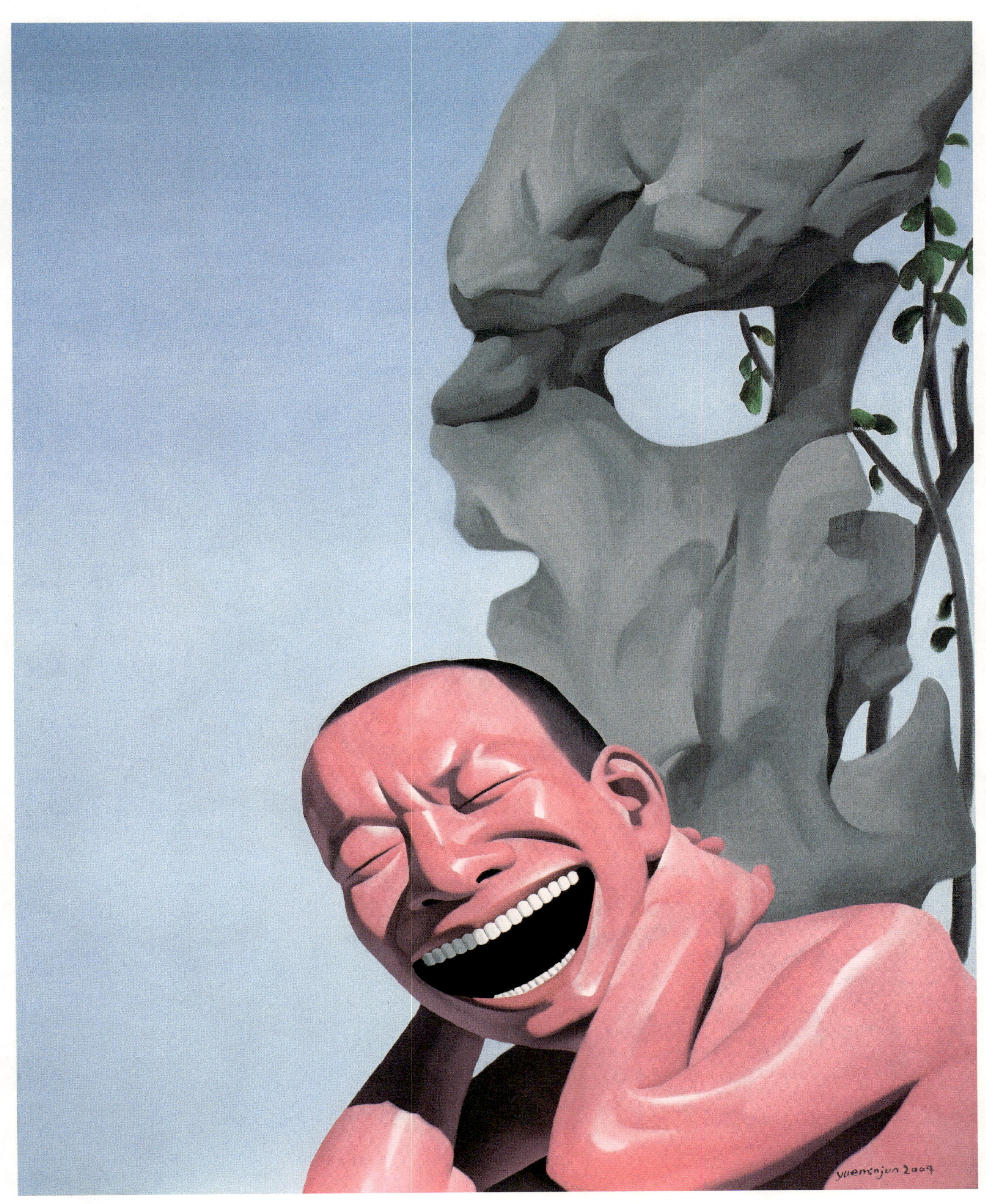

Taihu Lake Rockery * 太湖石 * 100 x 80cm * 2004 * oil on canvas * 布上油畫

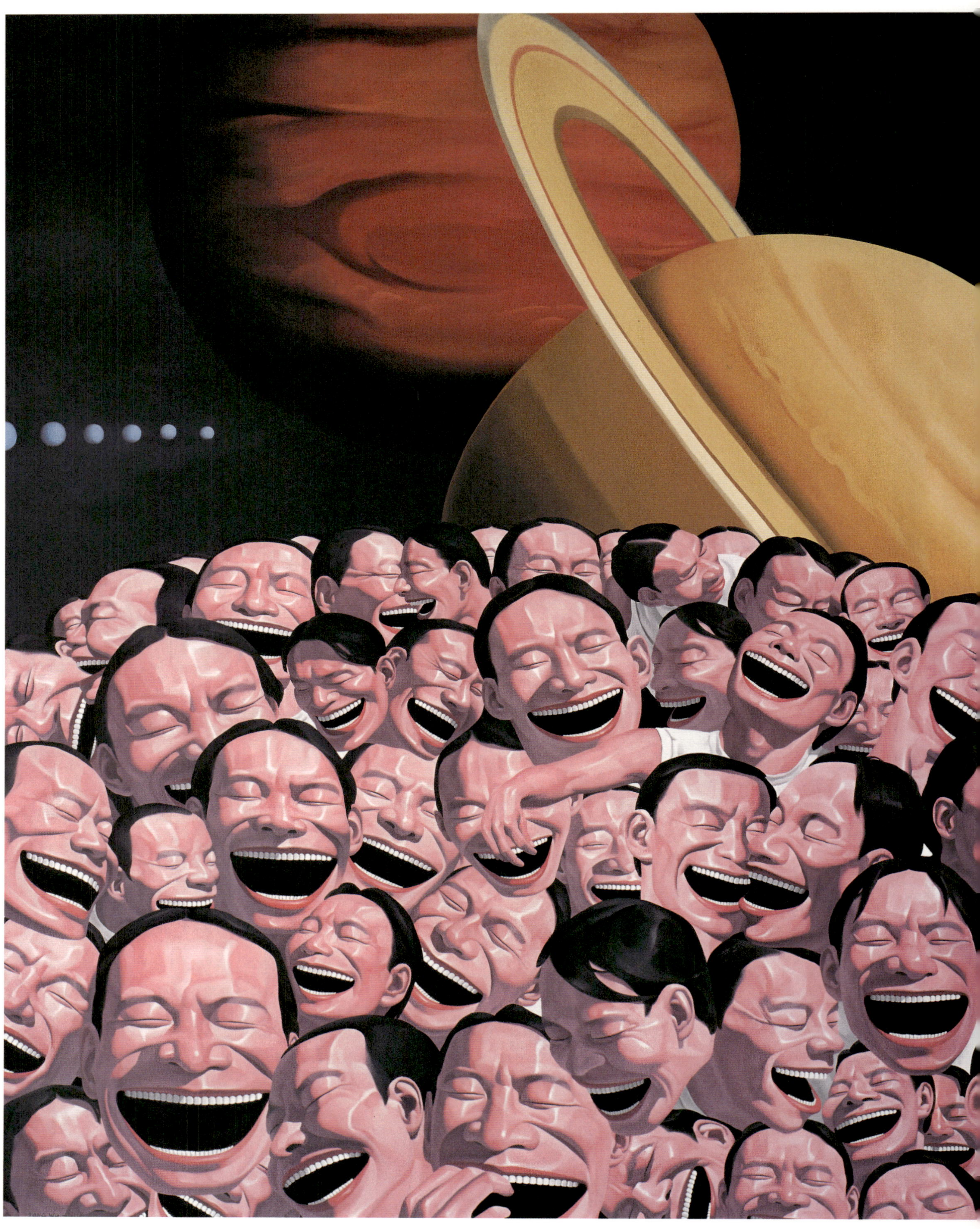

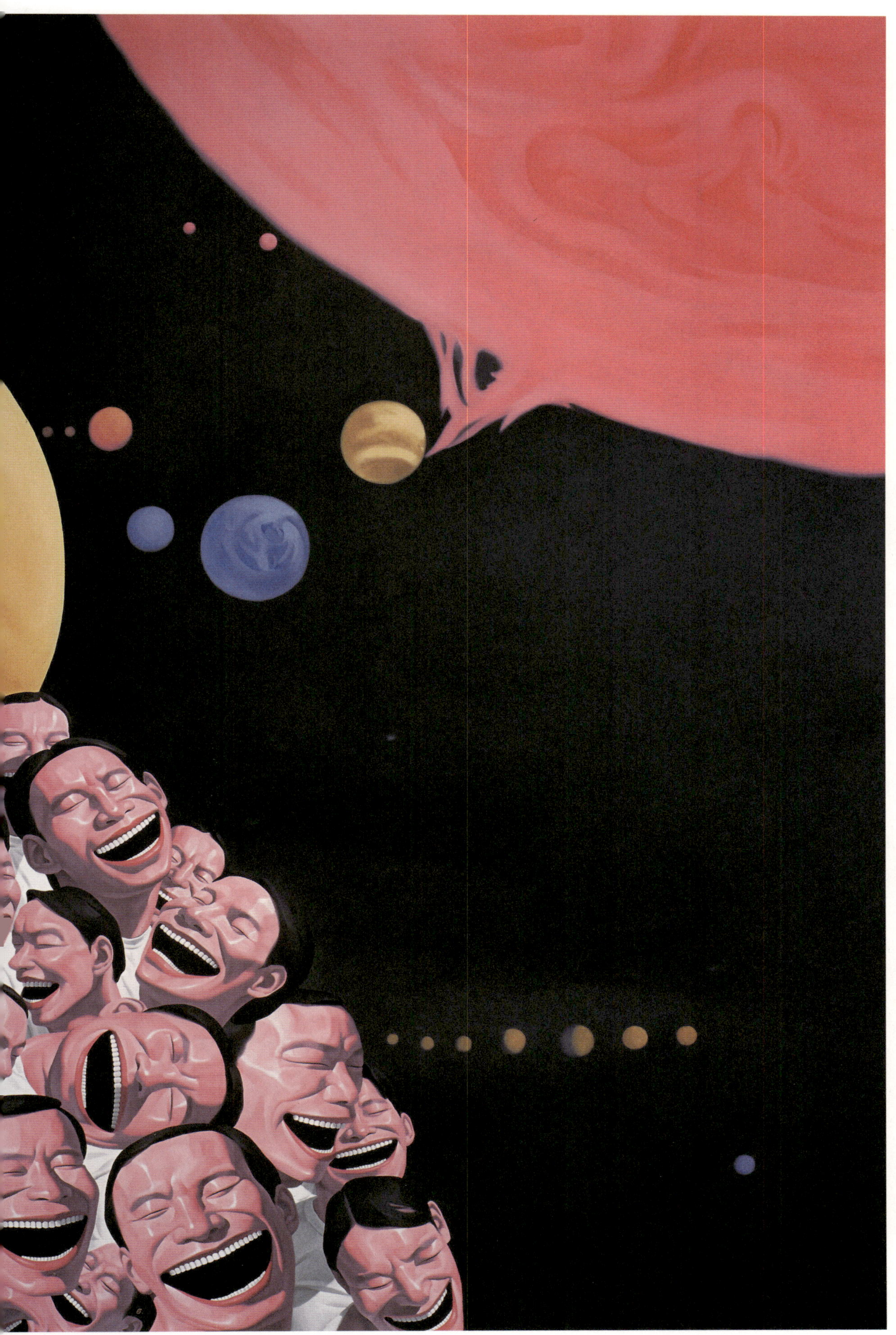

Starry Night *
星空 *
300 x 220cm *
2004 *
oil on canvas *
布上油畫

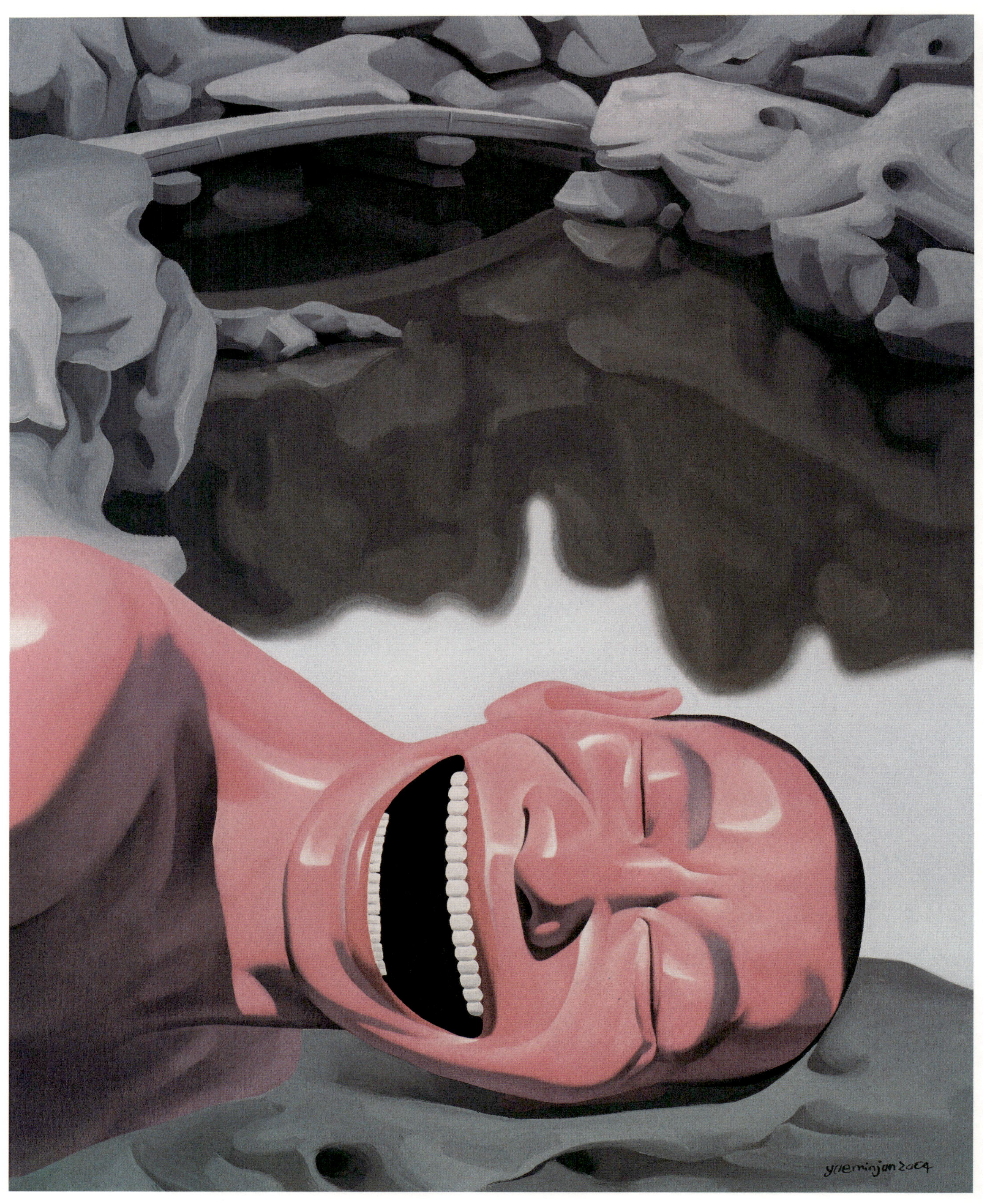

Garden * 園林 * 100 x 80cm * 2004 * oil on canvas * 布上油畫

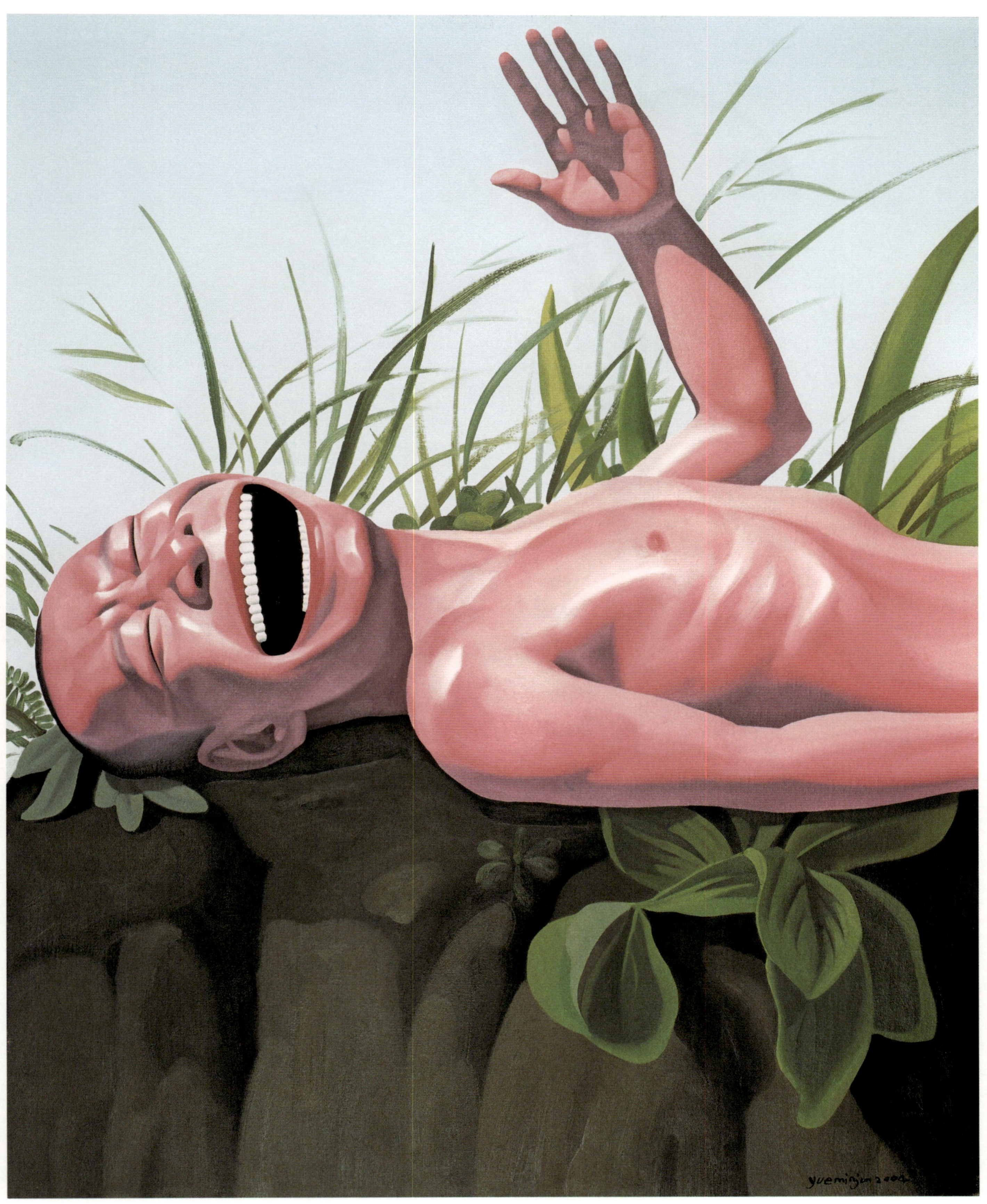

Hero Here * 英雄到了 * 100 x 80cm * 2004 * oil on canvas * 布上油畫

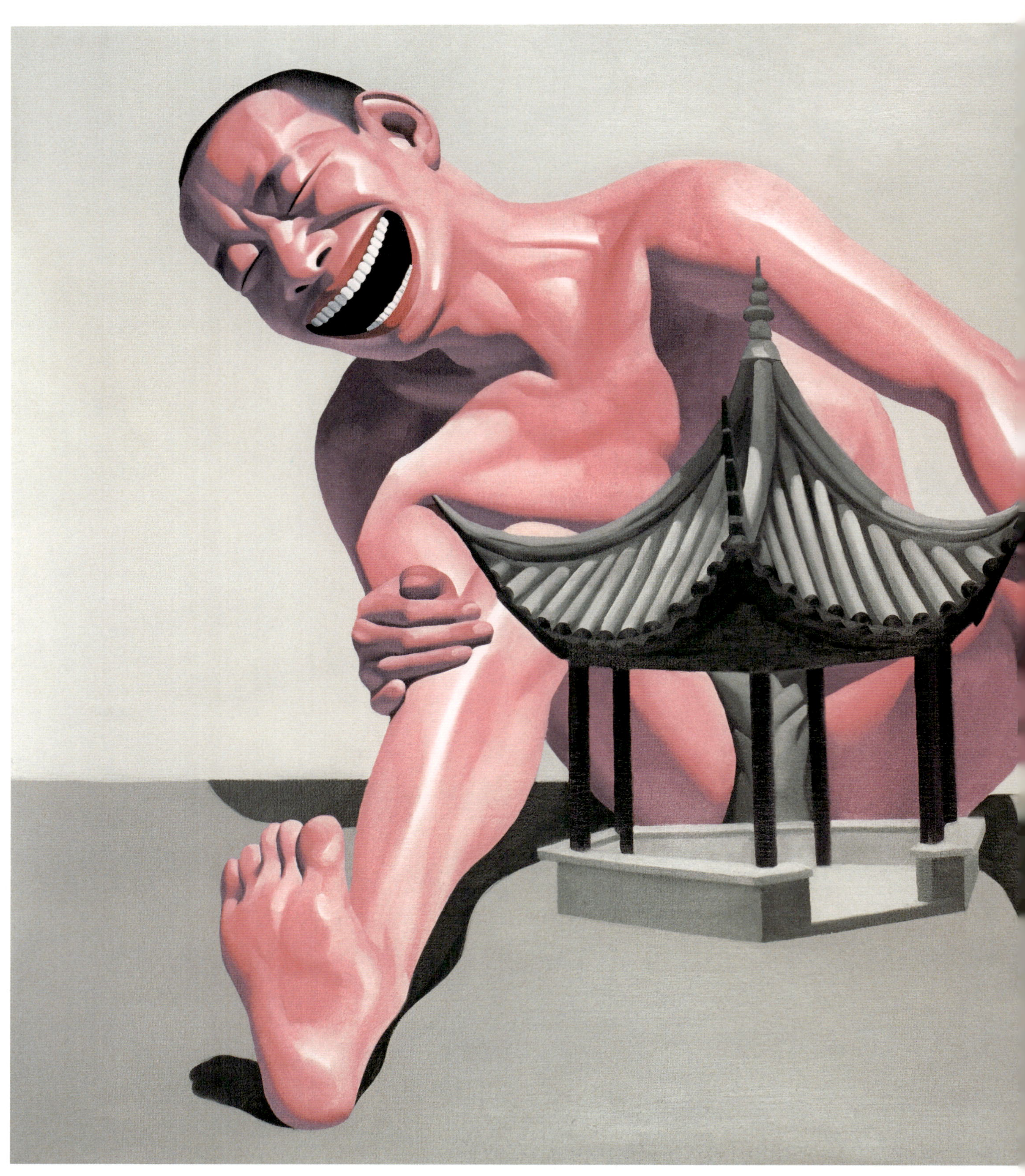

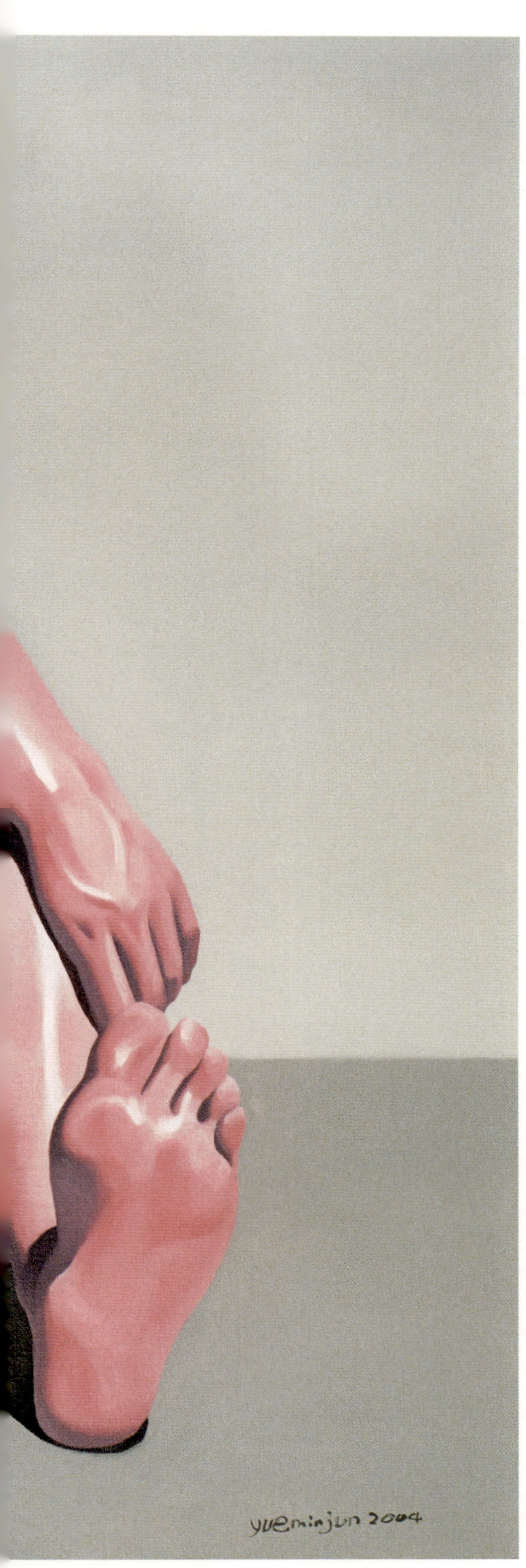

Chinese Pavilion *
中國亭子 *
100 x 80cm *
2004 *
oil on canvas *
布上油畫

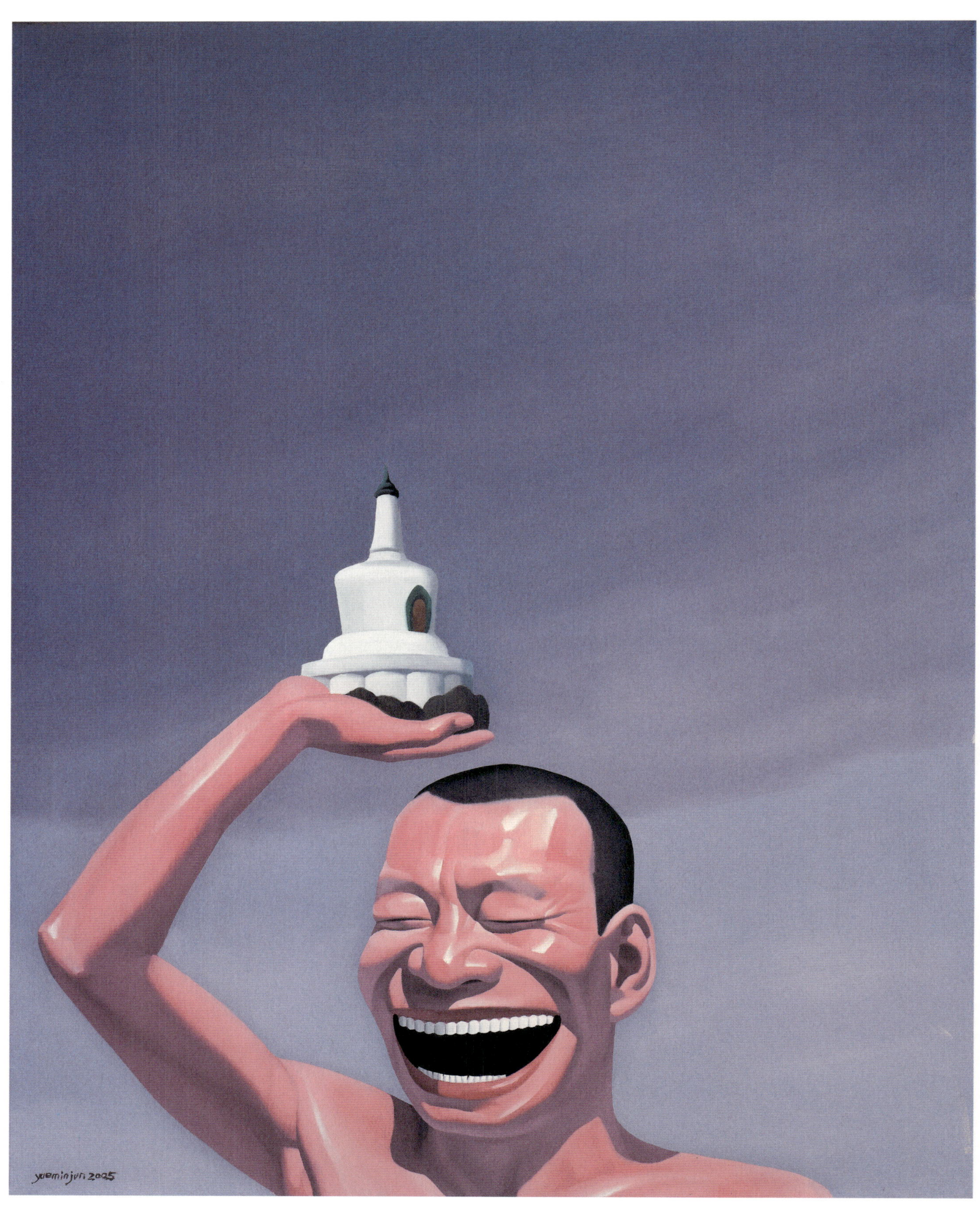

The North Sea * 北海 * 100 x 80cm * 2005 * oil on canvas * 布上油畫

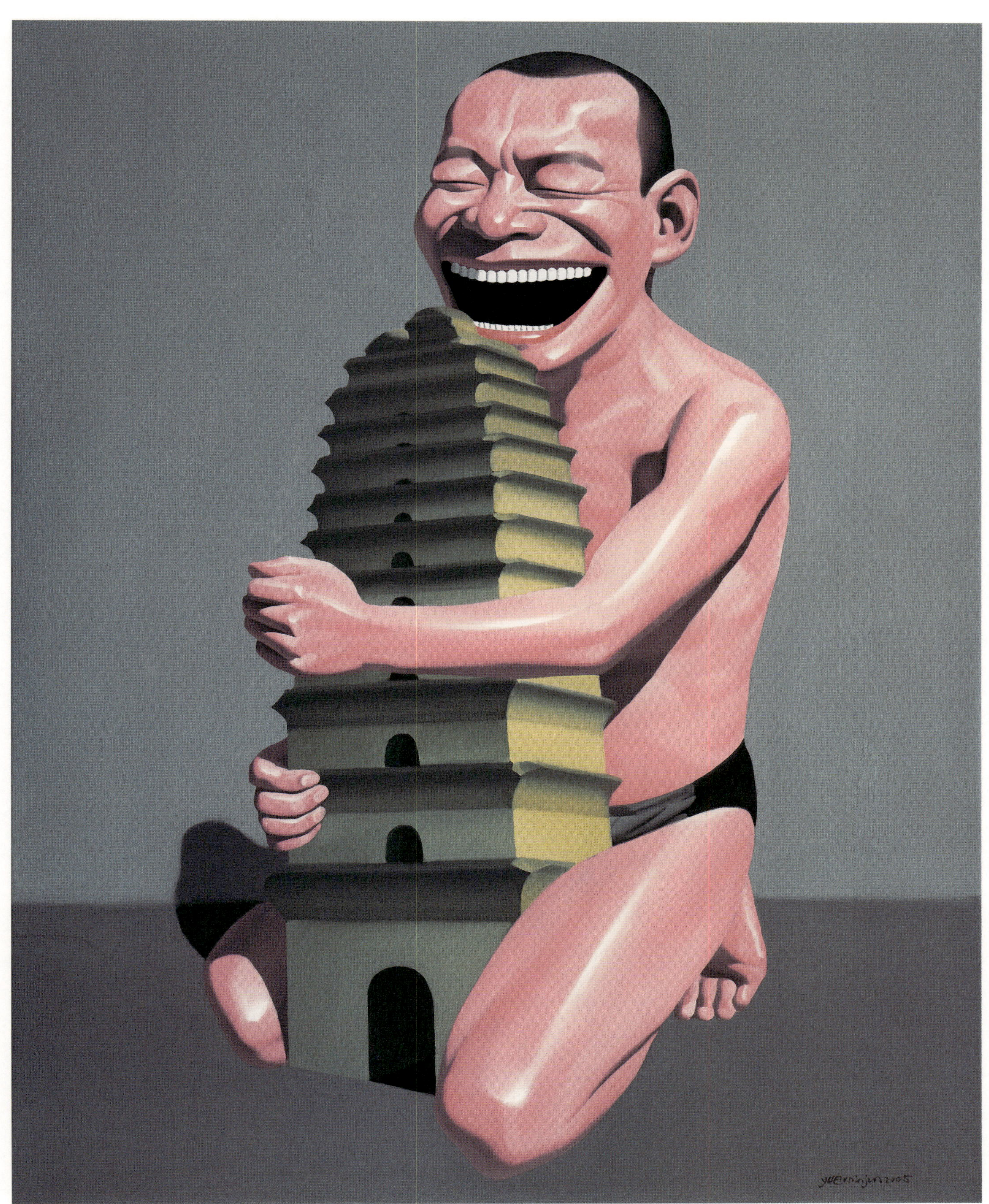

Big Wild Goose Pagoda * 大雁塔 * 100 x 80cm * 2005 * oil on canvas * 布上油畫

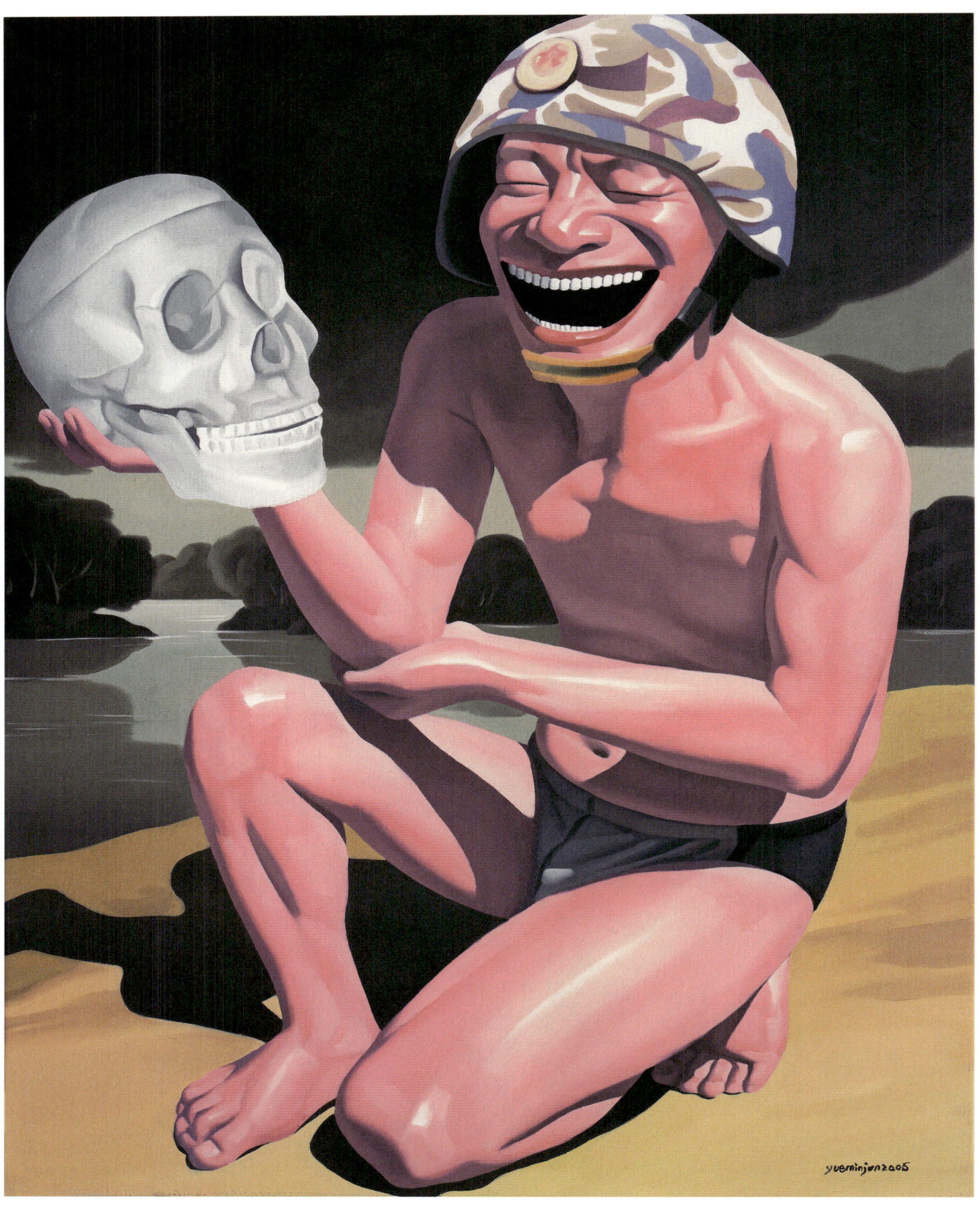

Archeologist * 考古 * 100 x 80cm * 2005 * oil on canvas * 布上油畫

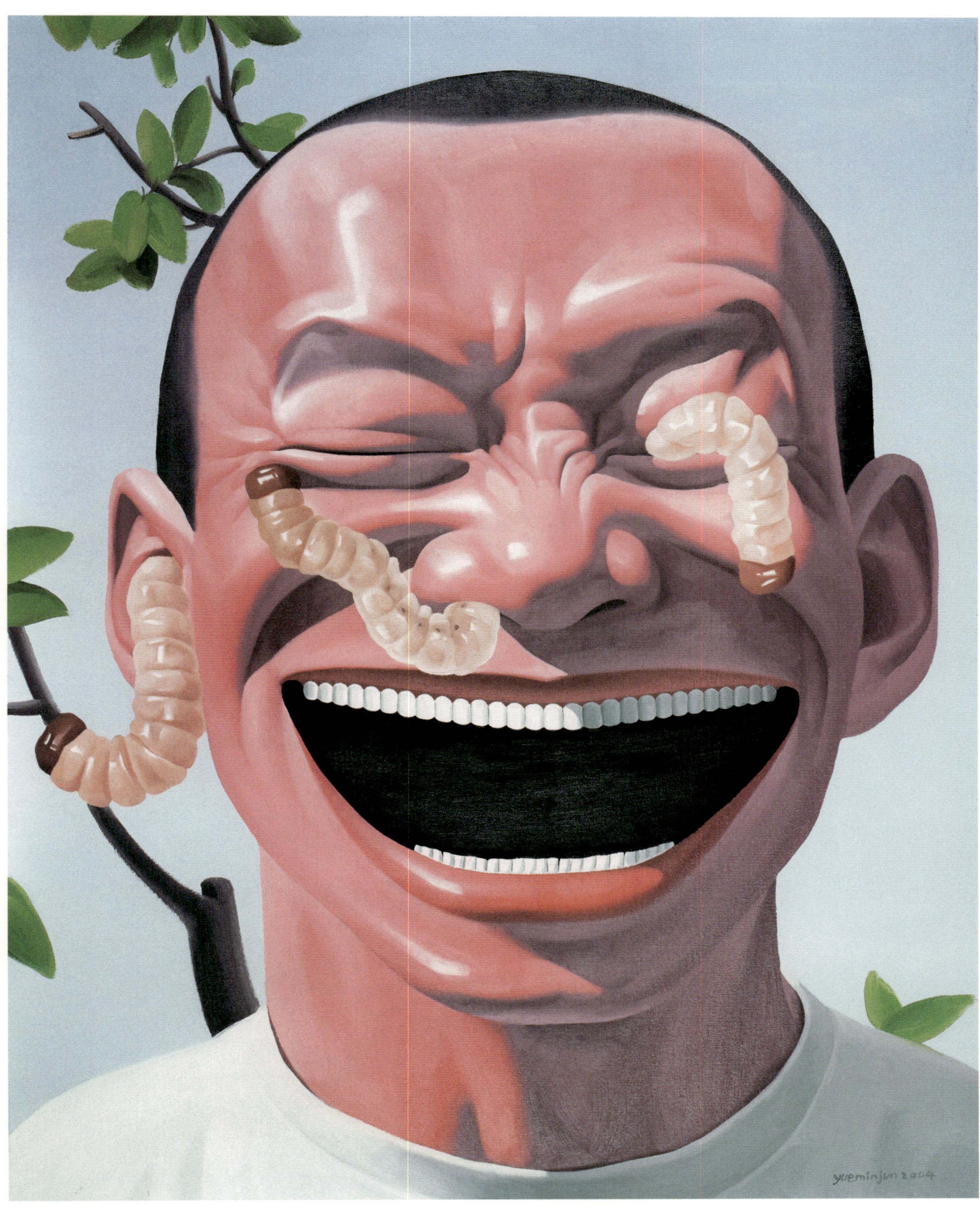

Dragon * 龍 * 100 x 80cm * 2005 * oil on canvas * 布上油畫

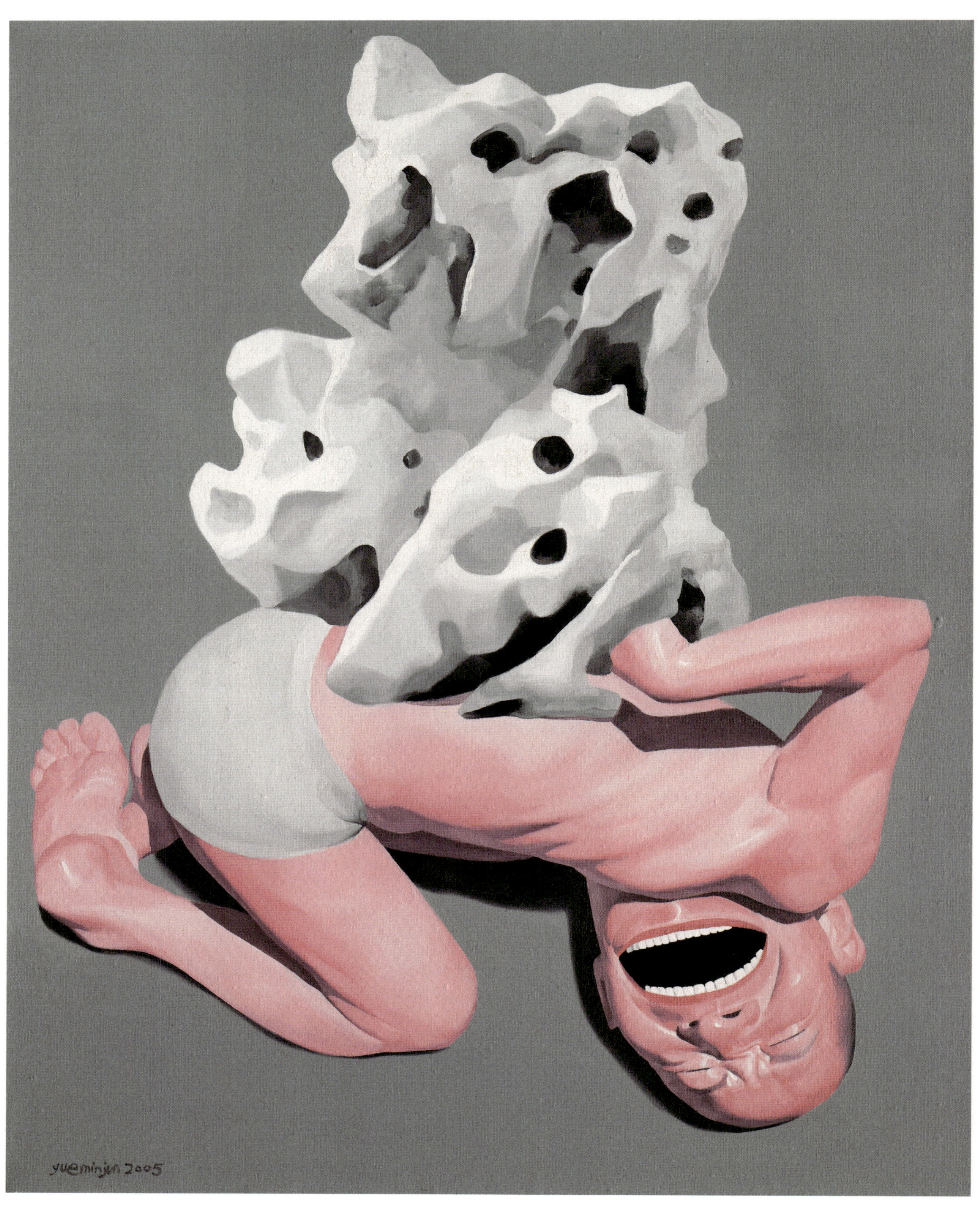

Chinese Stone * 中華奇石 * 100 x 80cm * 2005 * oil on canvas * 布上油畫

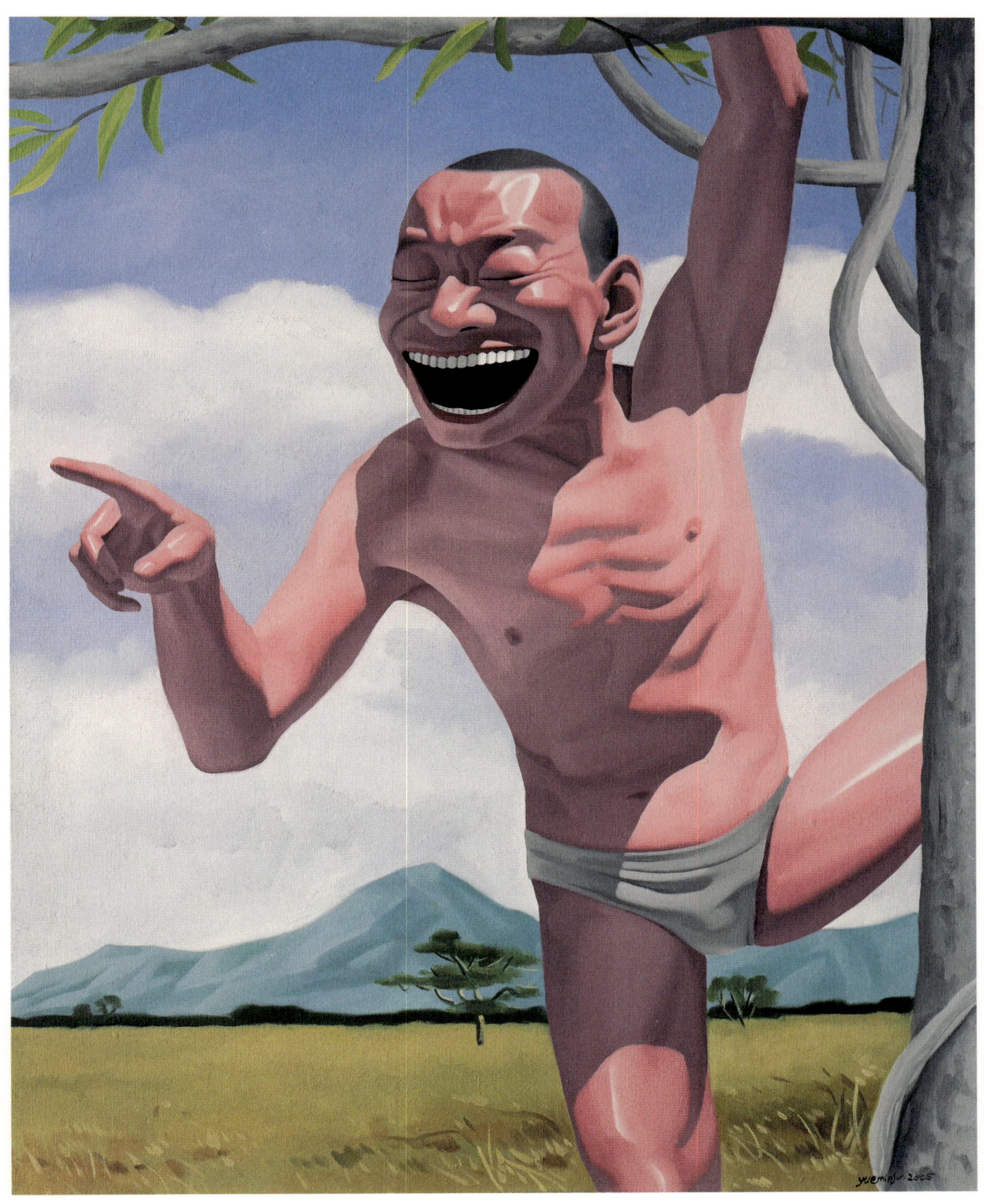

Untitled * 無題 * 100 x 80cm * 2005 * oil on canvas * 布上油畫

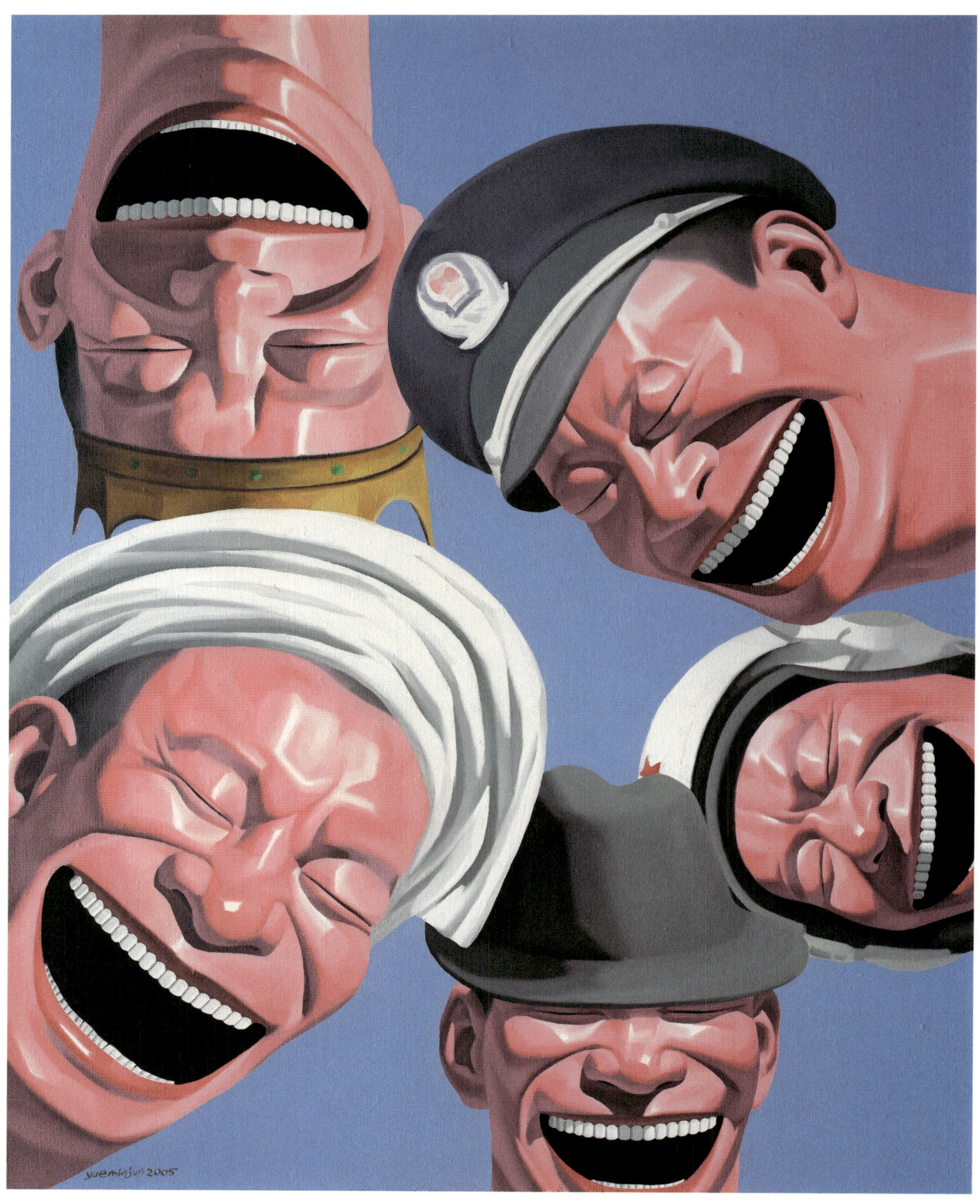

Untitled * 無題 * 100 x 80cm * 2005 * oil on canvas * 布上油畫

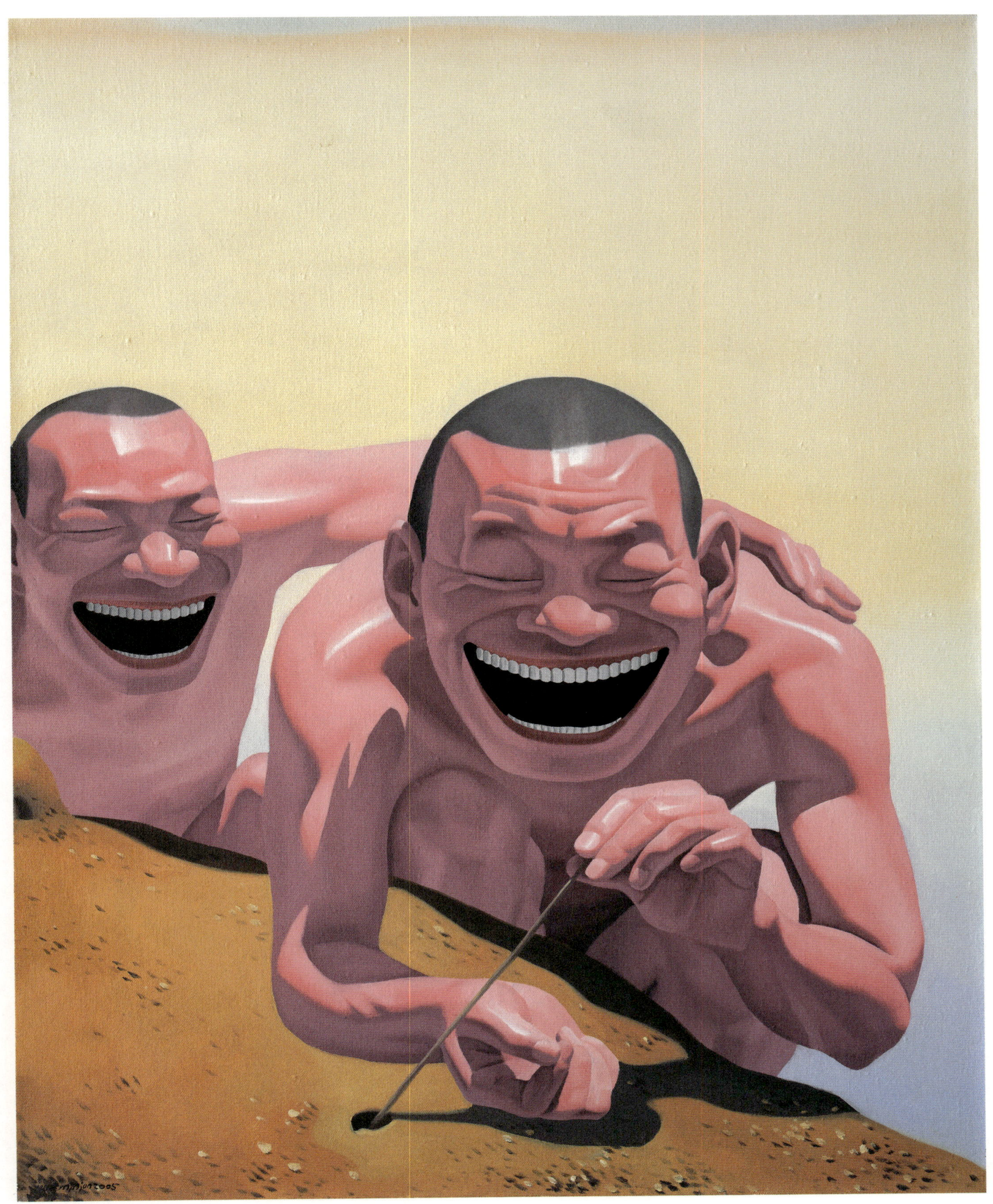

Untitled * 無題 * 100 x 80cm * 2005 * oil on canvas * 布上油畫

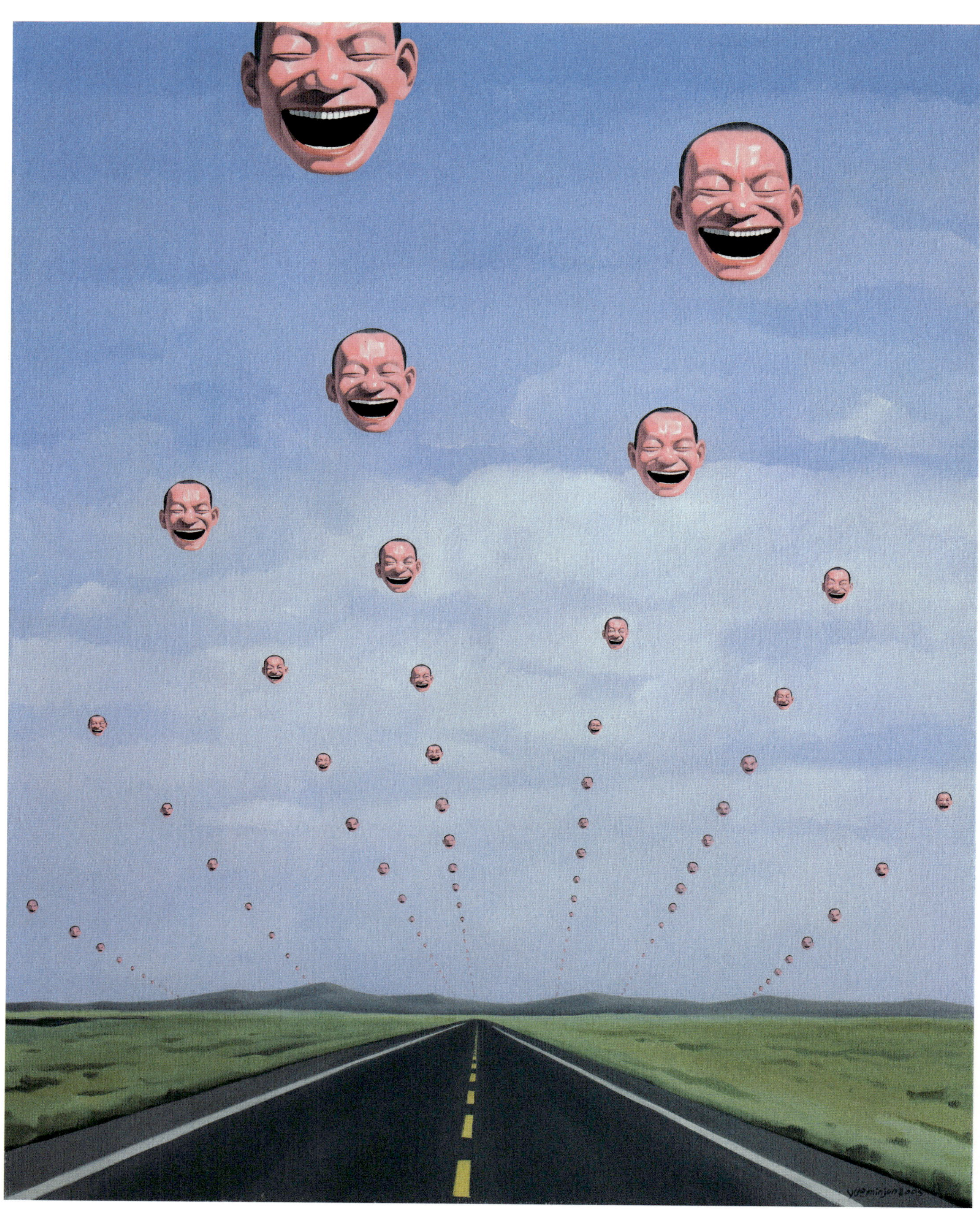

Untitled * 無題 * 100 x 80cm * 2005 * oil on canvas * 布上油畫

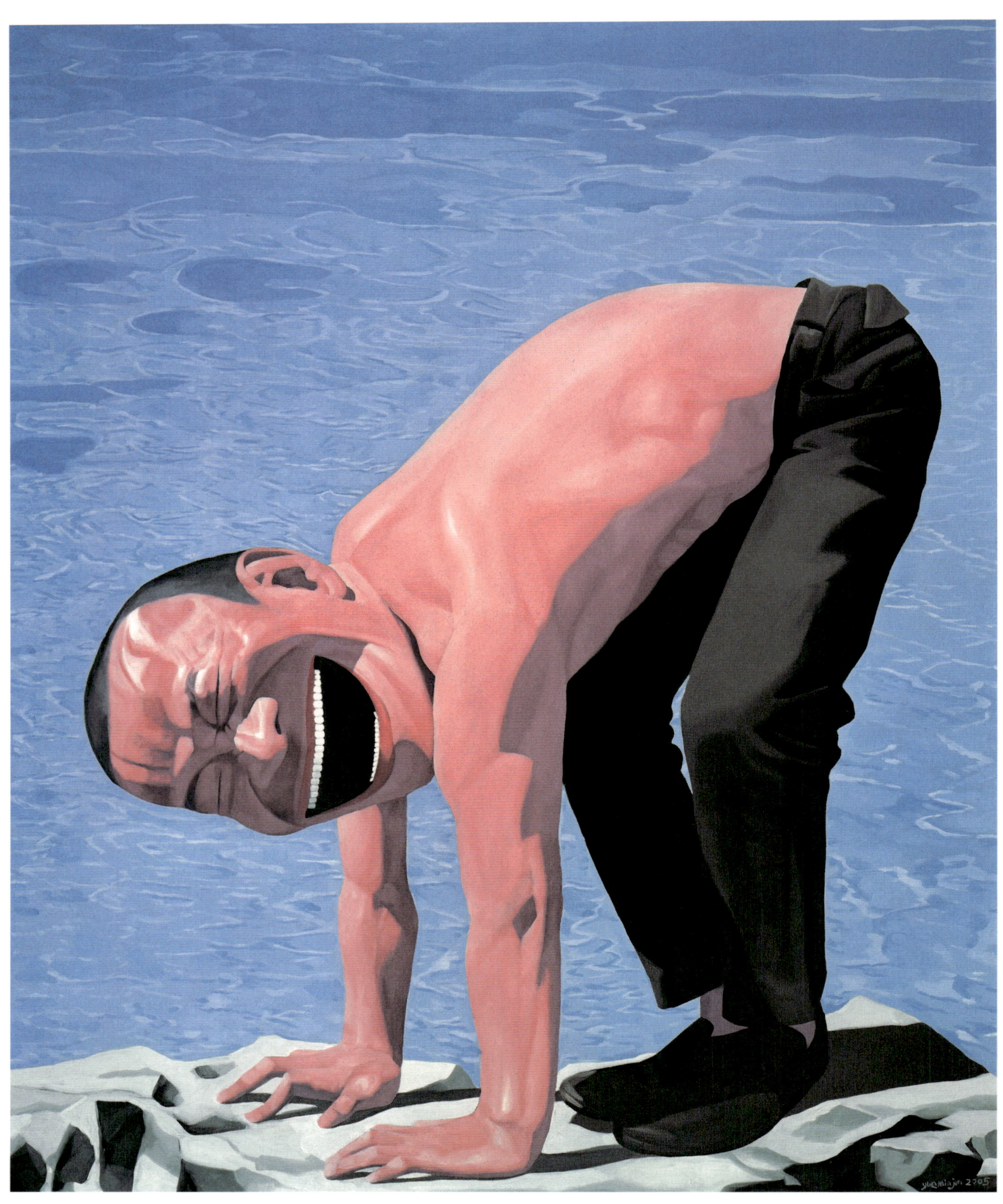

Backyard Garden * 後花園 * 170 x 140cm * 2005 * oil on canvas * 布上油畫

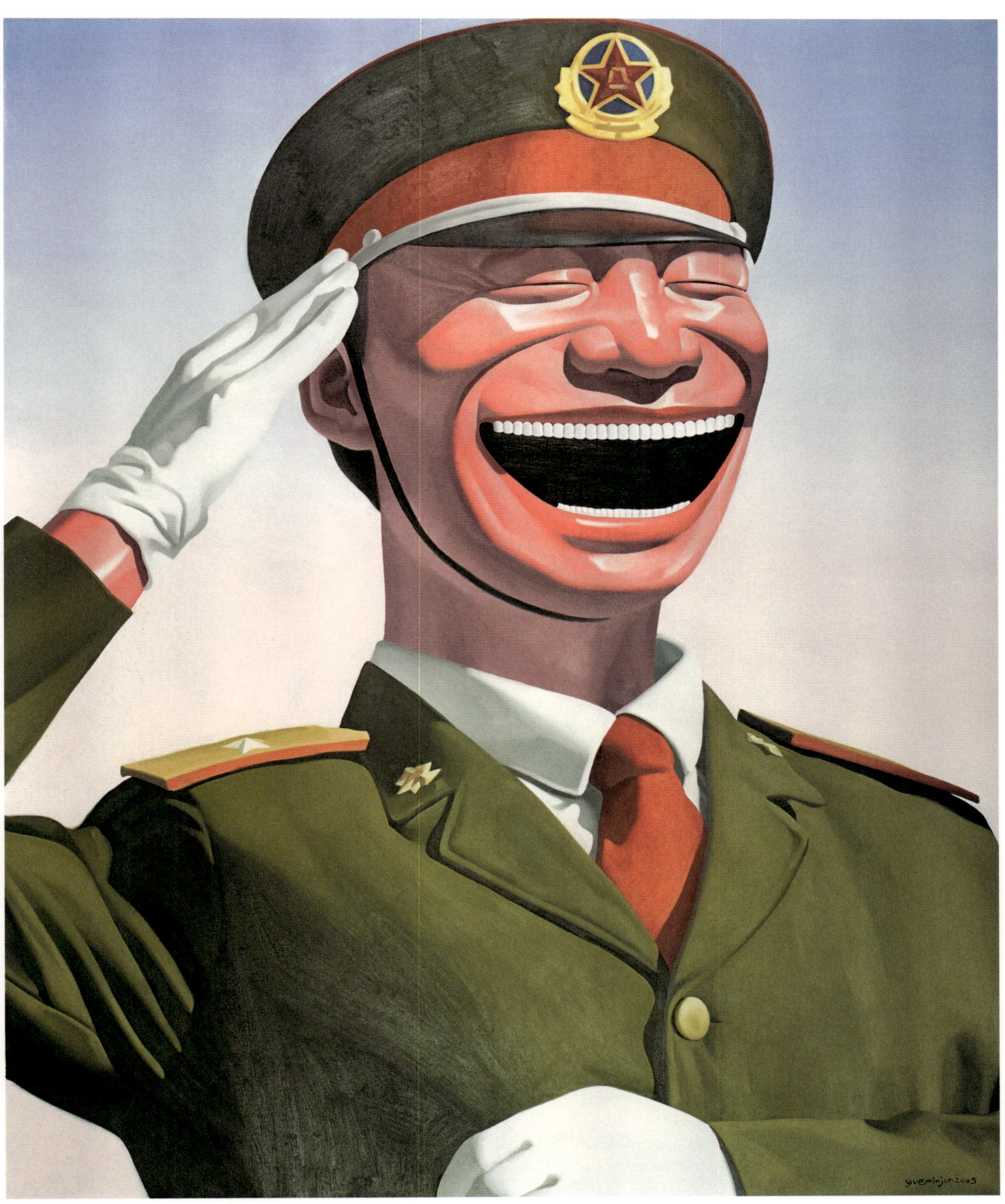

Salute * 敬禮 * 170 x 140cm * 2005 * oil on canvas * 布上油畫

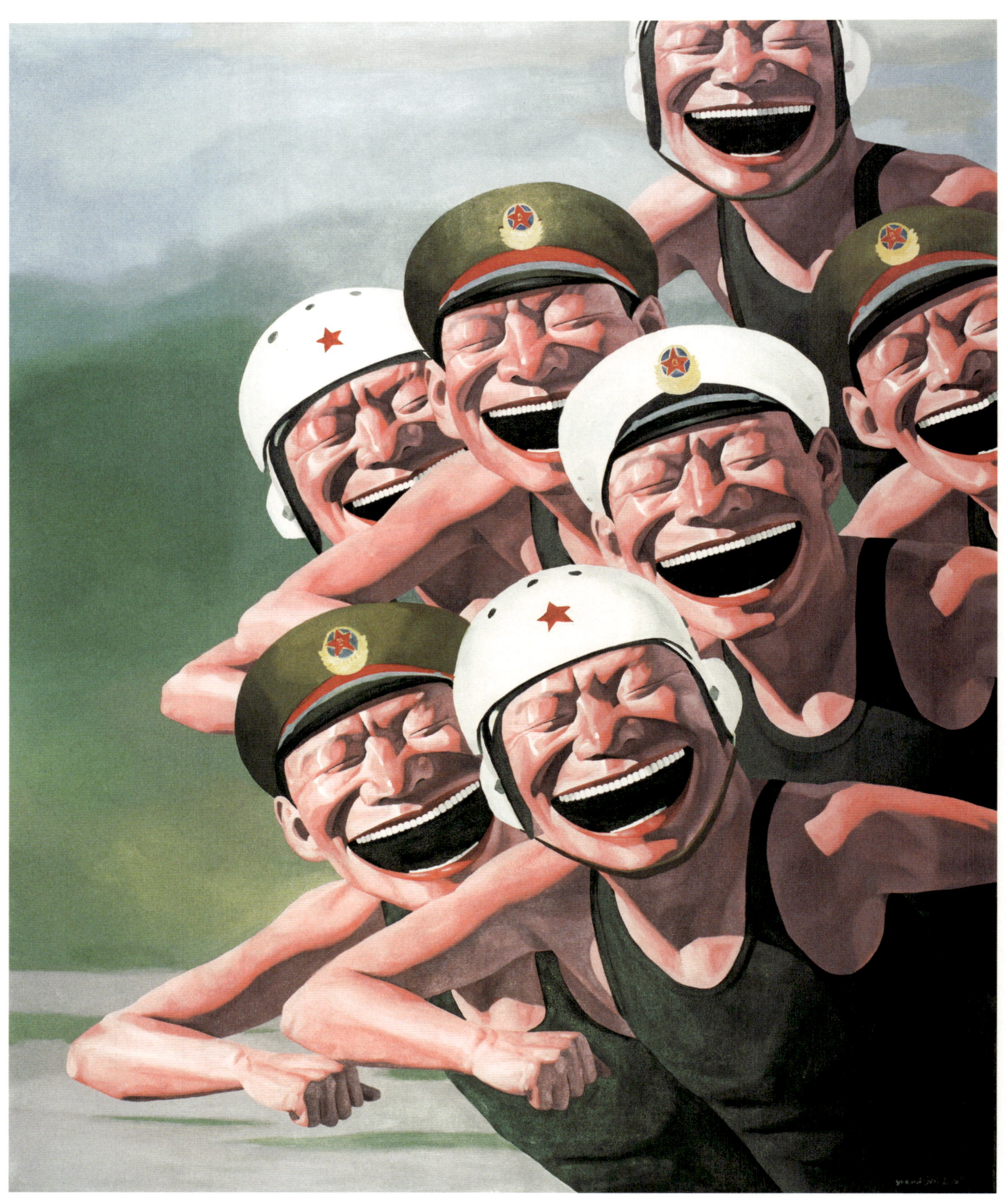

Armed Forces * 陸海空 * 170 x 140cm * 2005 * oil on canvas * 布上油畫

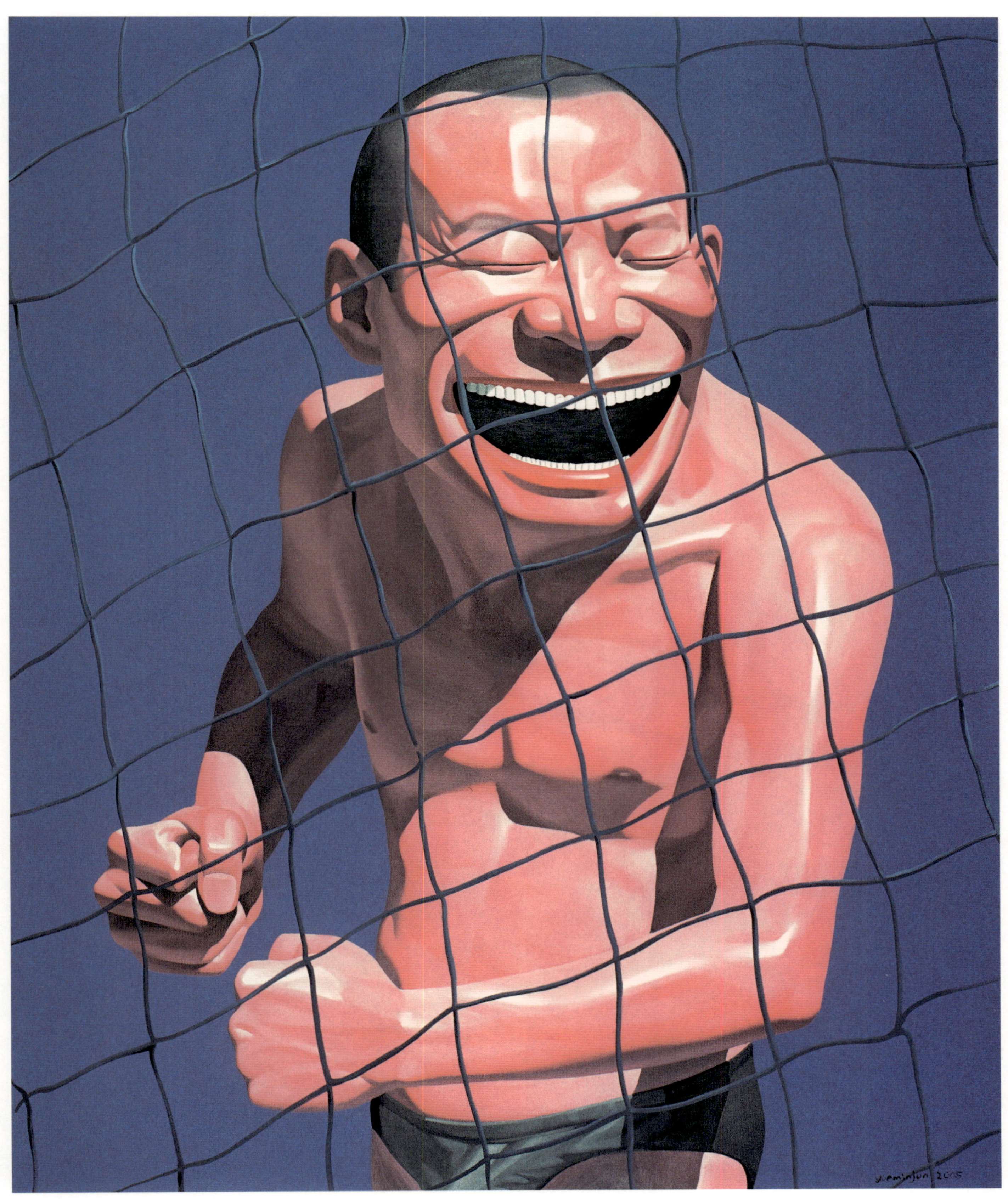

Fists * 拳頭 * 170 x 140cm * 2005 * oil on canvas * 布上油畫

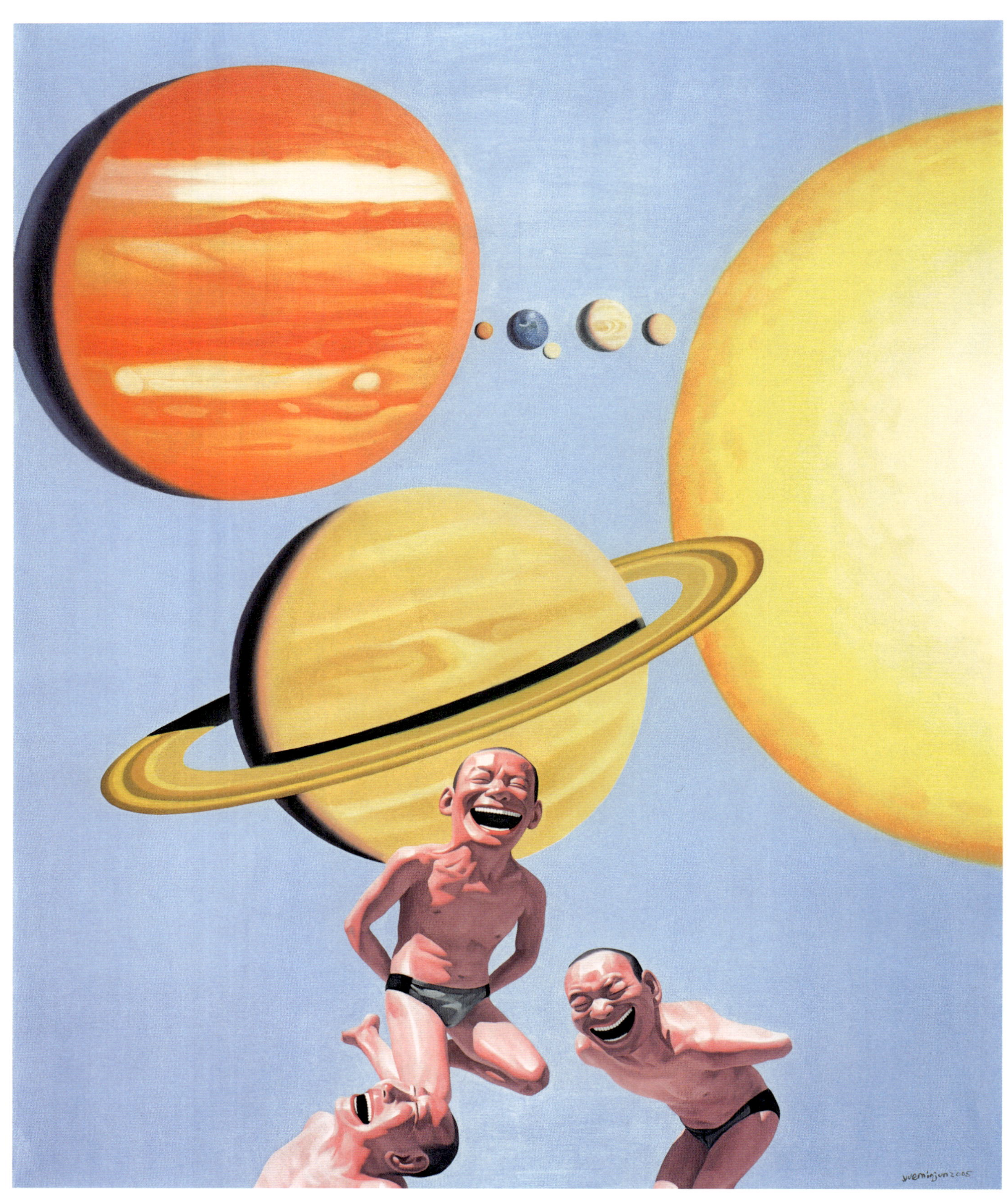

Solar System * 太陽系 * 170 x 140cm * 2005 * oil on canvas * 布上油畫

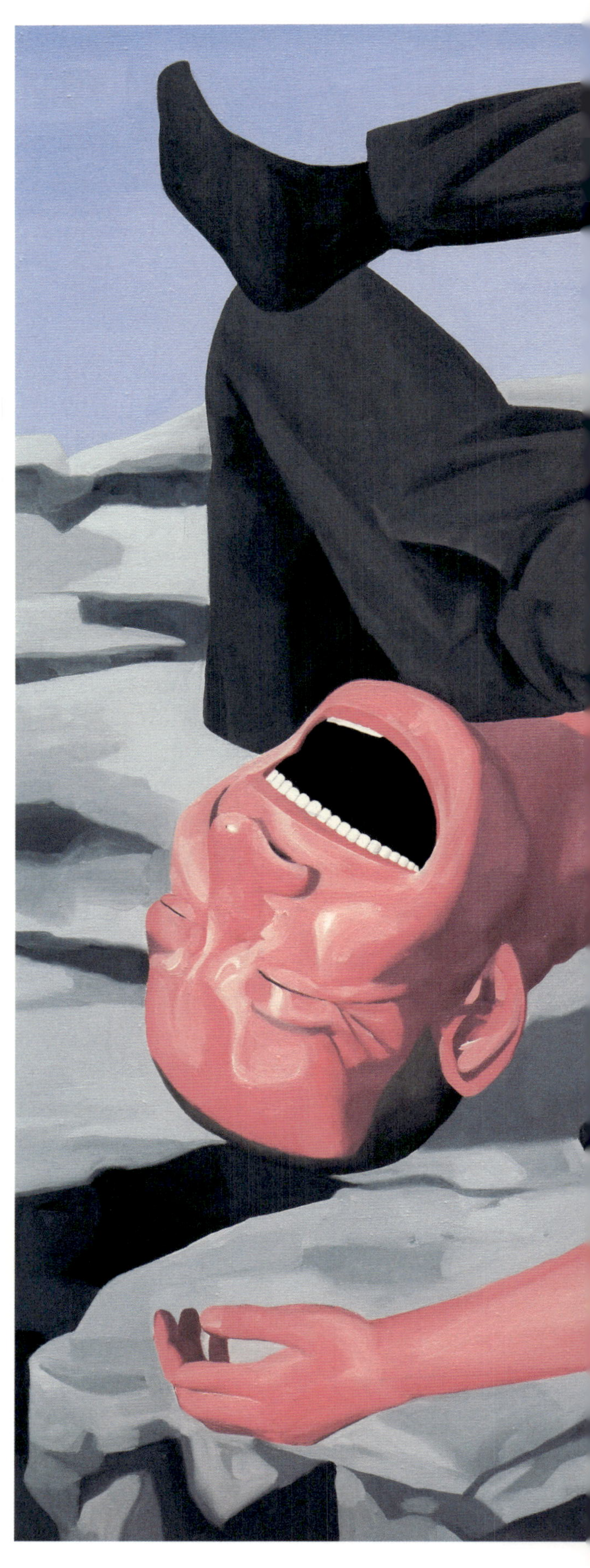

Untitled * 無題 * 140 x 170cm * 2005 * oil on canvas * 布上油畫

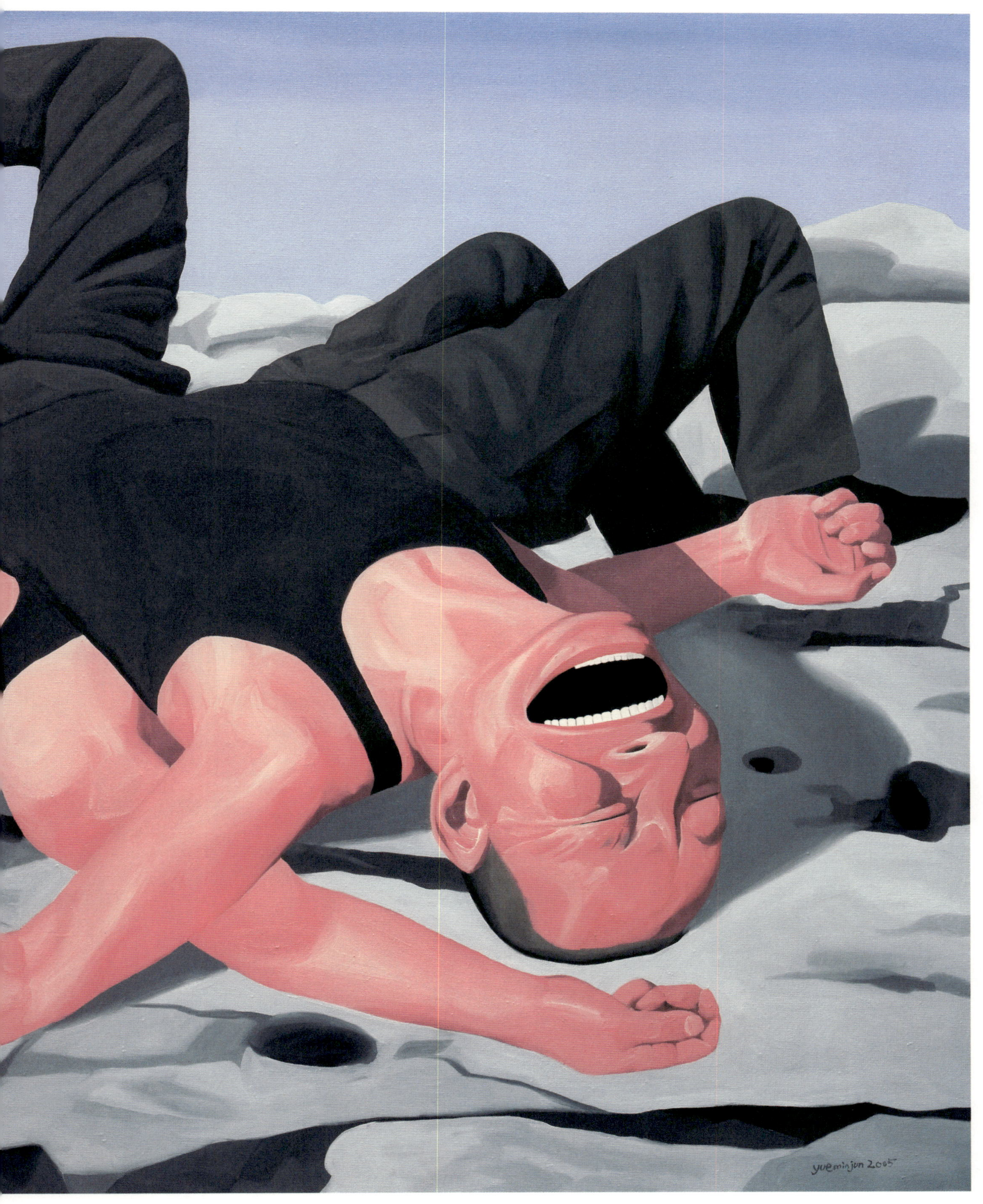
yueminjun 2005

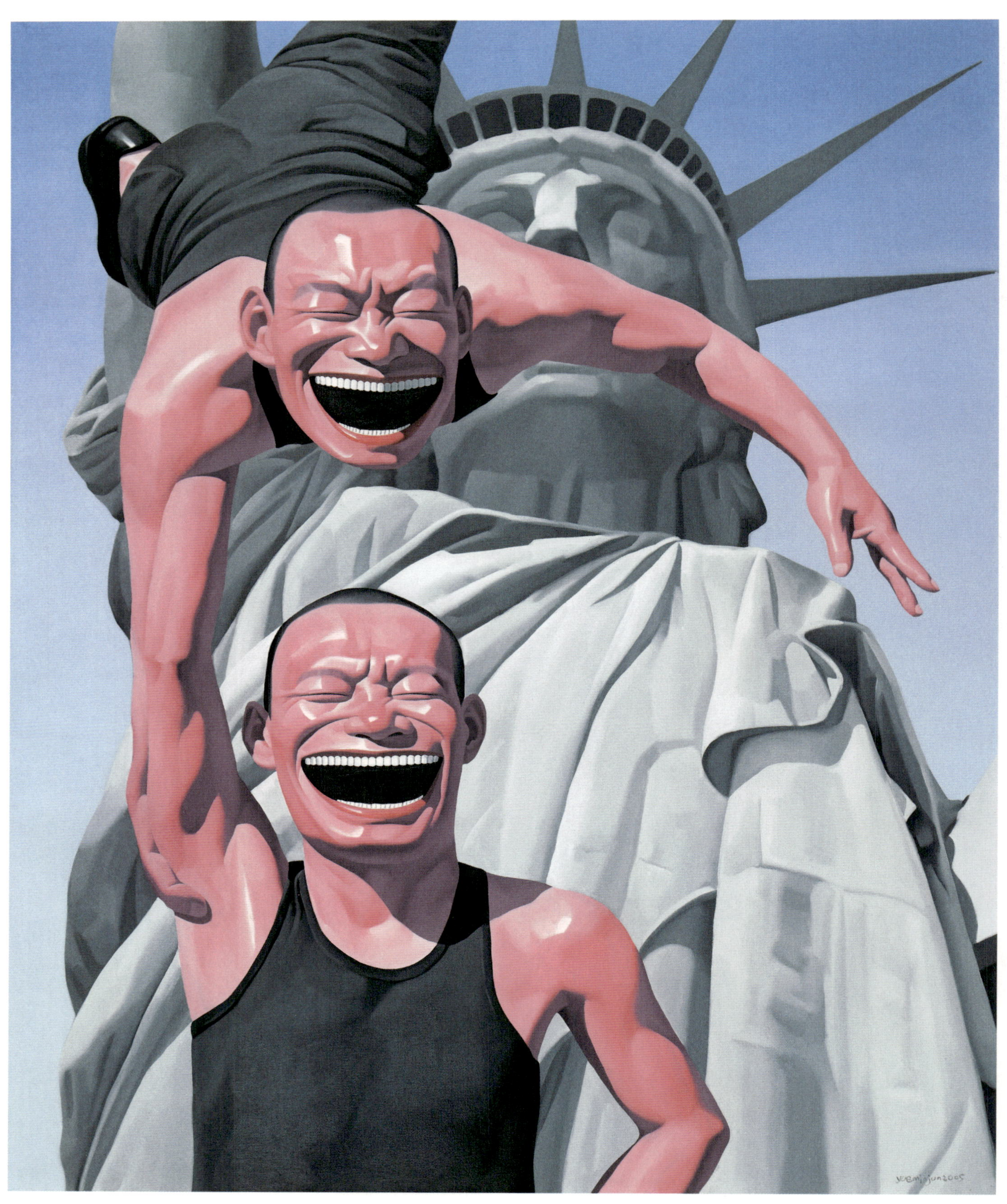

Untitled * 無題 * 170 x 140cm * 2005 * oil on canvas * 布上油畫

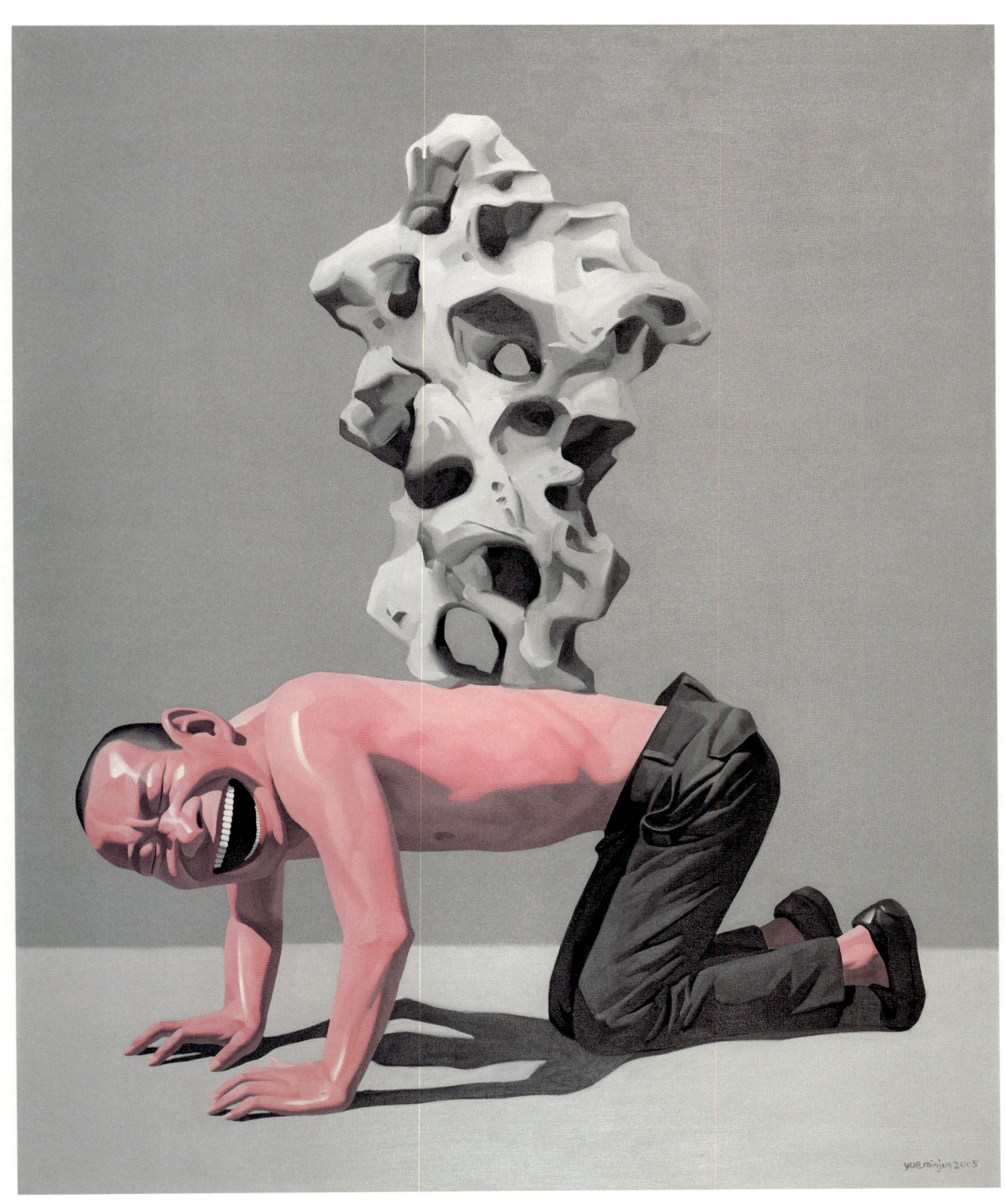

Untitled * 無題 * 170 x 140cm * 2005 * oil on canvas * 布上油畫

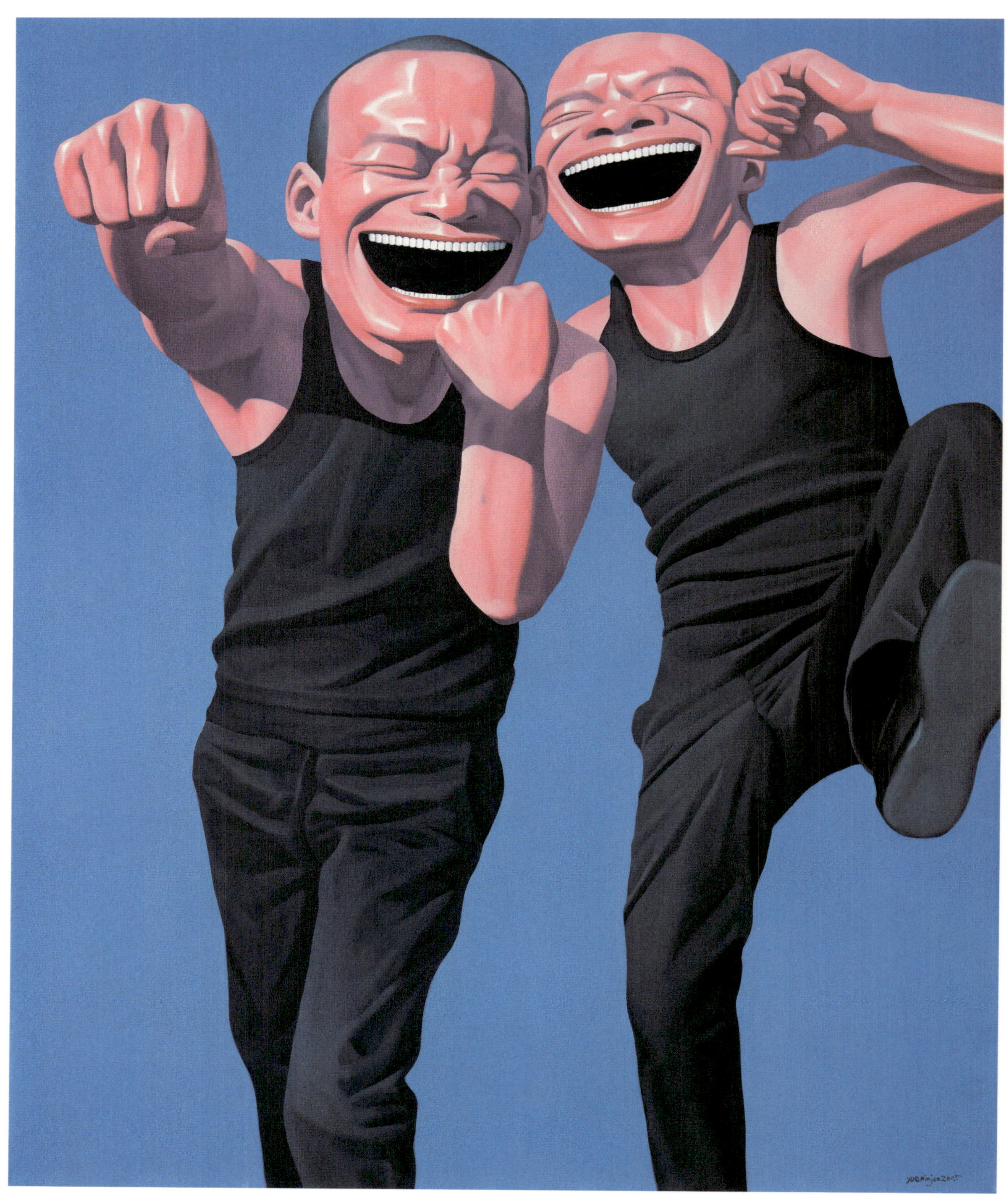

Untitled * 無題 * 170 x 140cm * 2005 * oil on canvas * 布上油畫

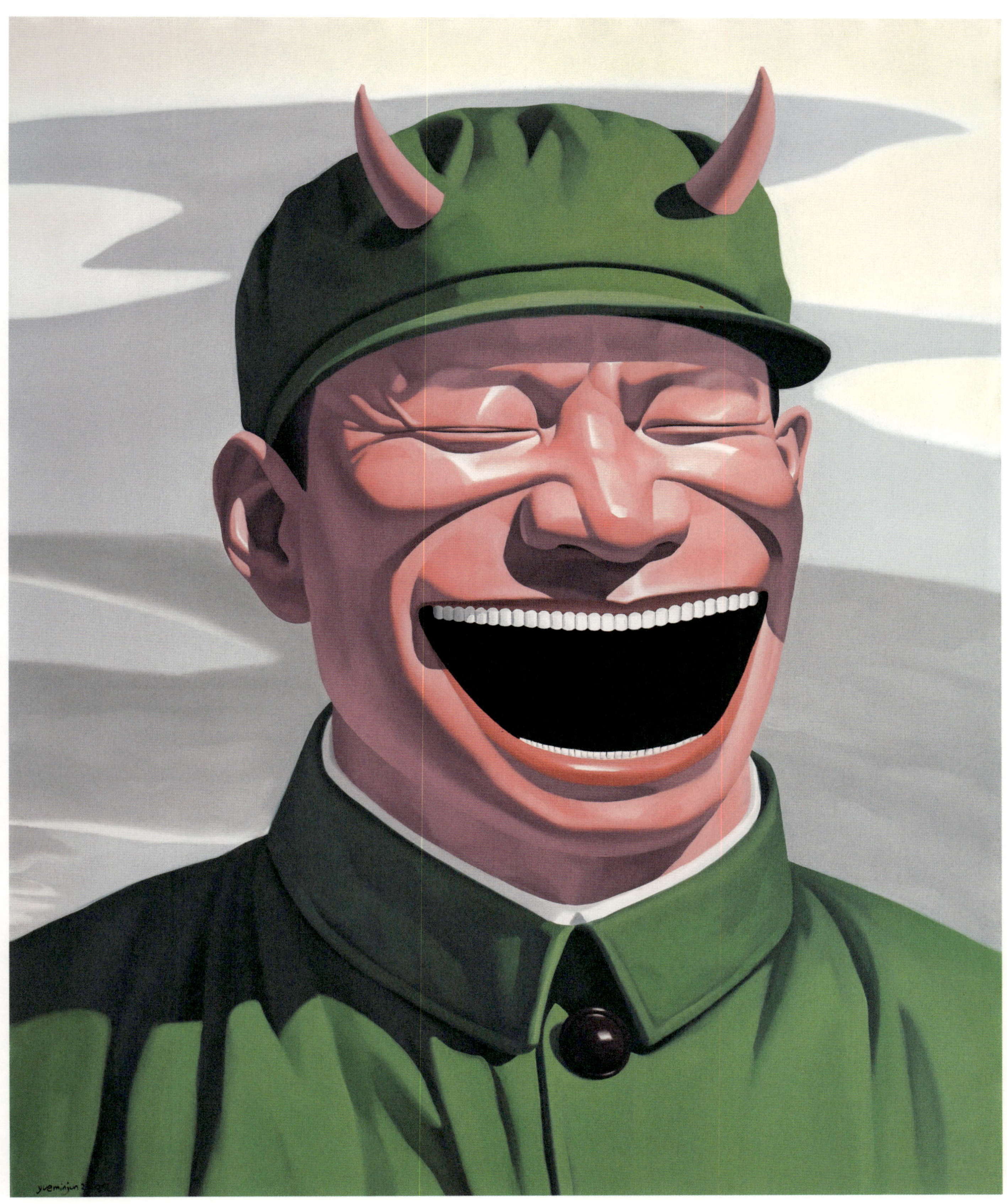

Untitled * 無題 * 170 x 140cm * 2005 * oil on canvas * 布上油畫

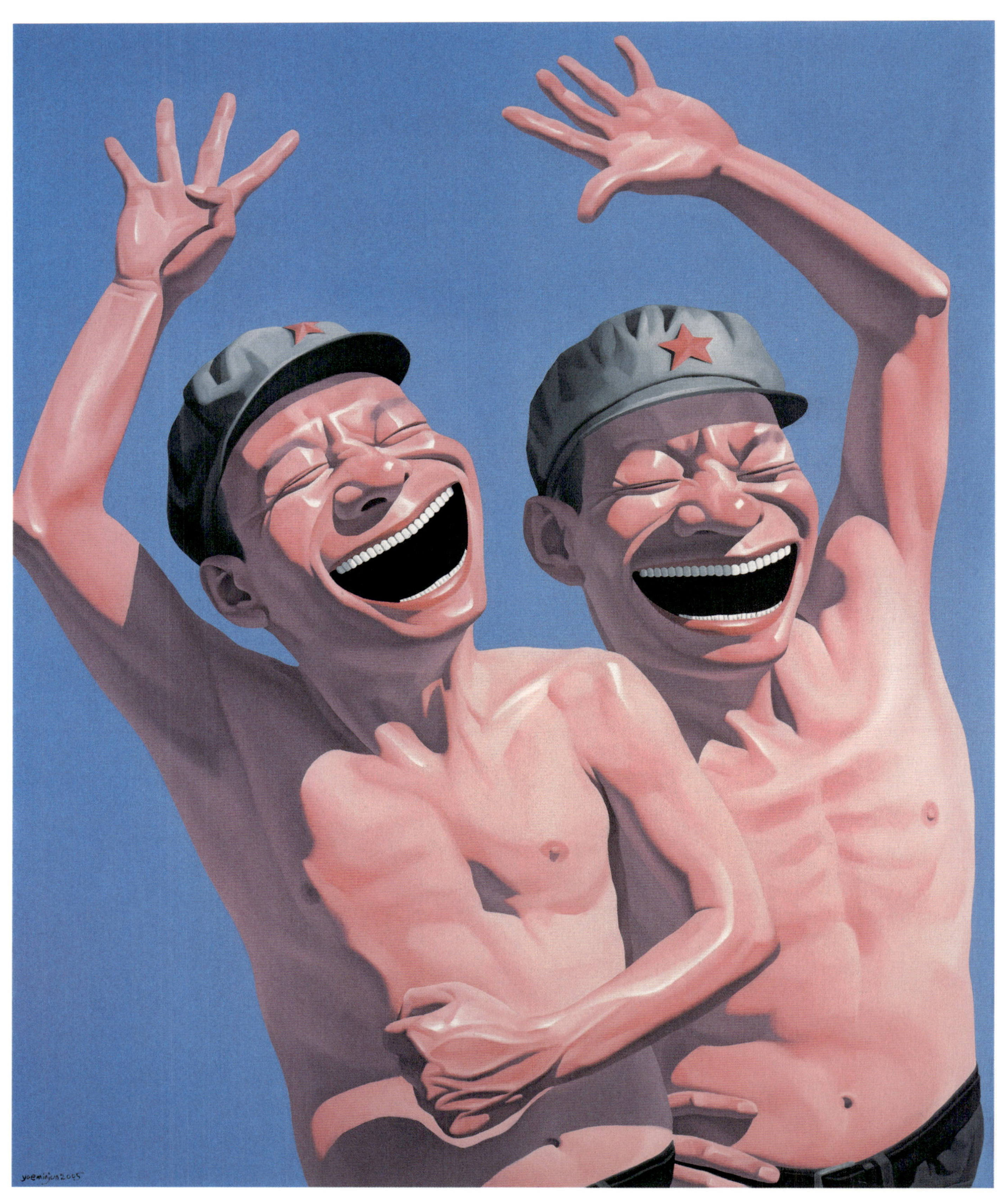

Untitled * 無題 * 170 x 140cm * 2005 * oil on canvas * 布上油畫

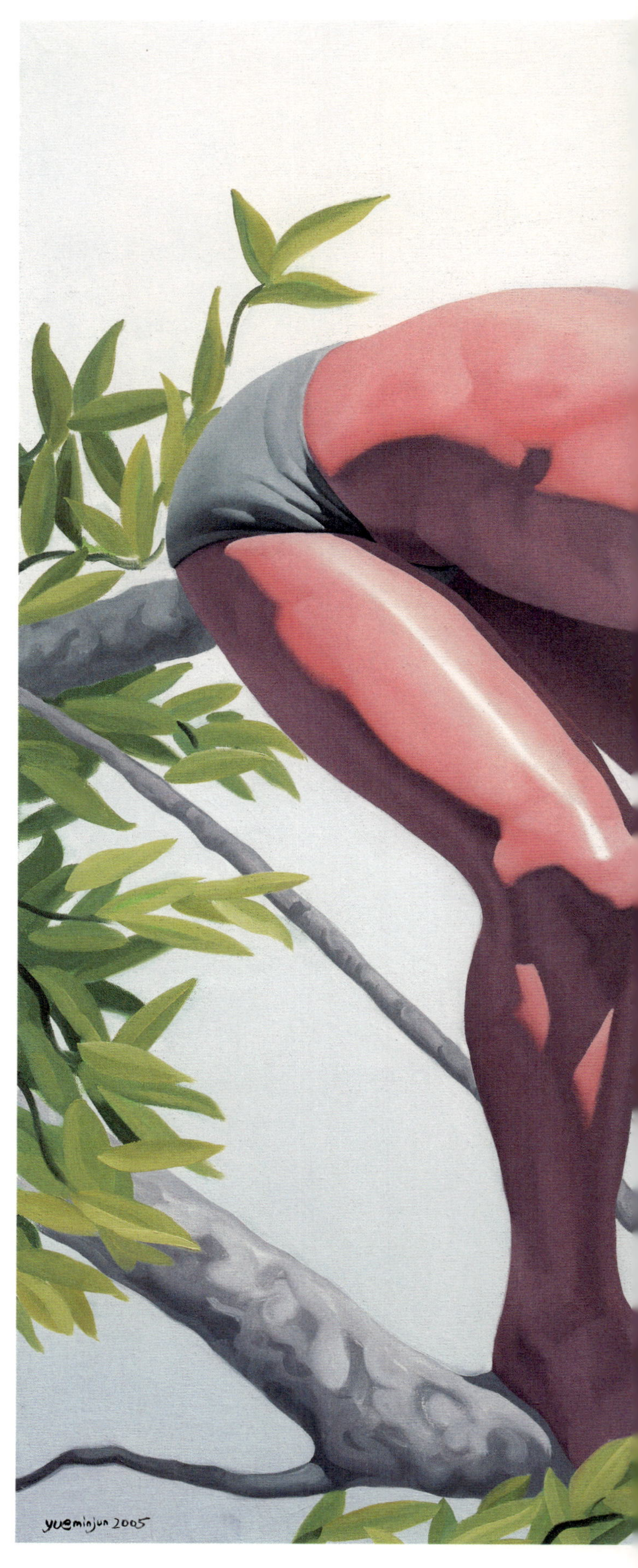

Untitled *
無題 *
170 x 140cm *
2005 *
oil on canvas *
布上油畫

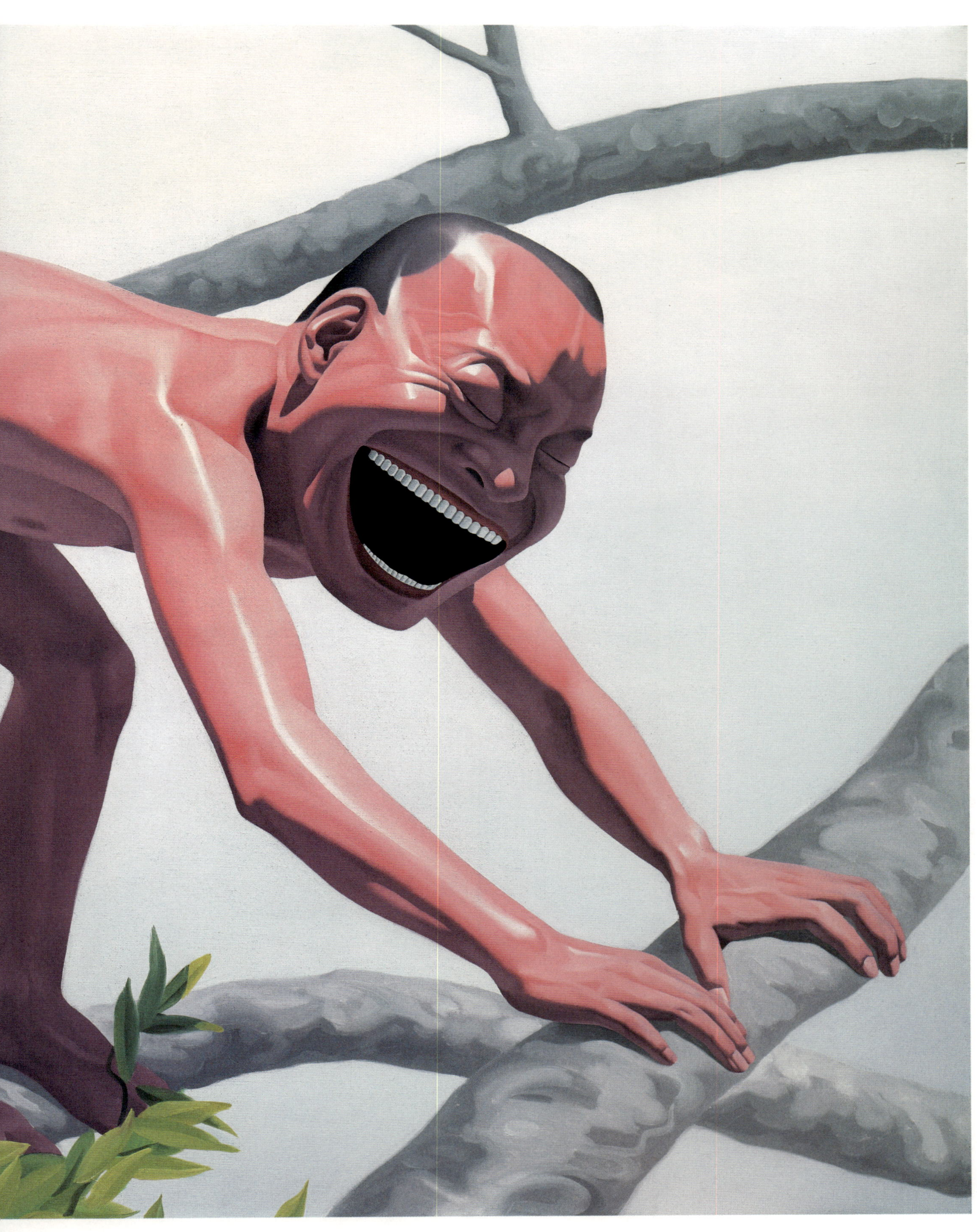

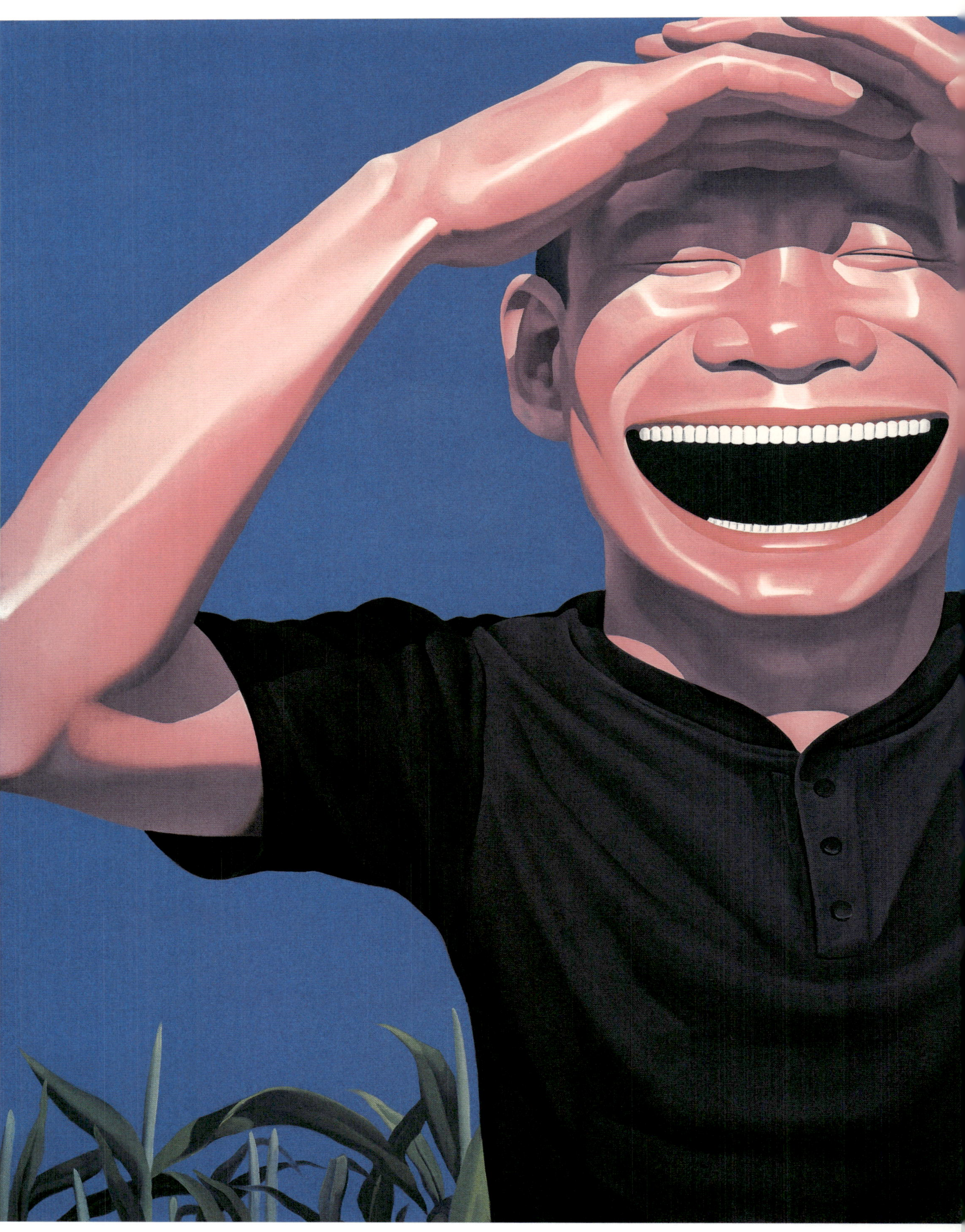

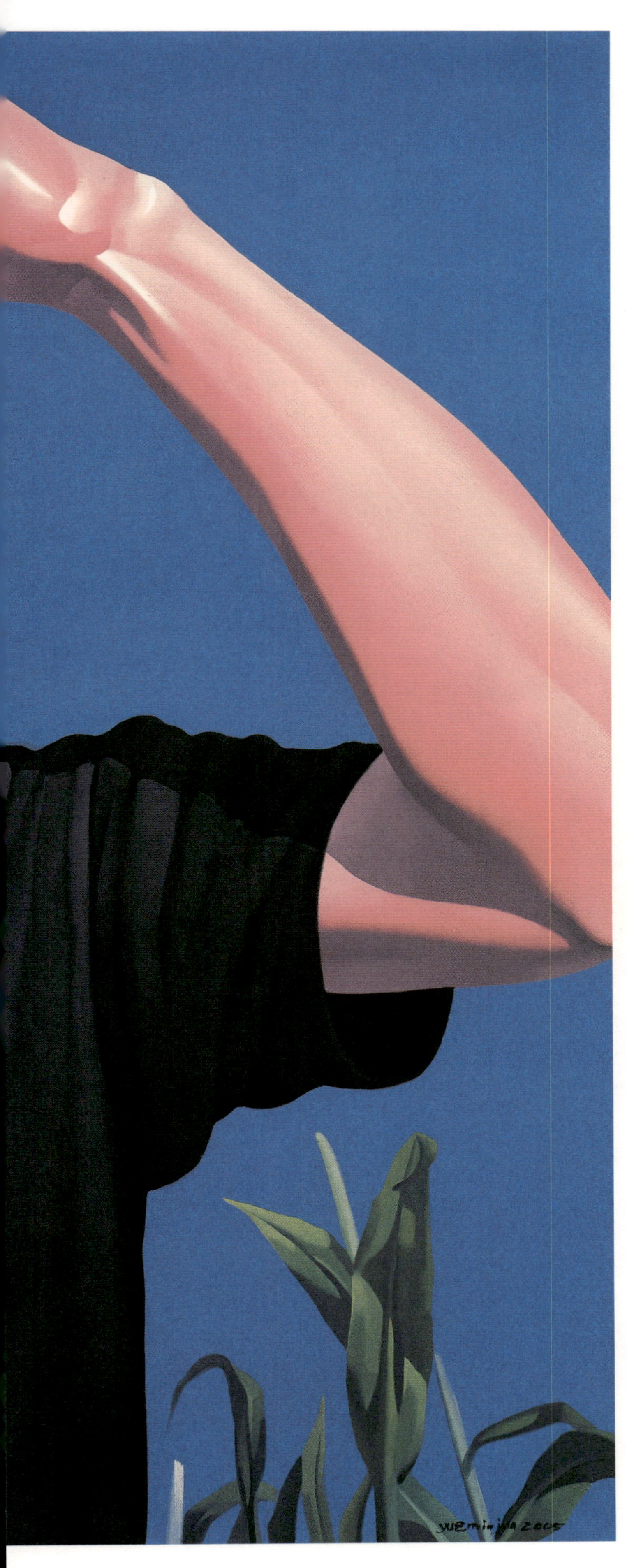

Hope *
希望 *
170 x 140cm *
2005 *
oil on canvas *
布上油畫

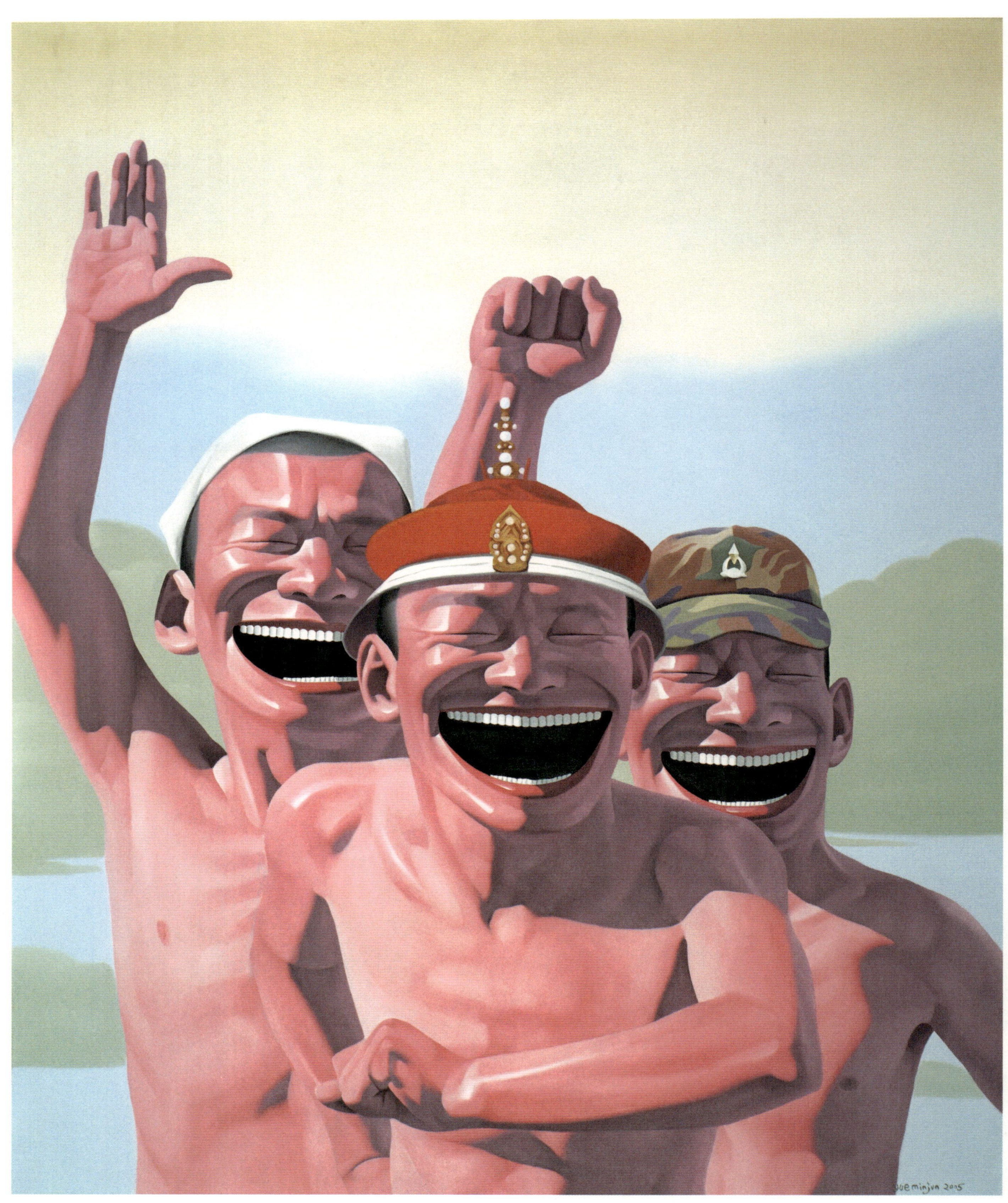

Overlook * 遠望 * 170 x 140cm * 2005 * oil on canvas * 布上油畫

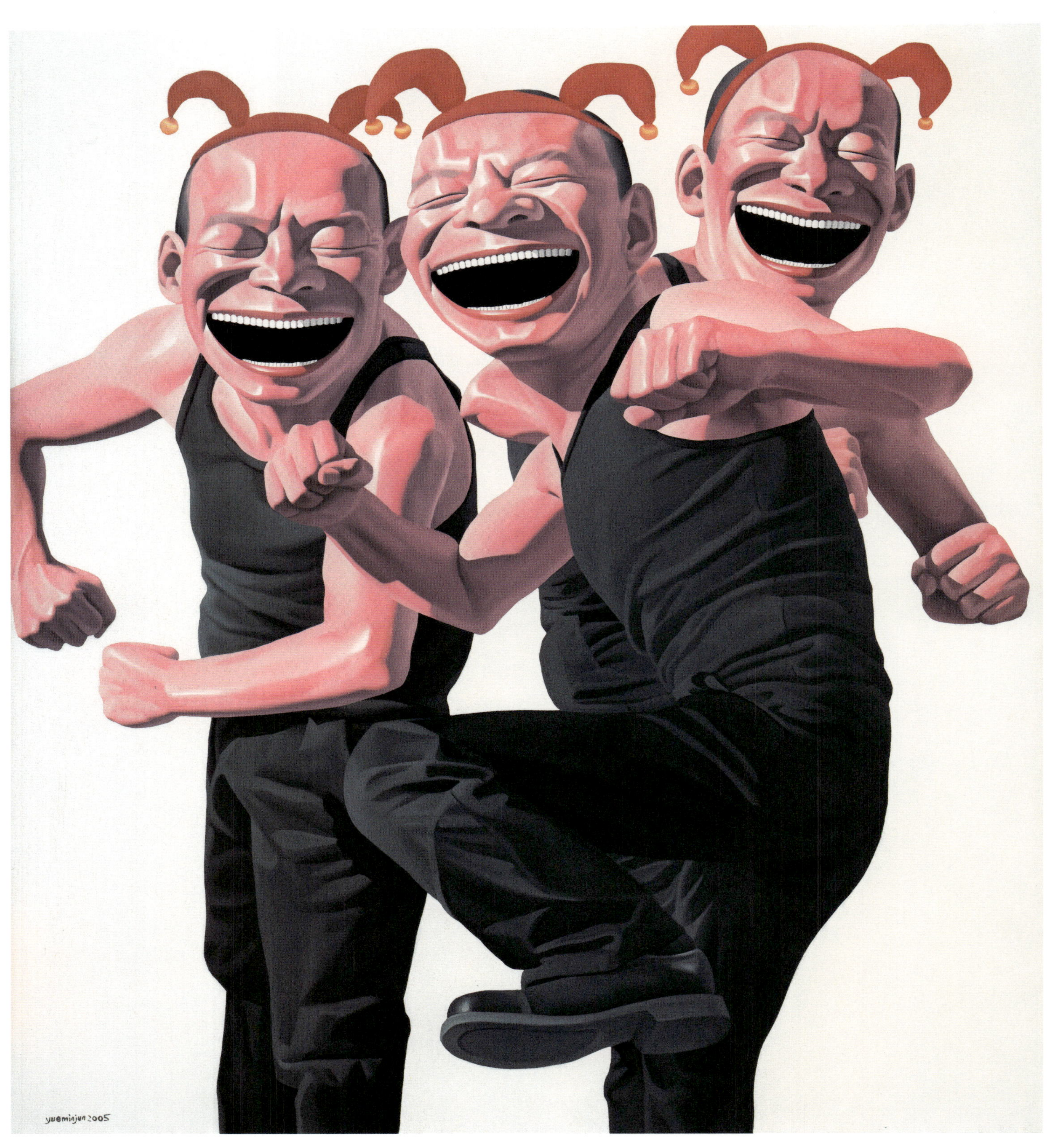

Kong Fu - I * 功夫 – I * 220 x 200cm * 2005 * oil on canvas * 布上油畫

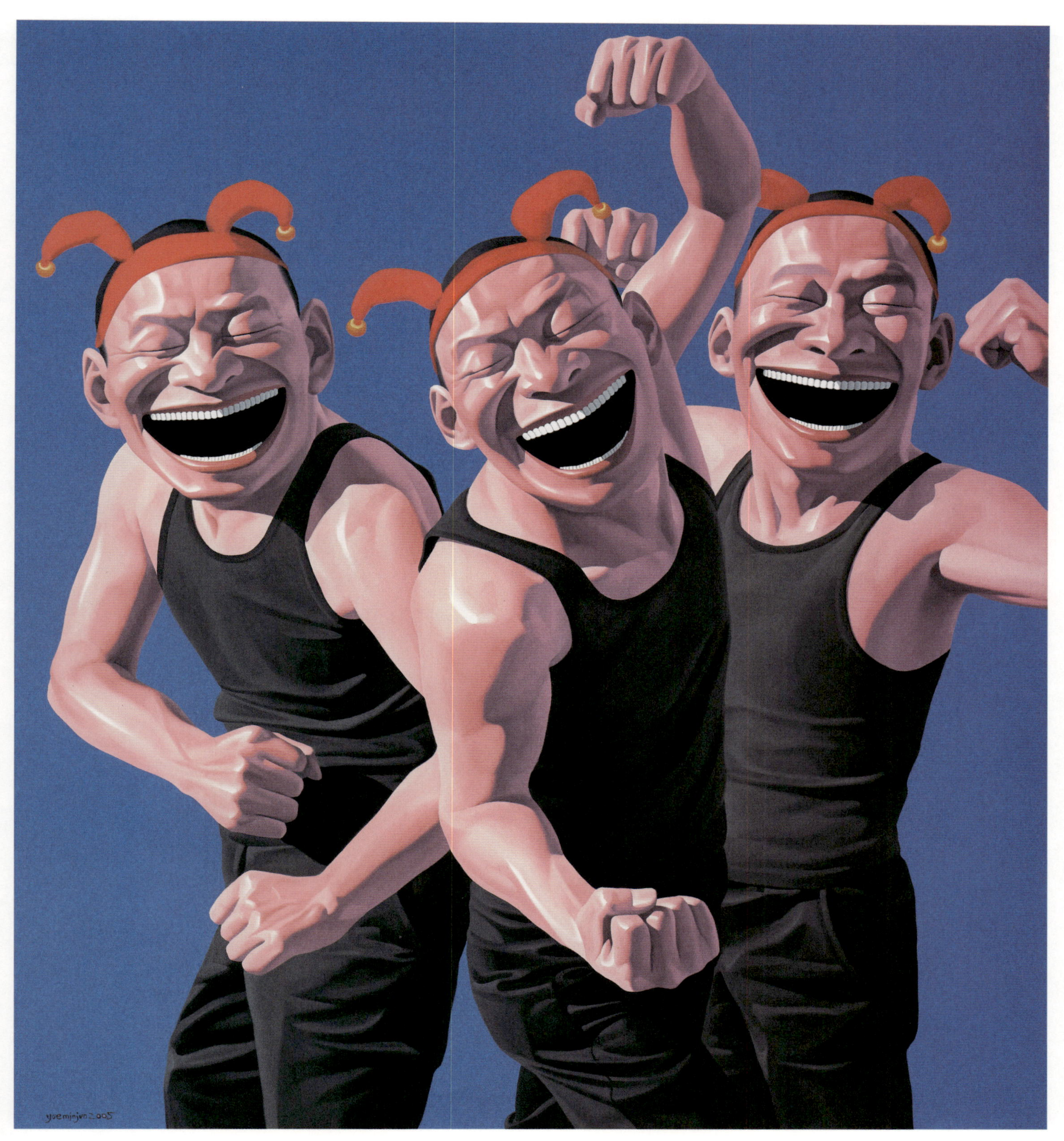

Kong Fu - II * 功夫 – II * 220 X 200cm * 2005 * oil on canvas * 布上油畫

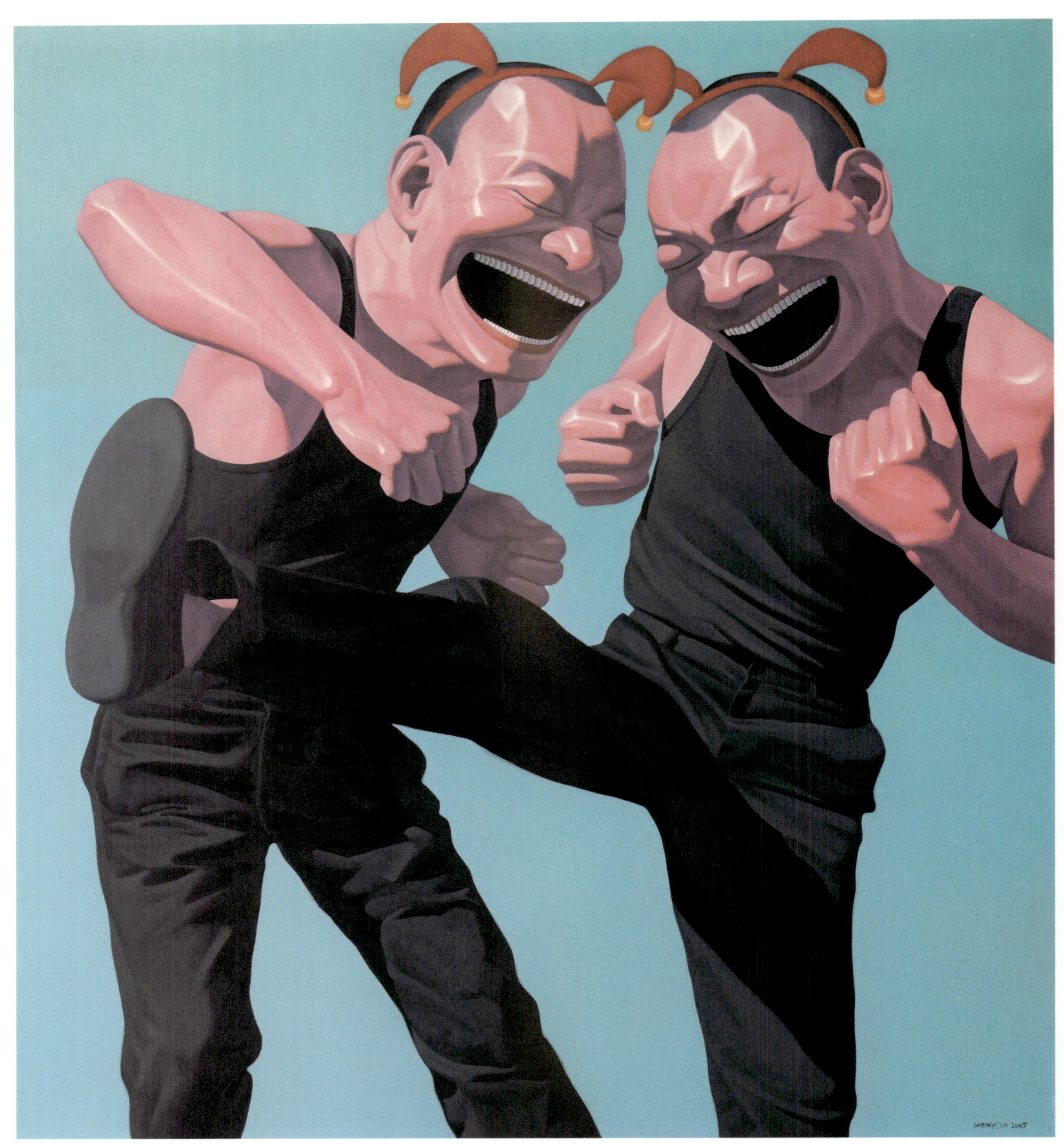

Kong Fu - III * 功夫 – III * 220 x 200cm * 2005 * oil on canvas * 布上油畫

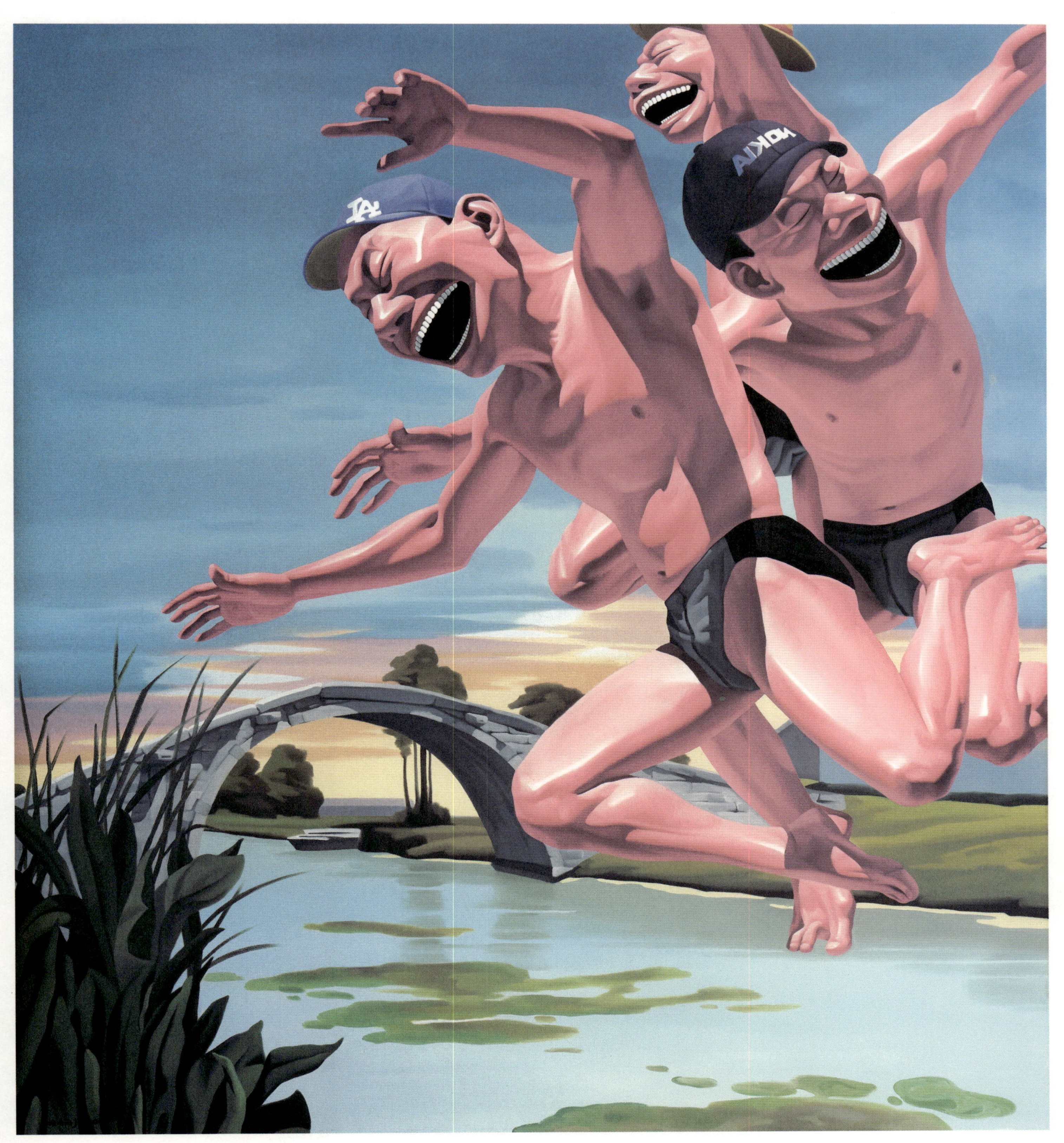

Hometown * 故鄉 * 220 x 200cm * 2005 * oil on canvas * 布上油畫

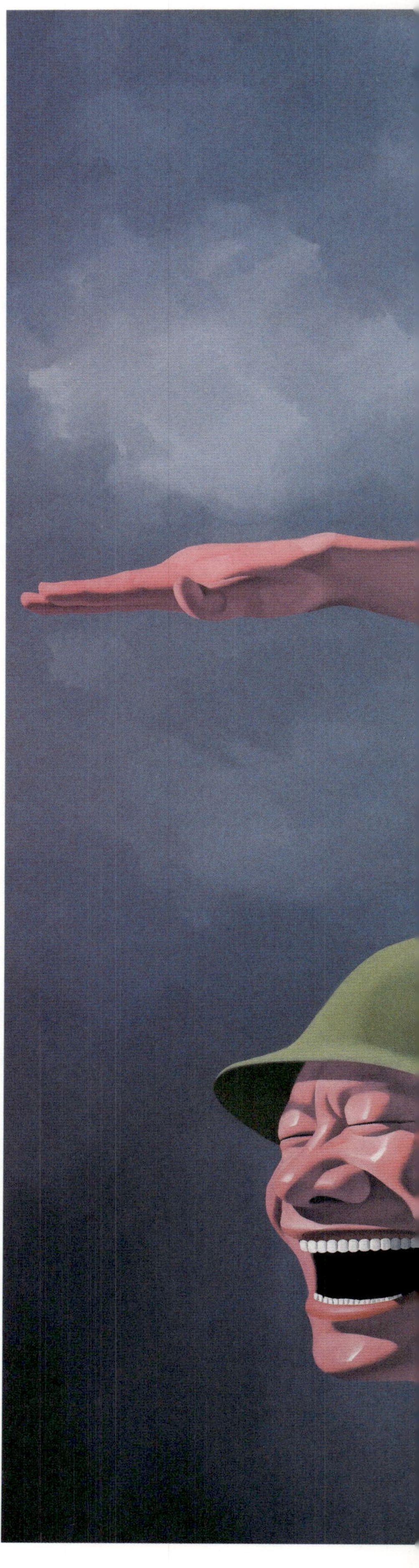

Untitled *
無題 *
200 x 220cm *
2005 *
oil on canvas *
布上油畫

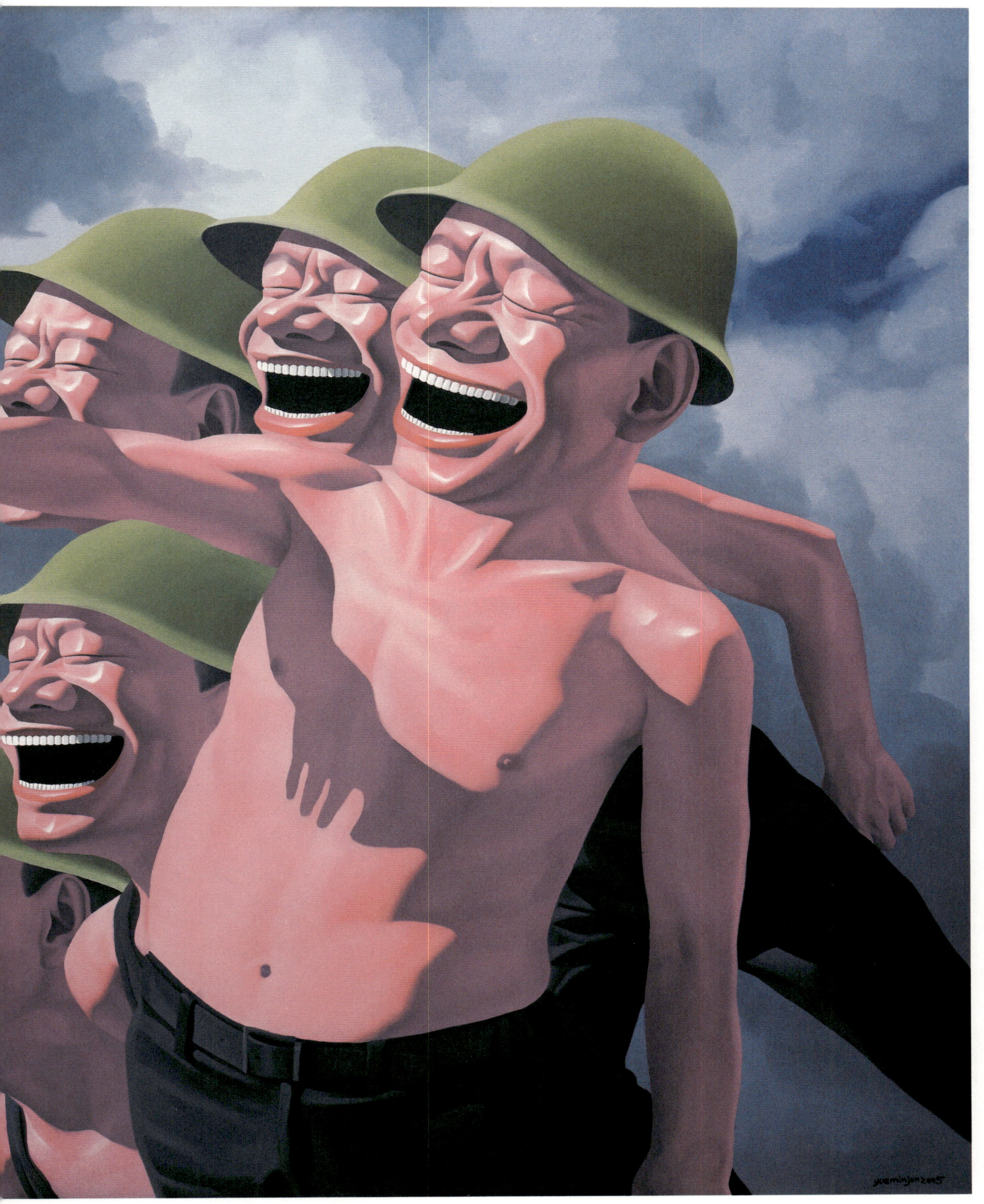
yueminjun2005

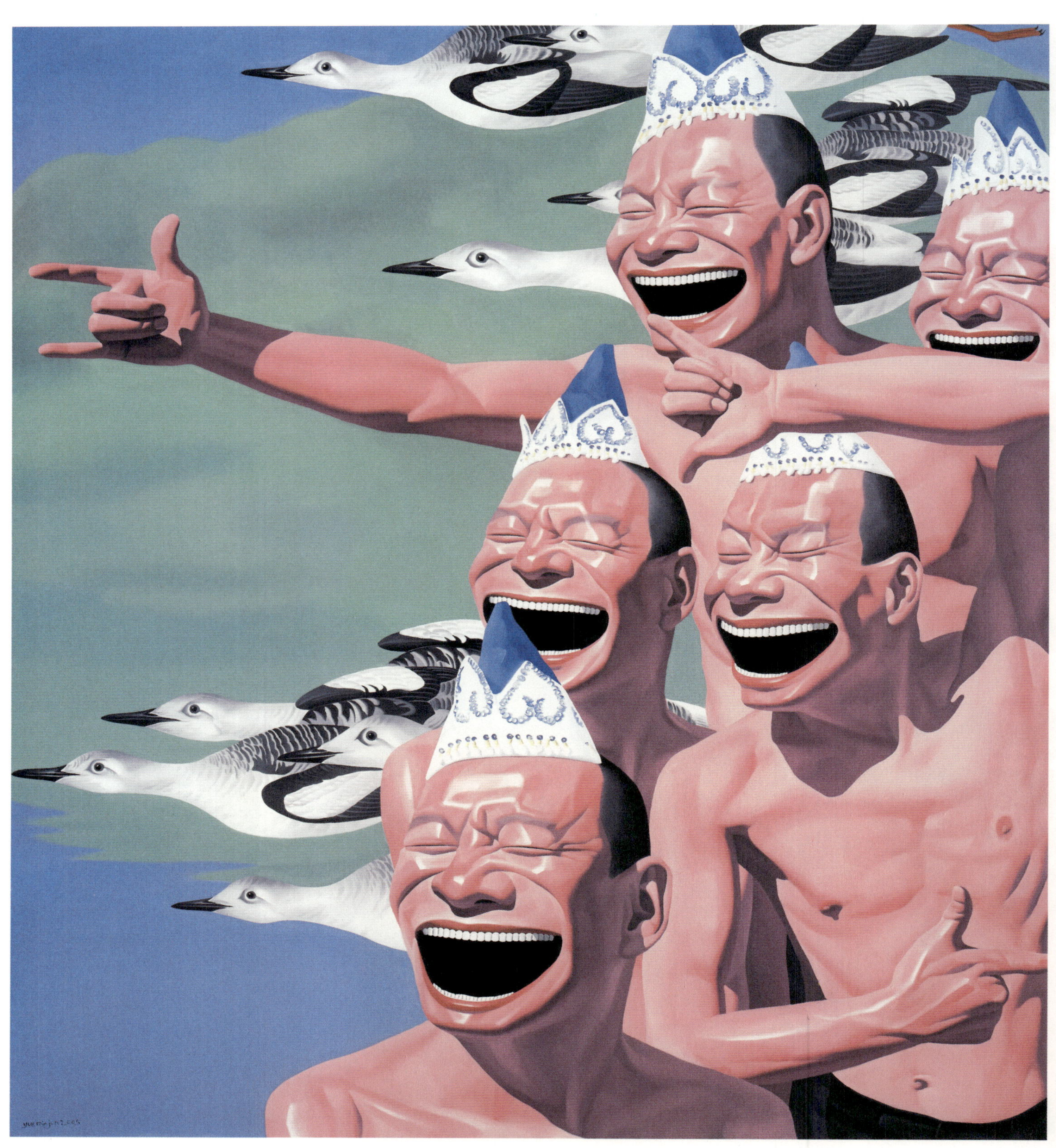

Untitled * 無題 * 220 x 200cm * 2005 * oil on canvas * 布上油畫

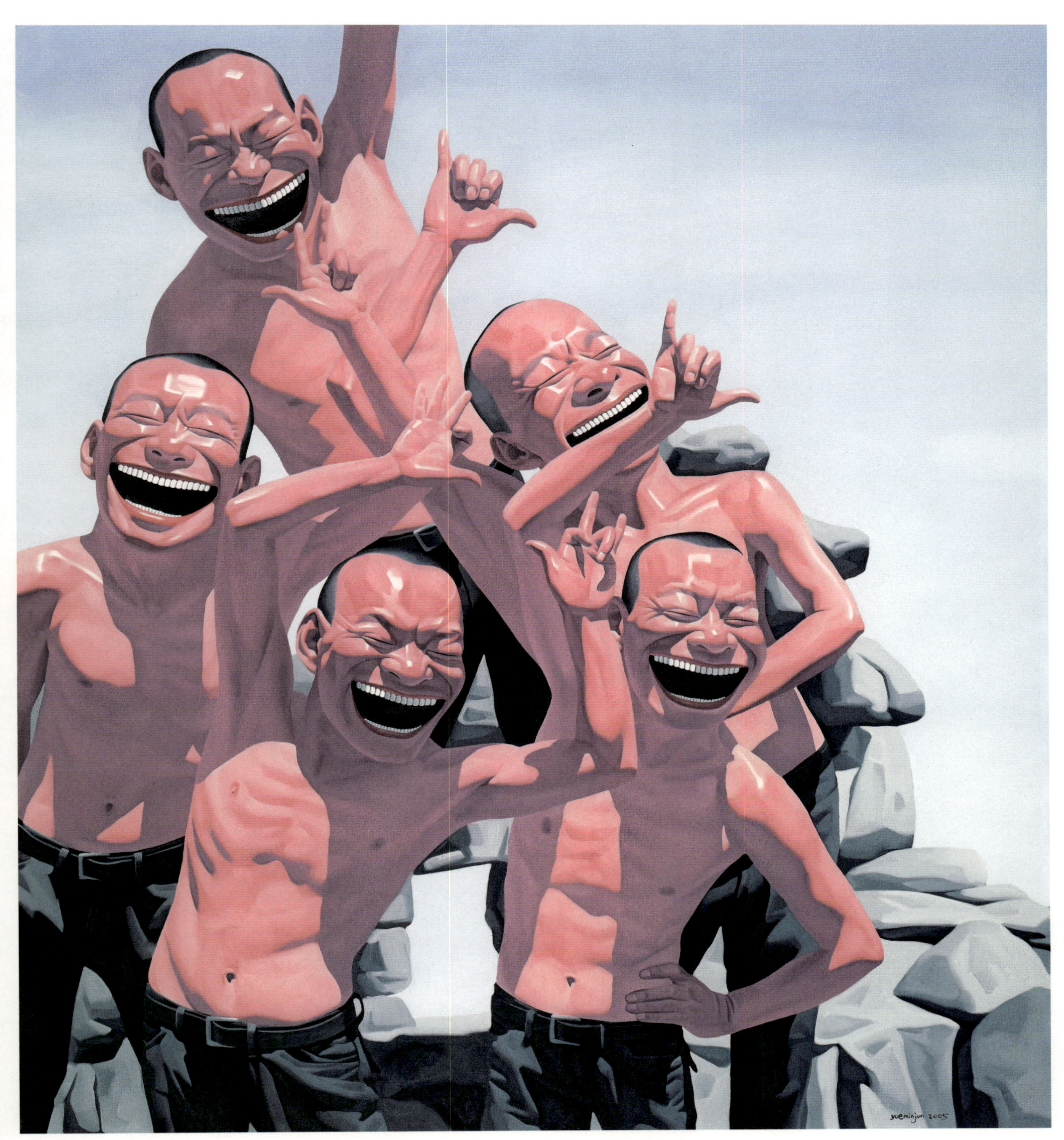

Untitled * 無題 * 220 x 200cm * 2005 * oil on canvas * 布上油畫

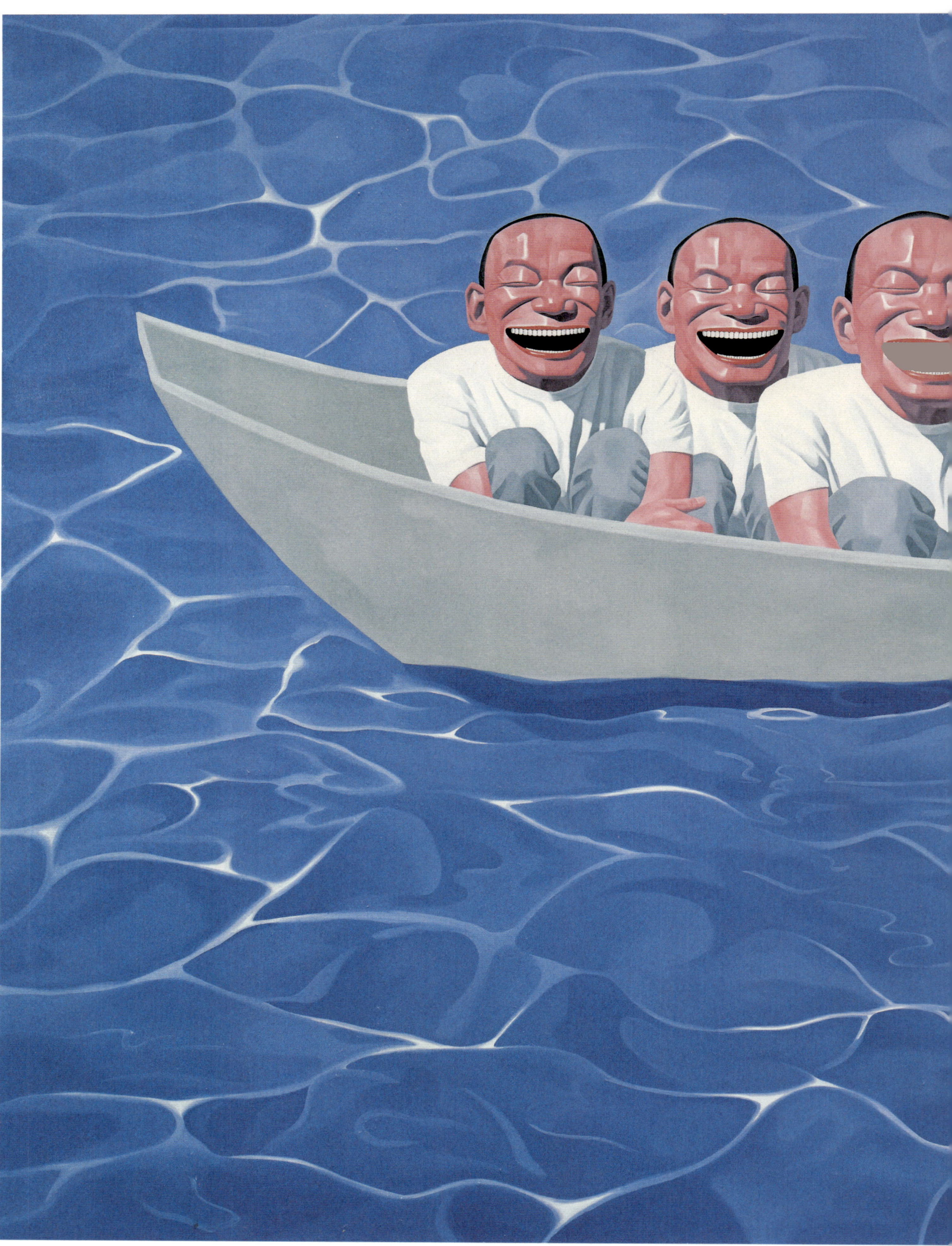

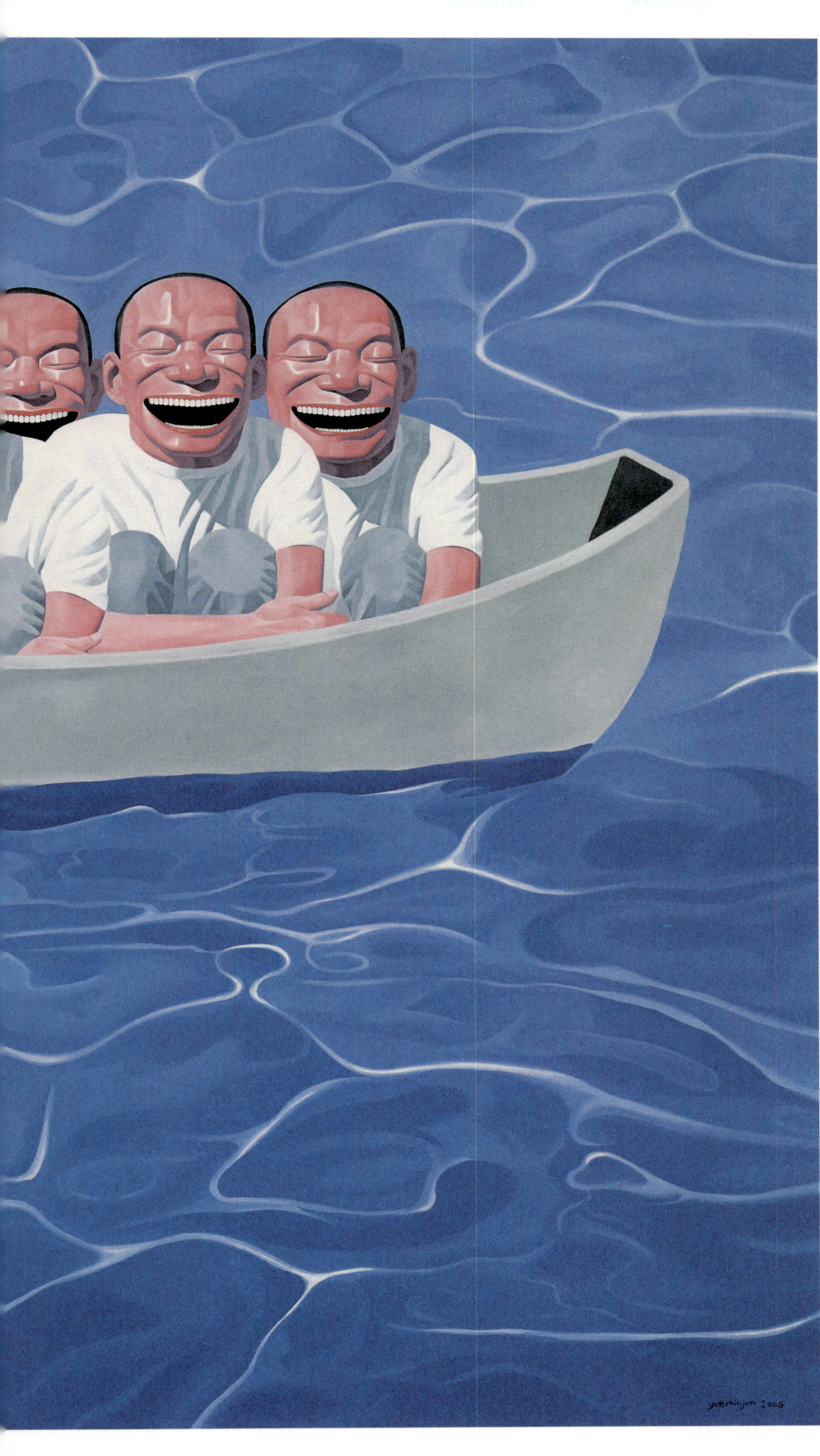

Noah's Ark *
諾亞方舟 *
300 x 220cm *
2005 *
oil on canvas *
布上油畫

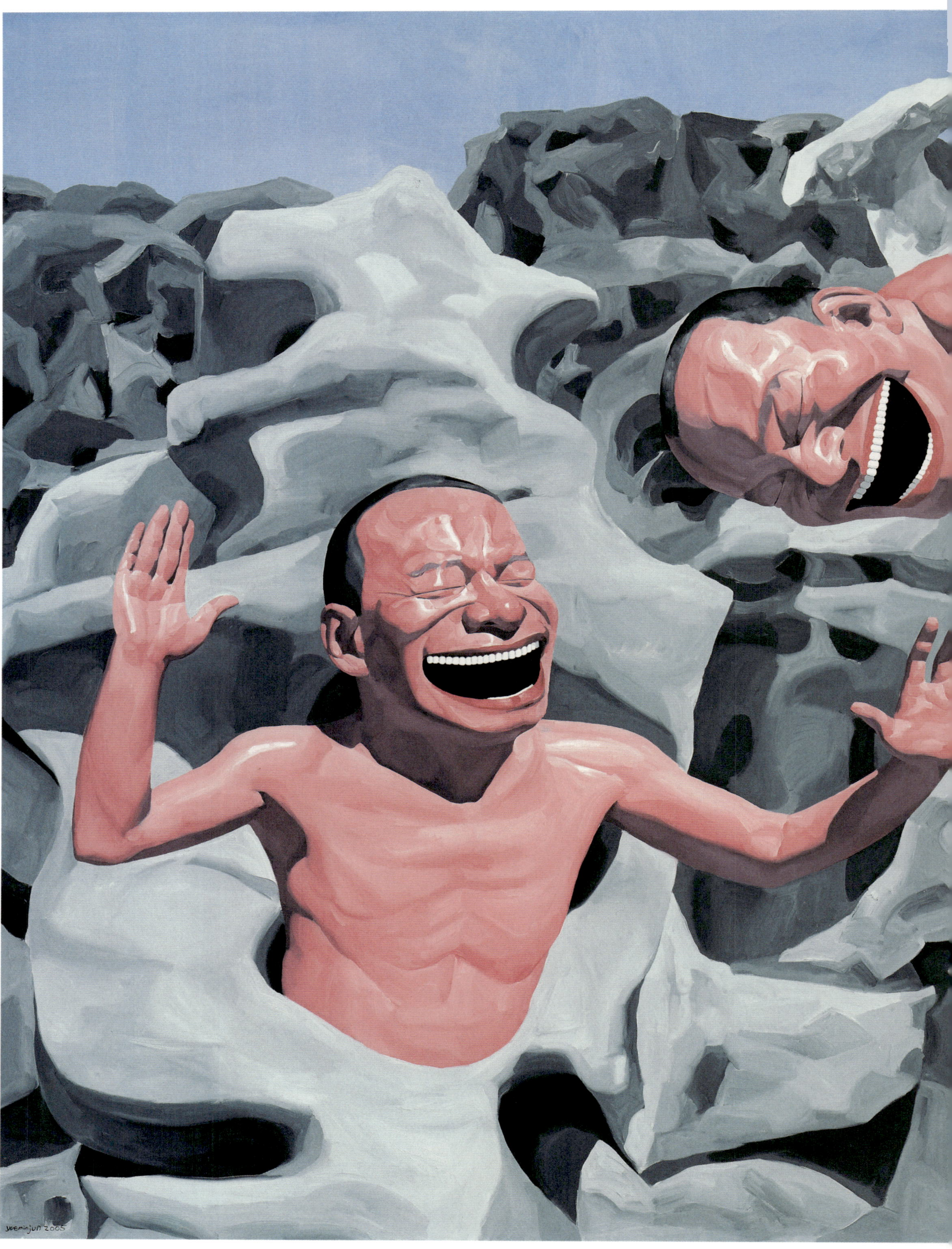
yueminjun 2005

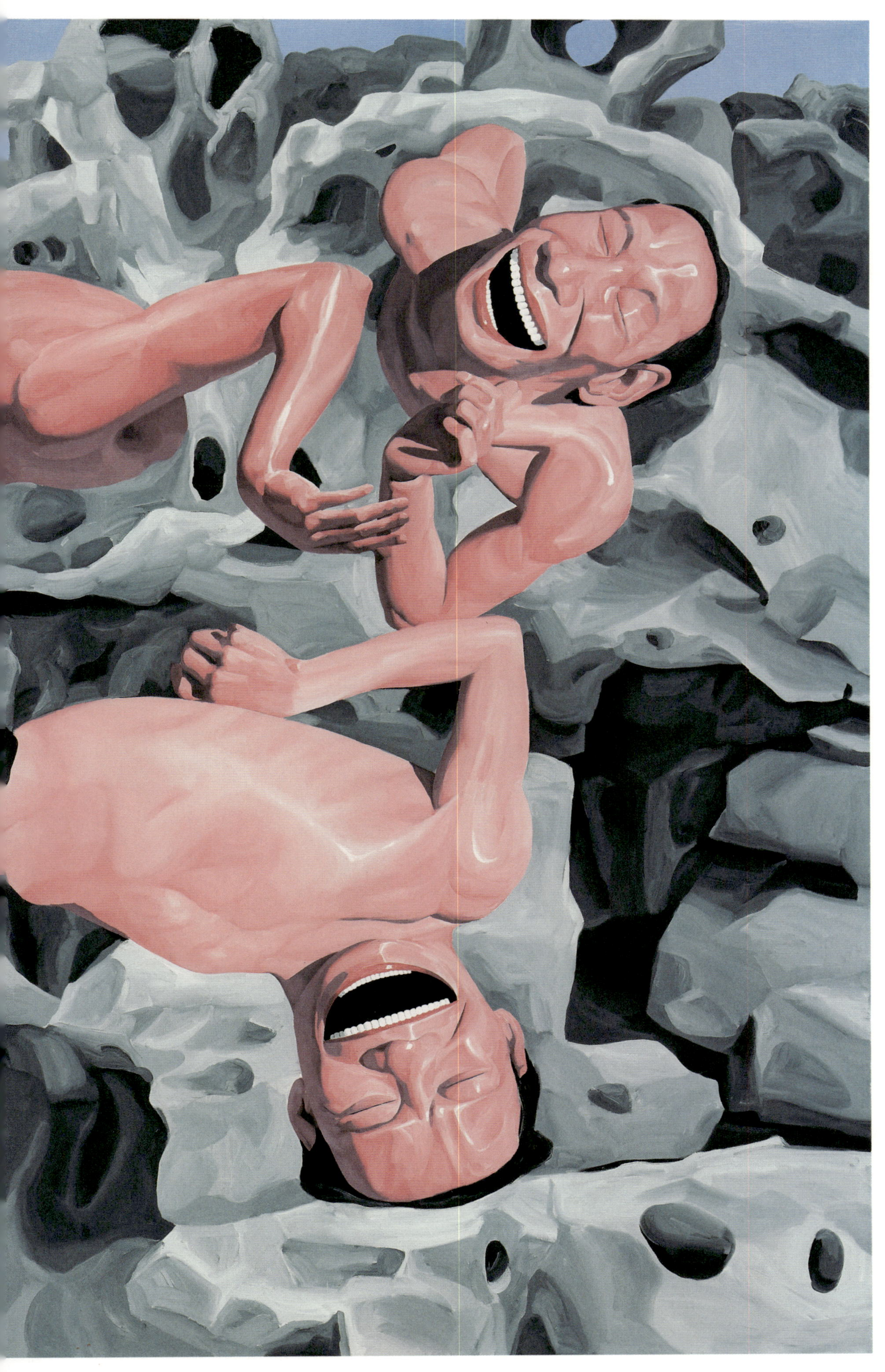

Backyard Garden *
後花園 *
280 x 400cm *
2005 *
oil on canvas *
布上油畫

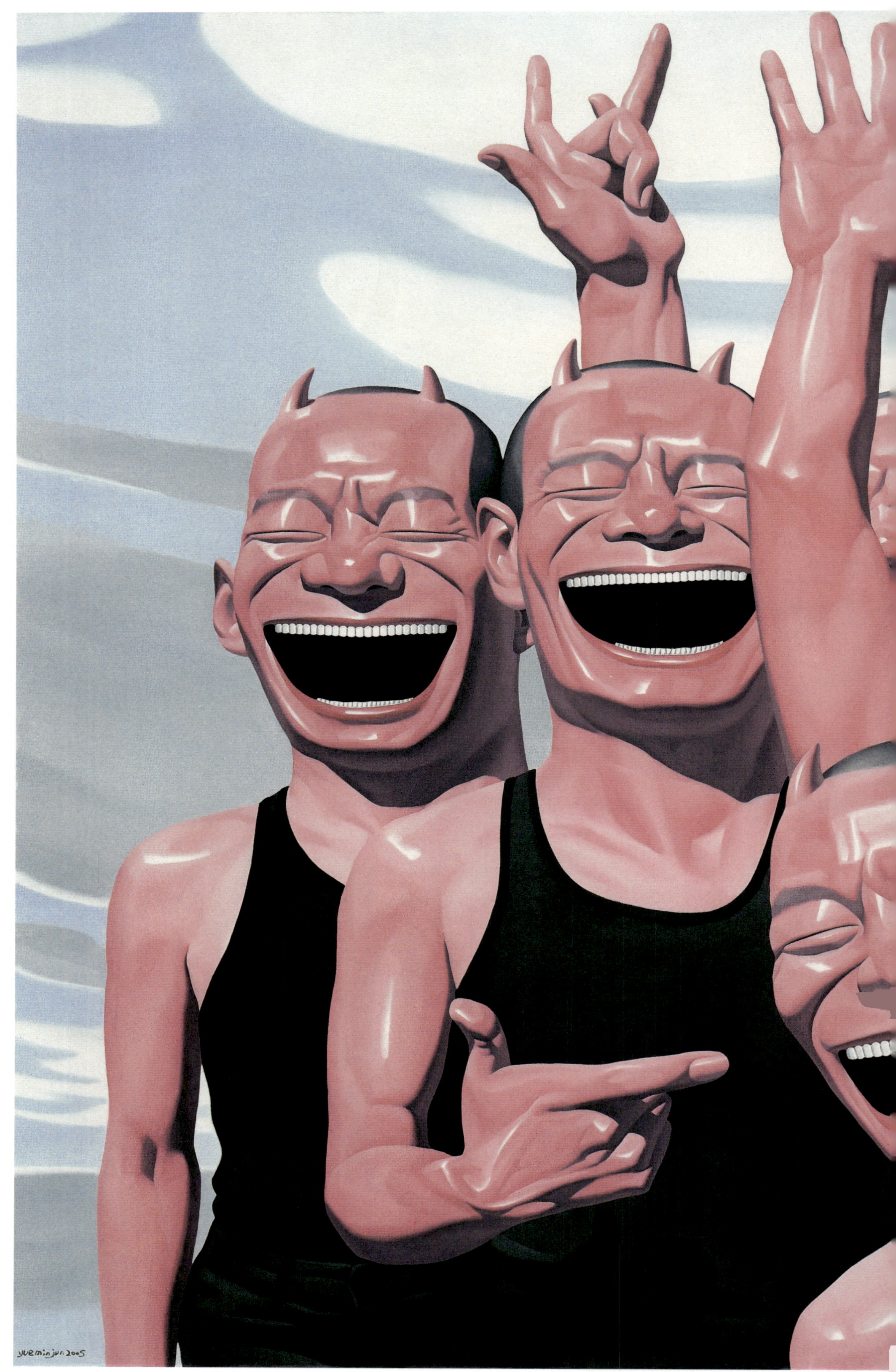

Between Men and Animal *
人獸之間 *
280 x 400cm *
2005 *
oil on canvas *
布上油畫

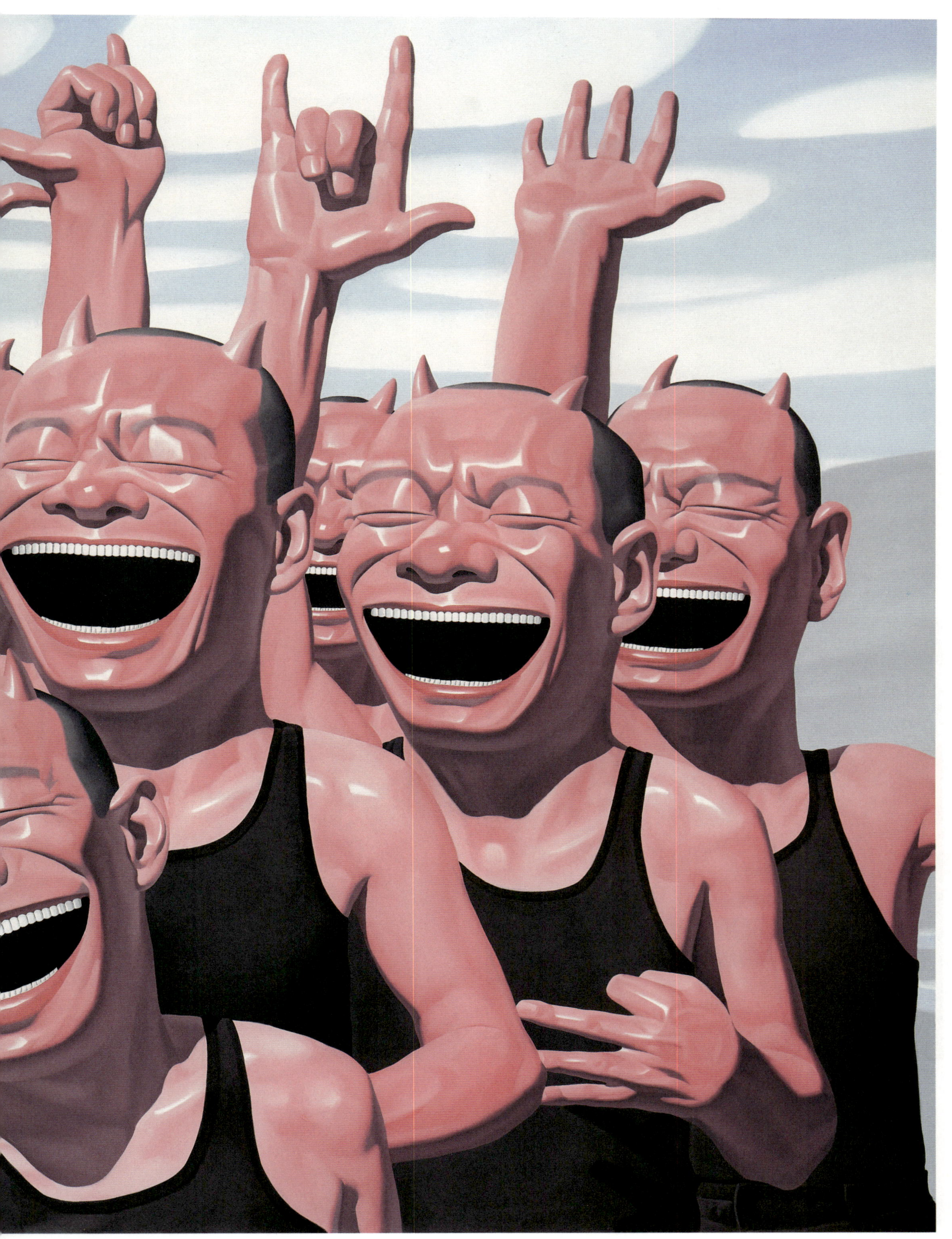

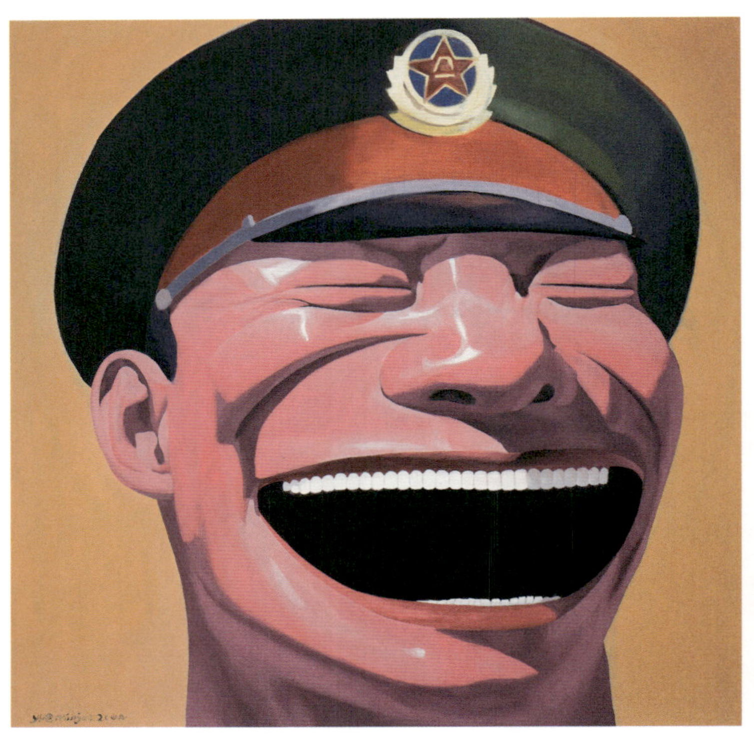

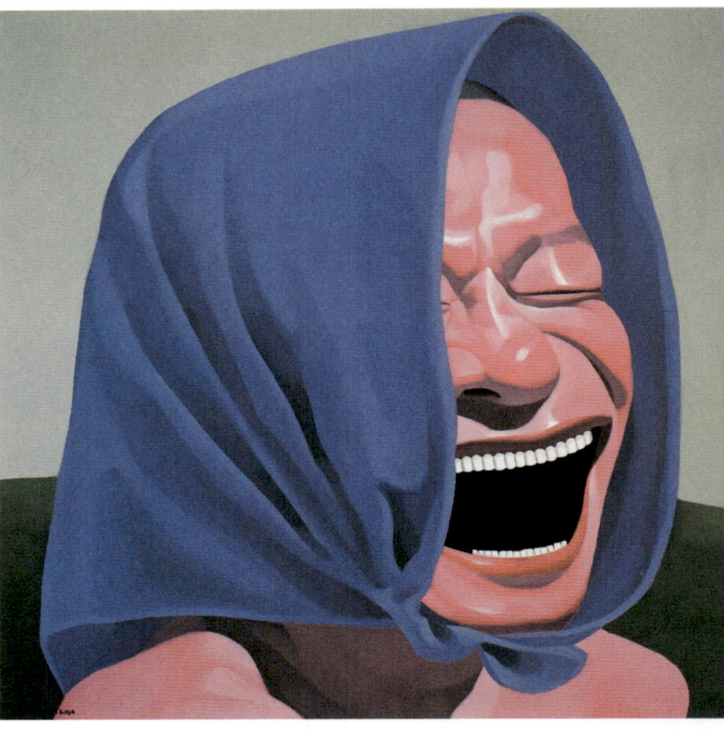

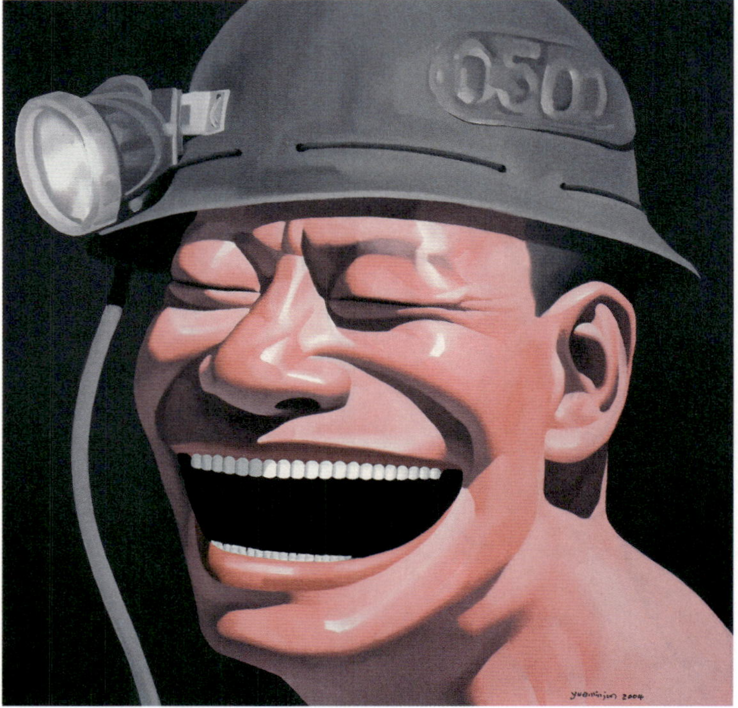

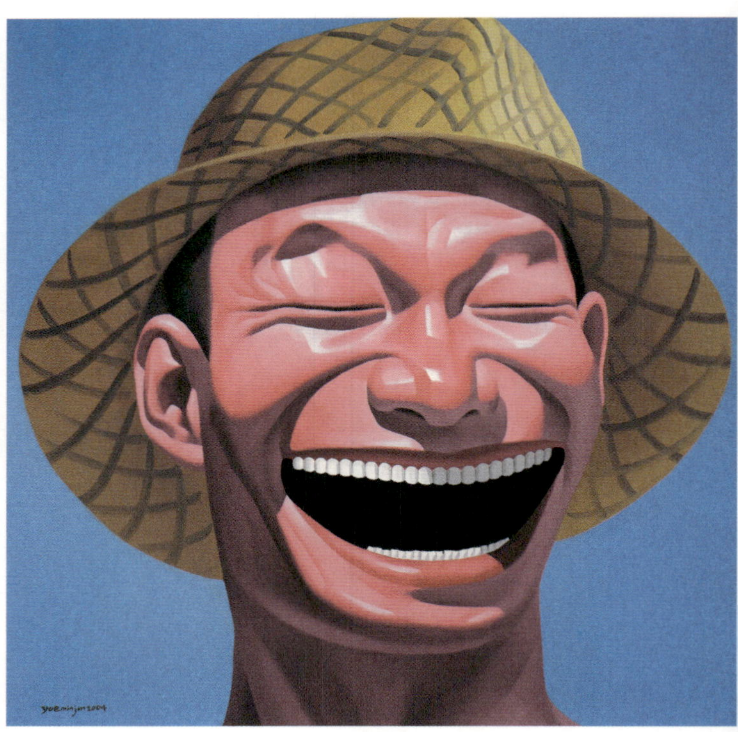

Hats * 帽子 * 82 x 82cm x 10pcs * 2004 * oil on canvas * 布上油畫

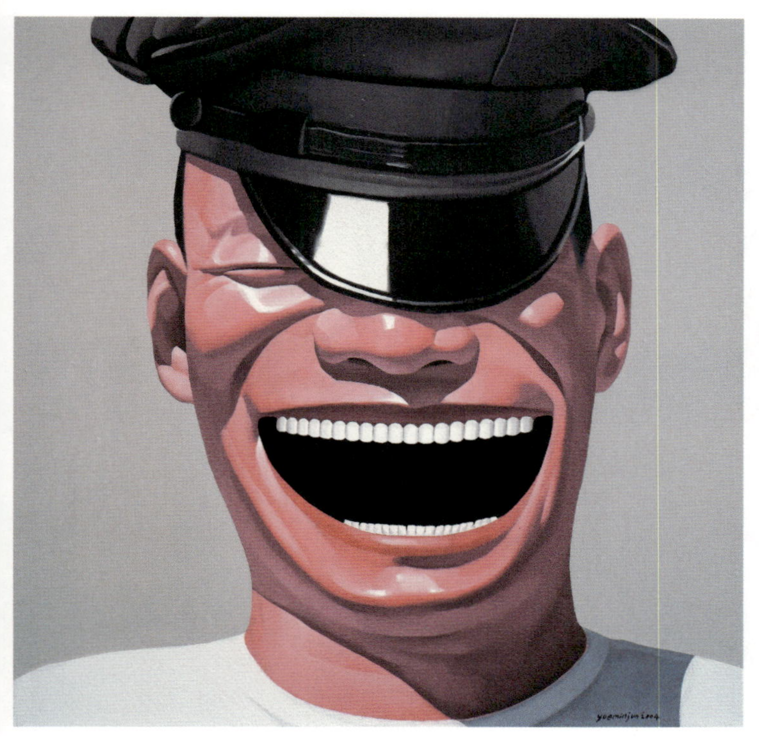

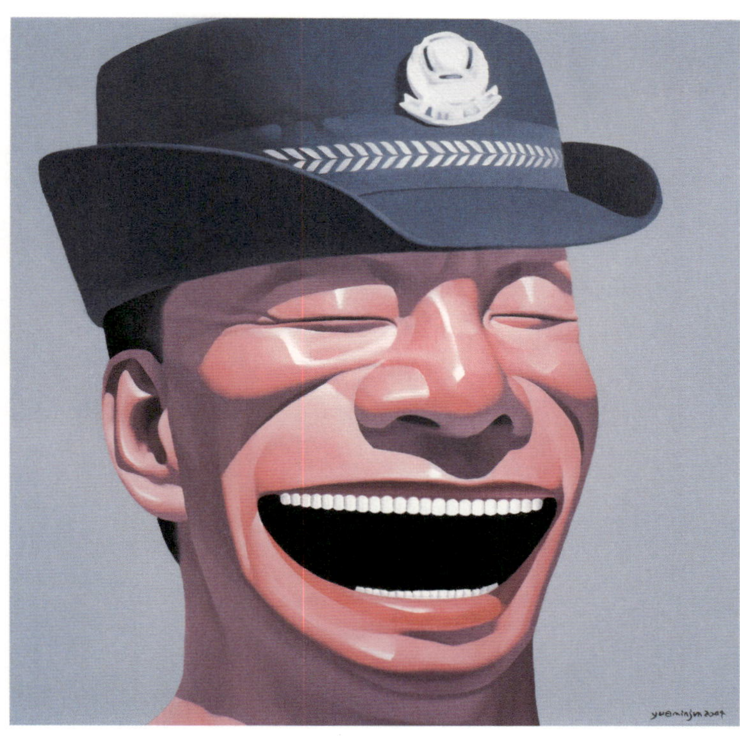

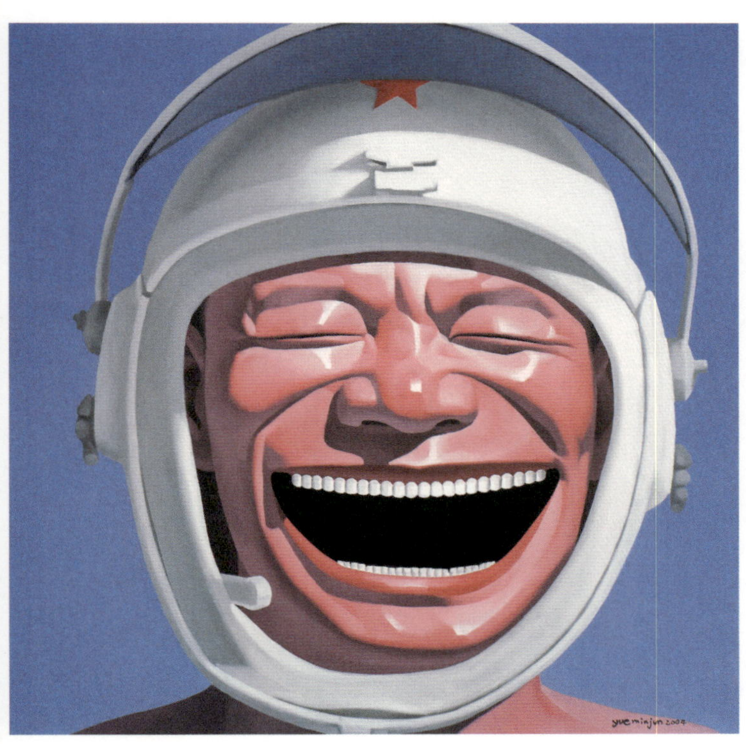

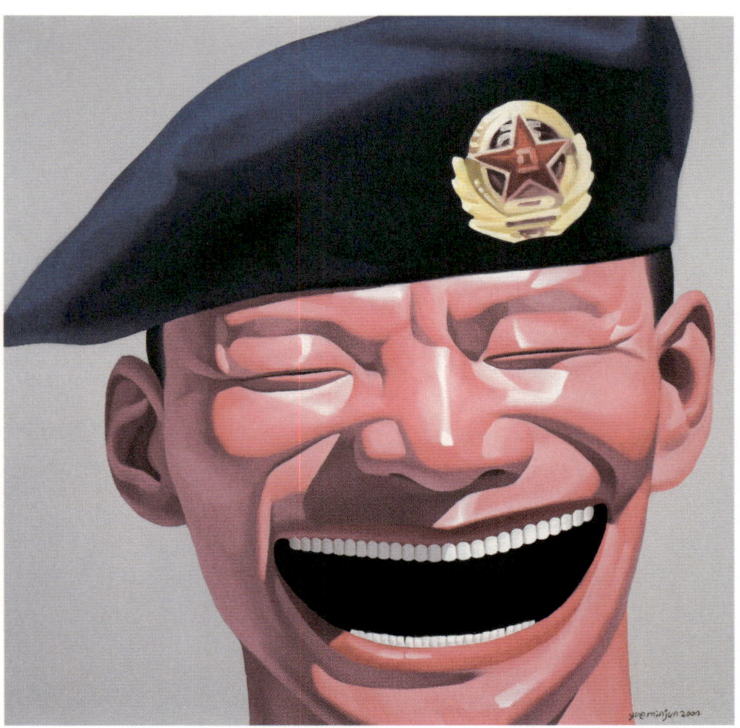

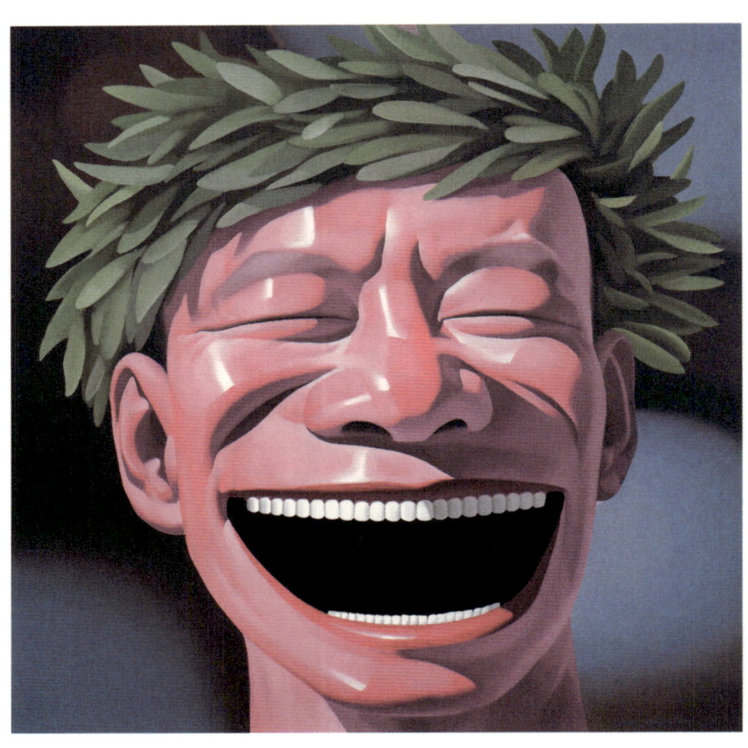

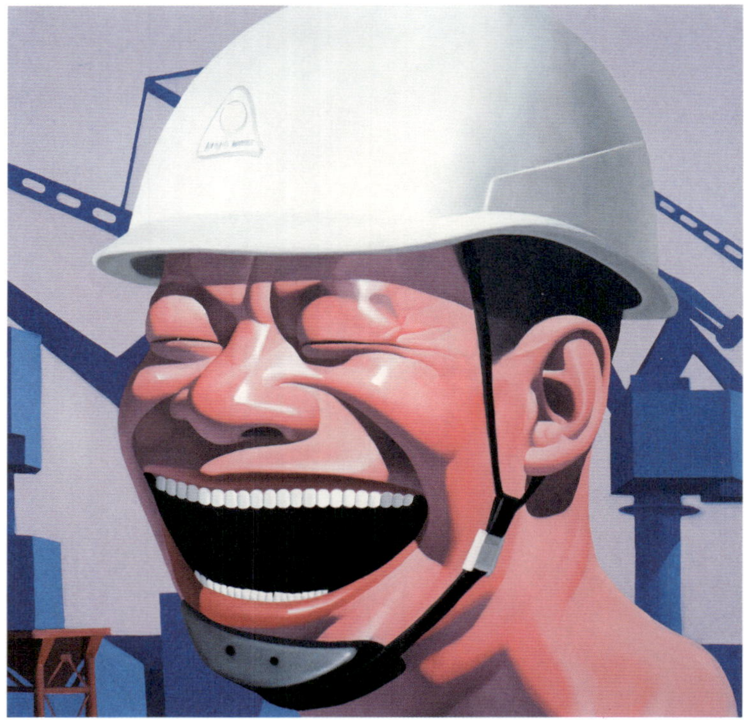

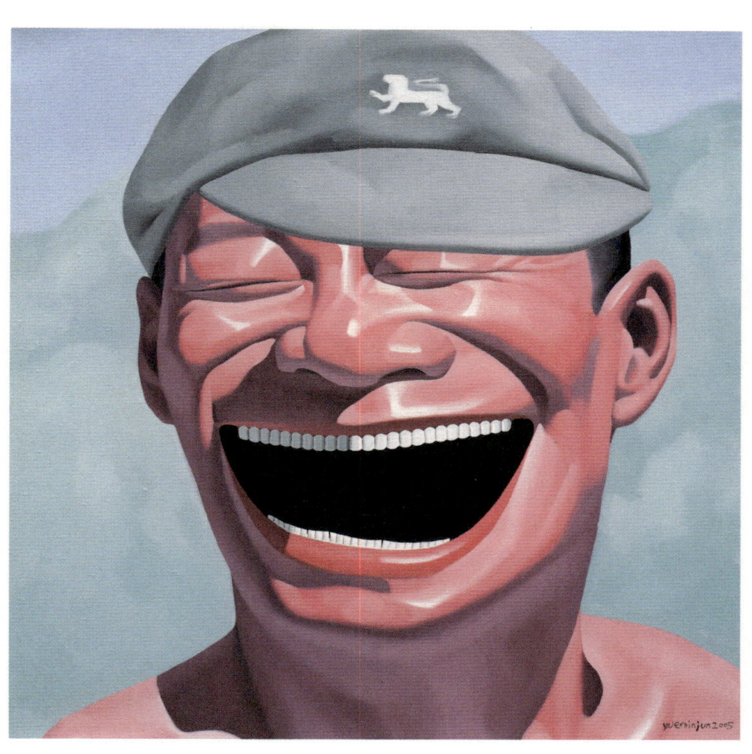

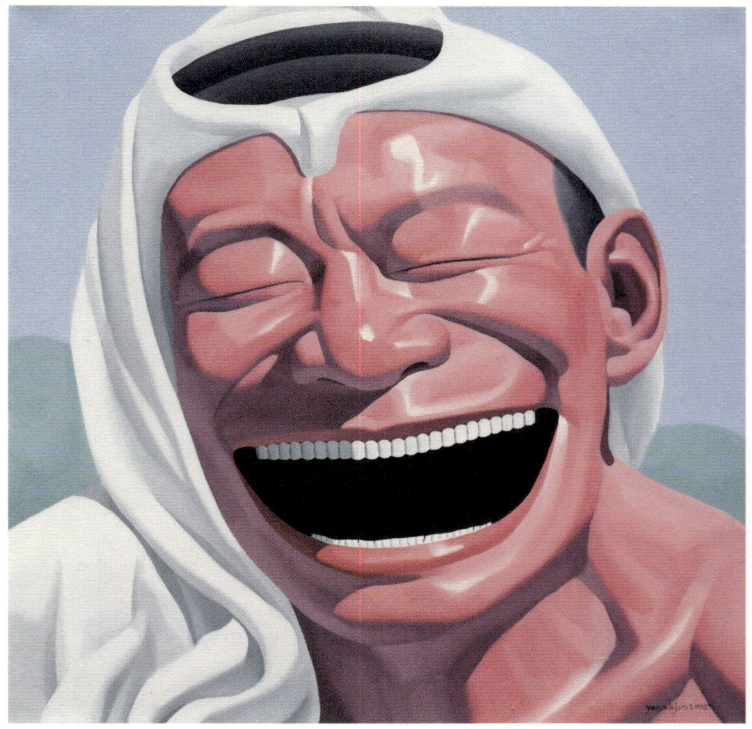

Hats * 帽子 * 80 x 80cm x 10pcs * 2005 * oil on canvas * 布上油畫

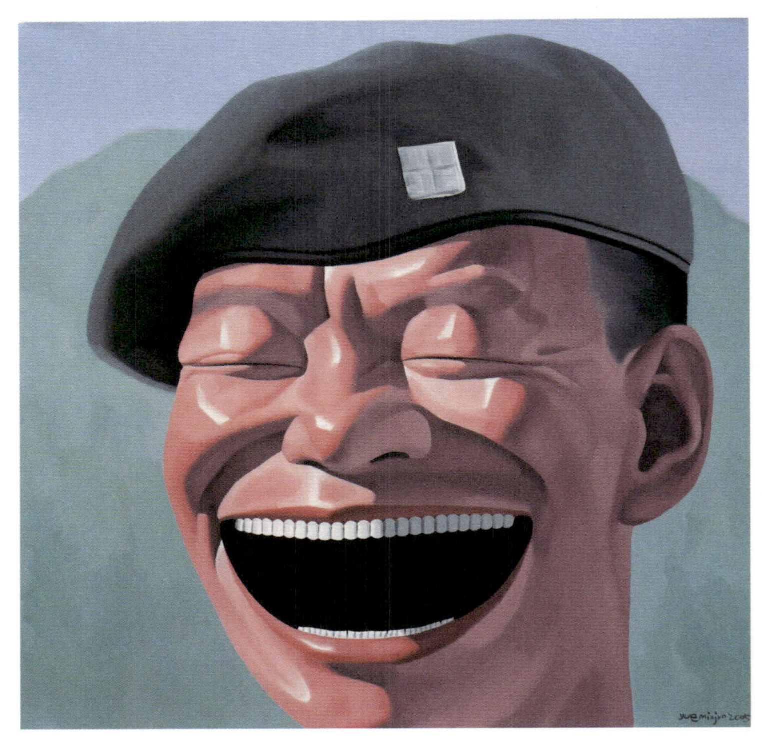

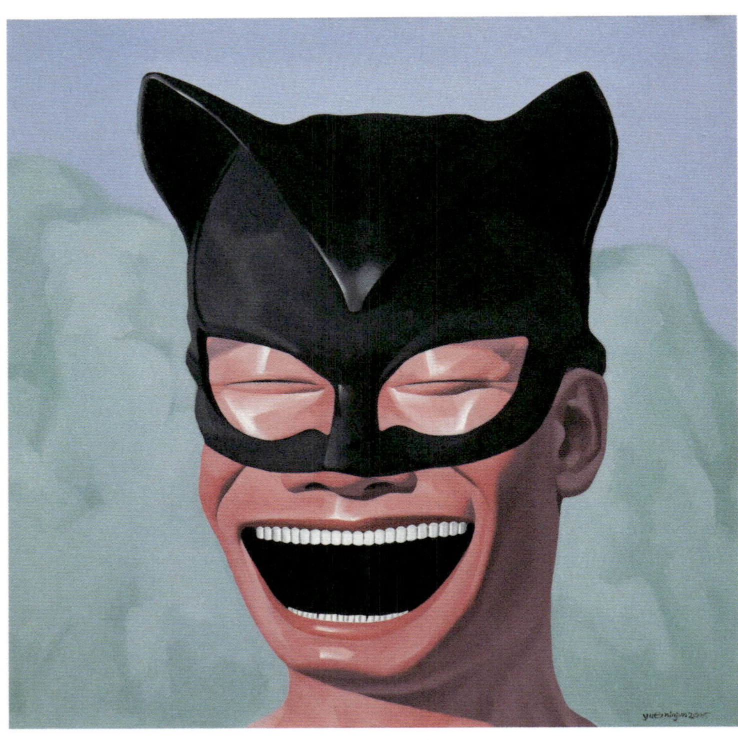

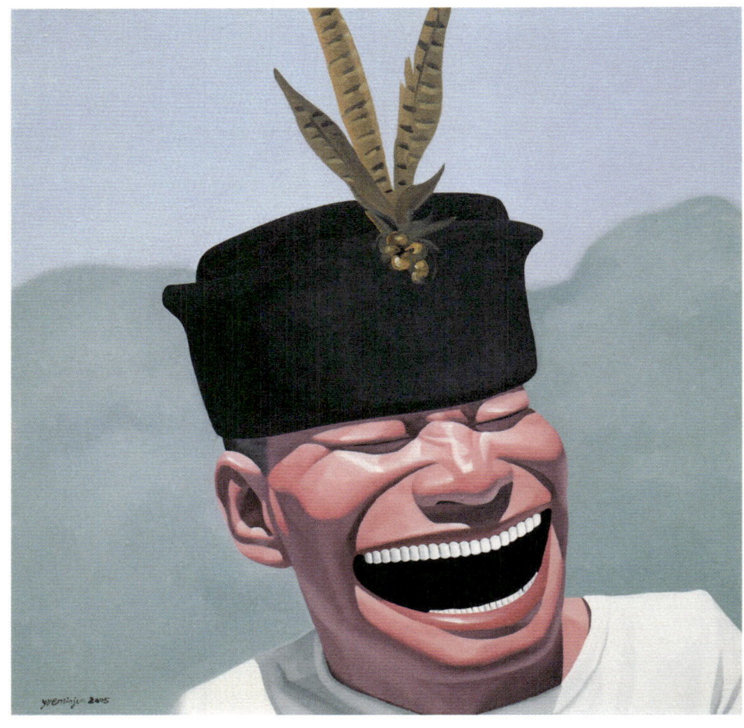

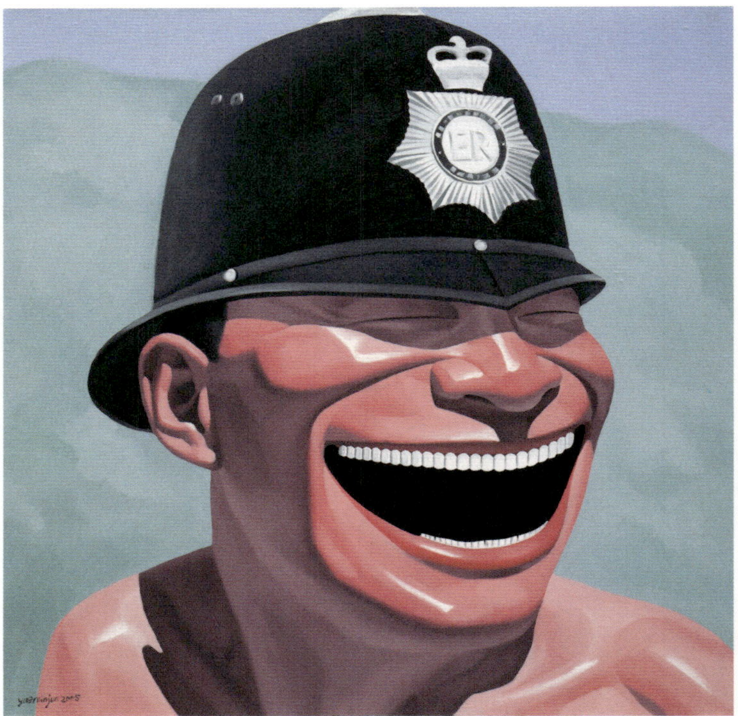

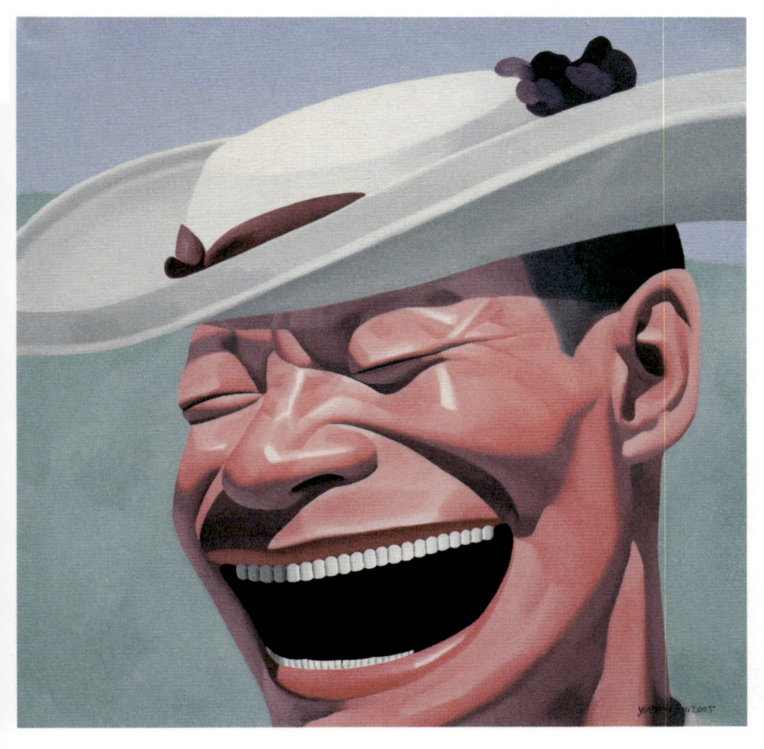

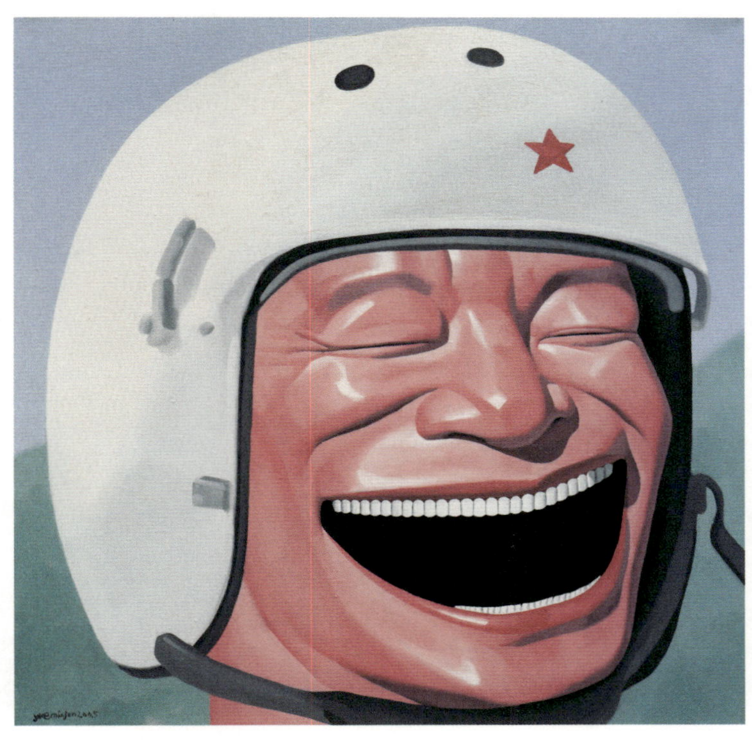

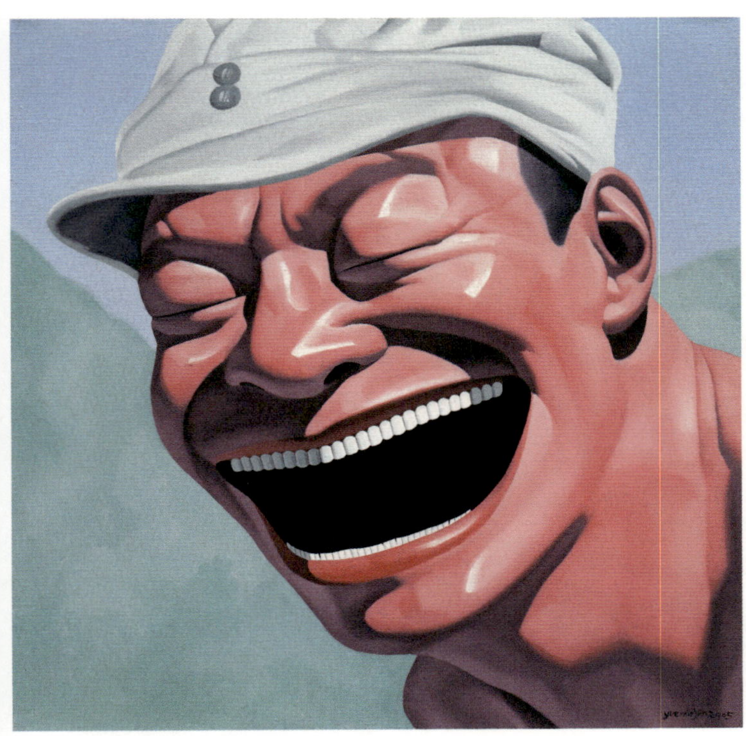

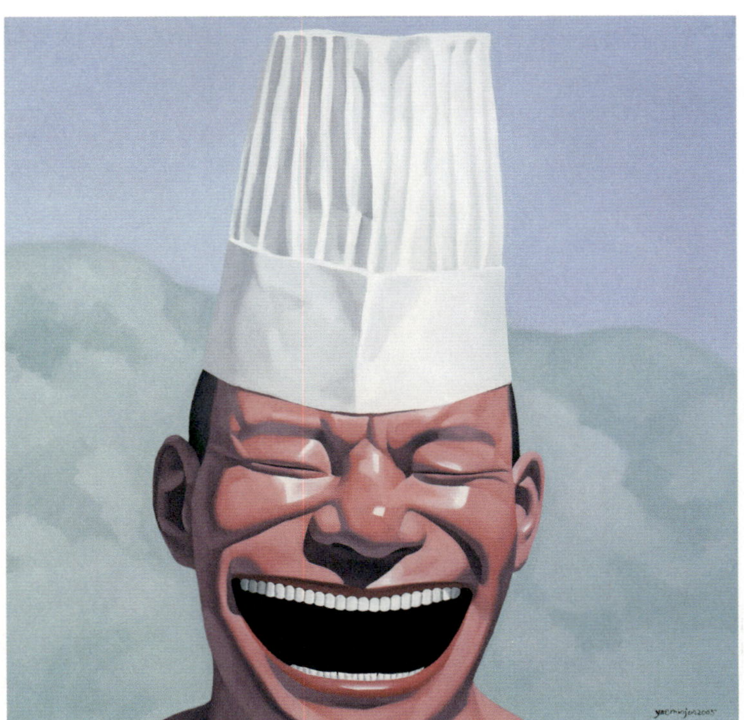

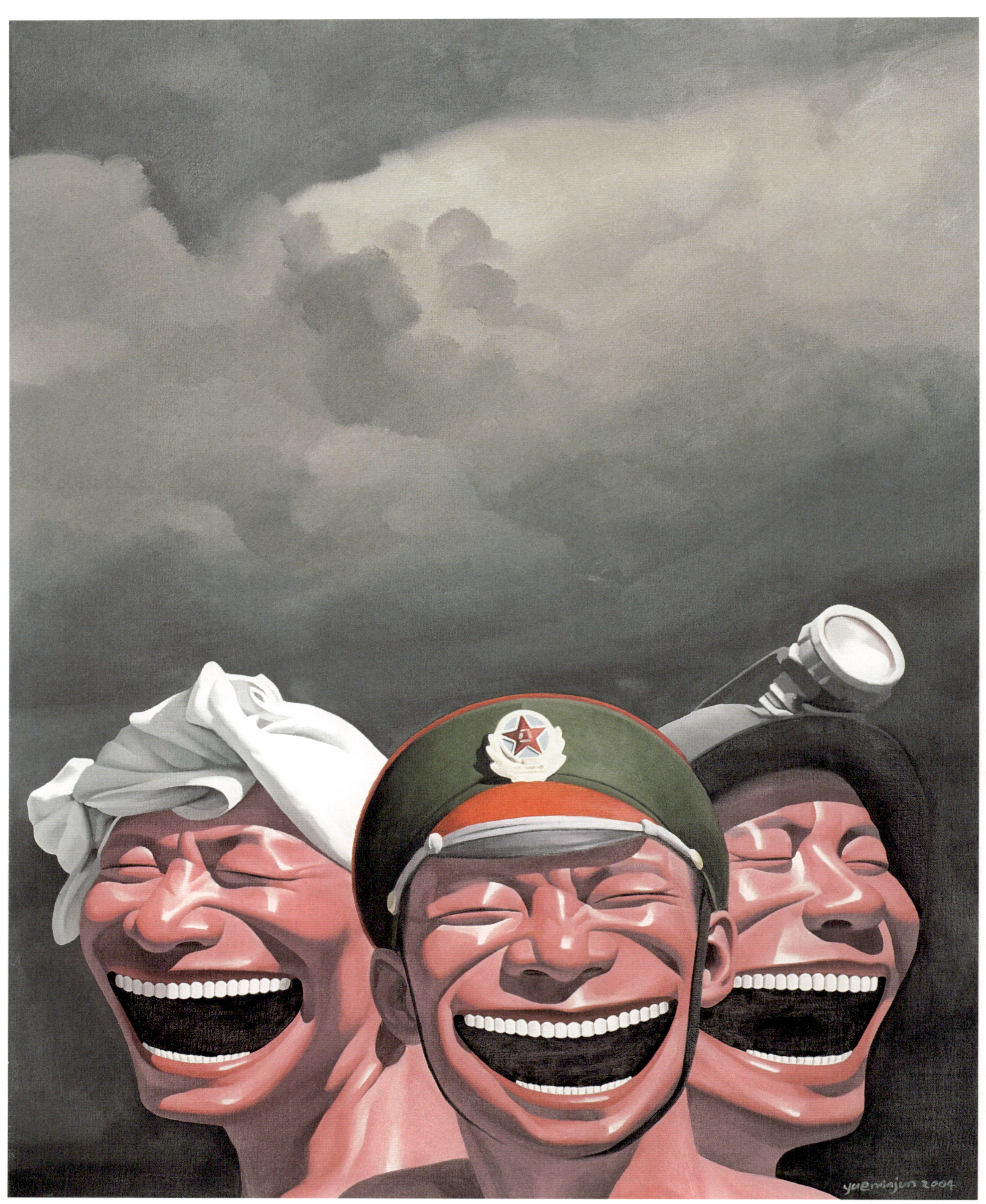

Hats Series No.1 * 帽子系列 No.1 * 100 x 80cm * 2004 * oil on canvas * 布上油畫

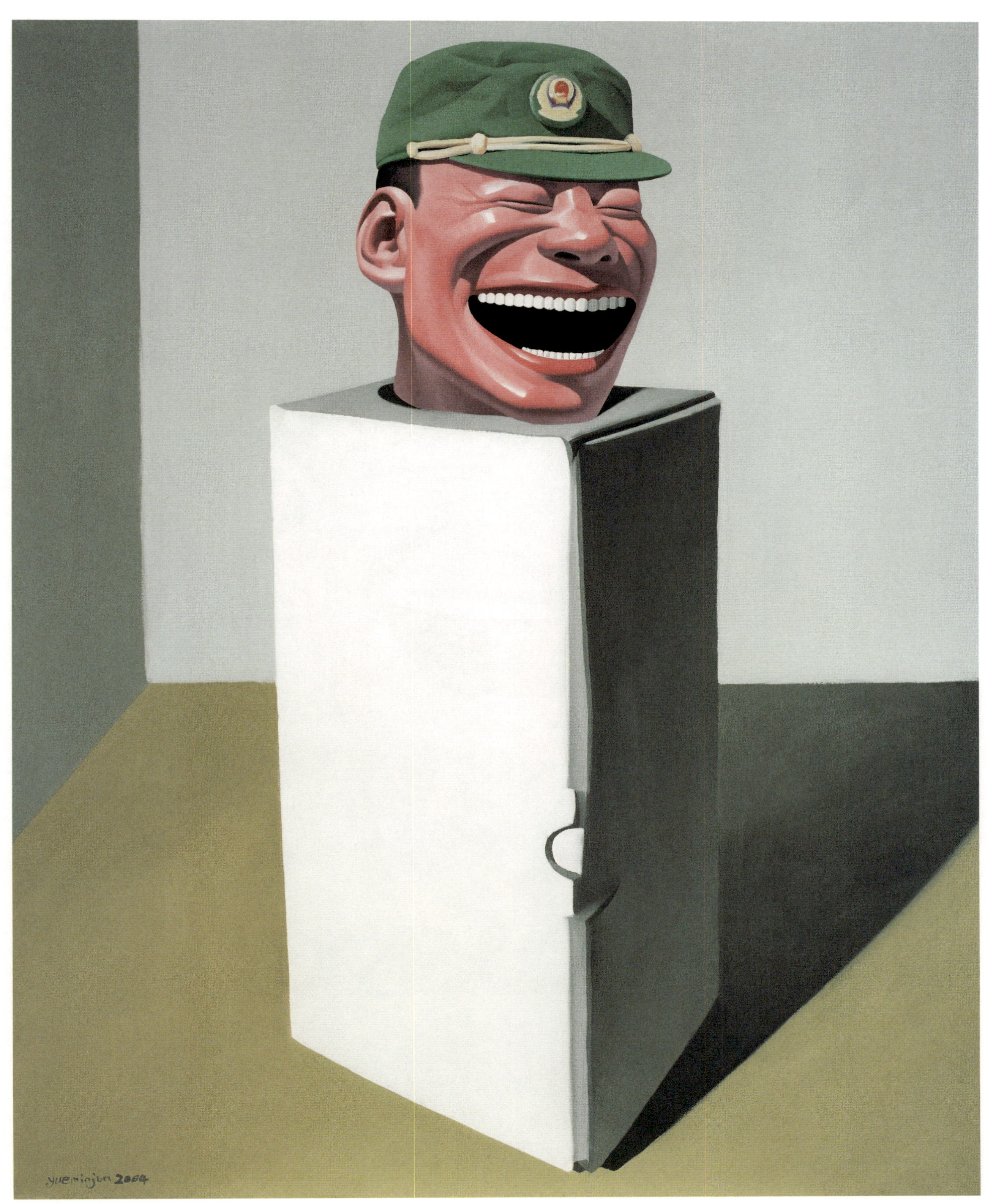

Hats Series No.2 * 帽子系列 No.2 * 100 x 80cm * 2004 * oil on canvas * 布上油畫

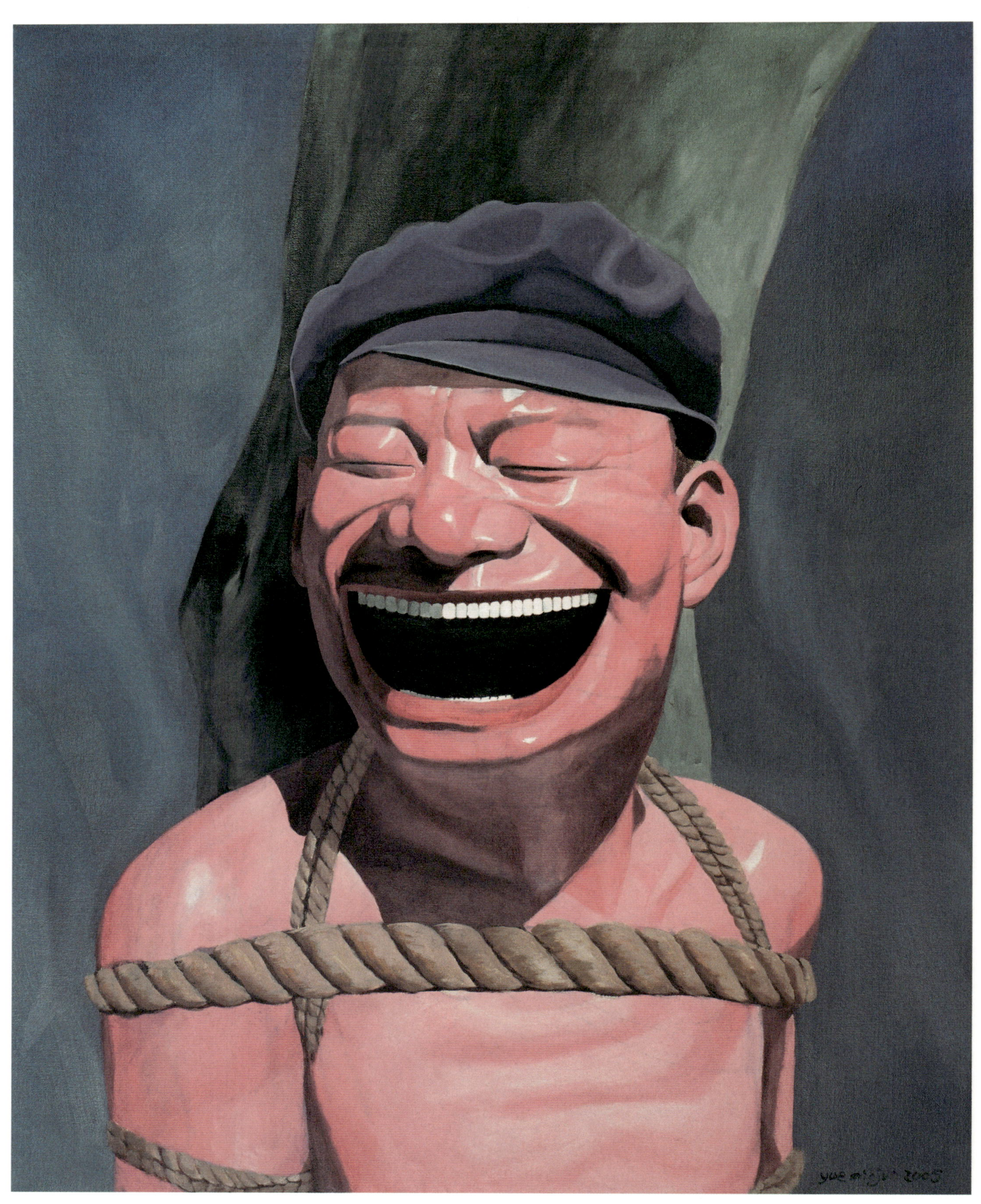

Hats Series No.3 Storm * 帽子系列 No.3 風暴 * 100 x 80cm * 2005 * oil on canvas * 布上油畫

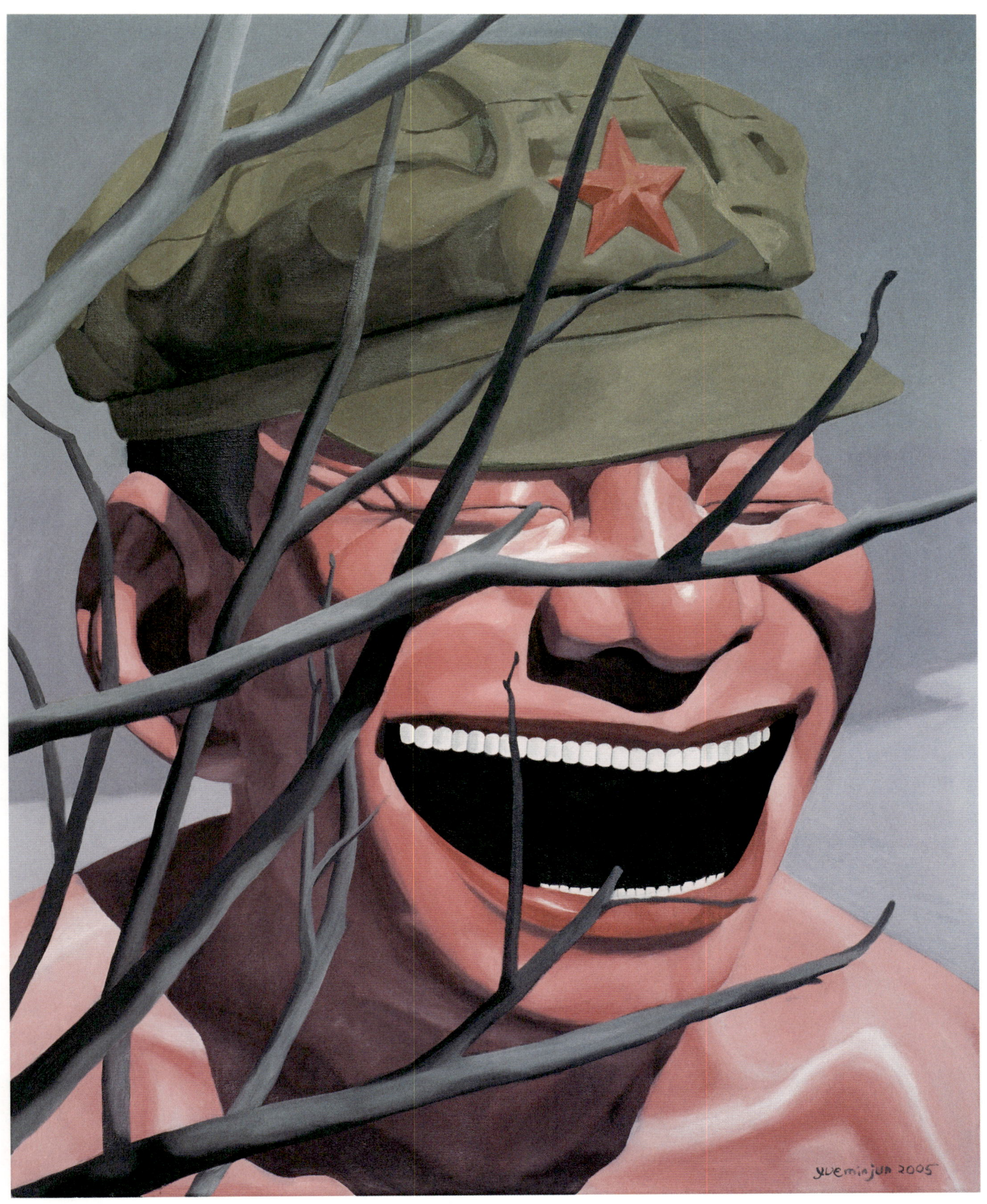

Hats Series No.4 Laughter in Bosk * 帽子系列 No.4 他在叢中笑 * 100 x 80cm * 2005 * oil on canvas * 布上油畫

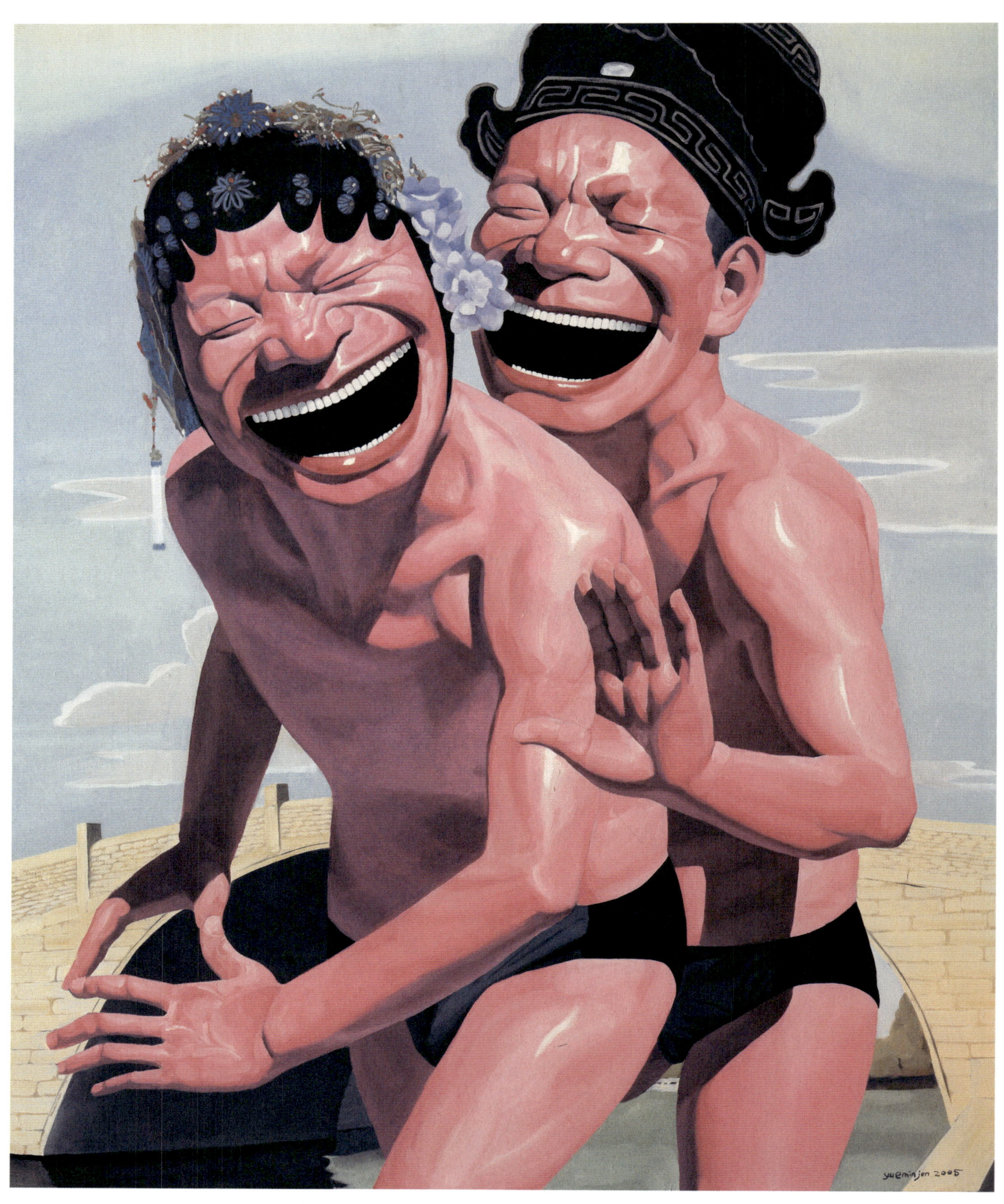

Hats Series – The Lovers * 帽子系列 — 才子佳人 * 170 x 140cm * 2005 * oil on canvas * 布上油畫

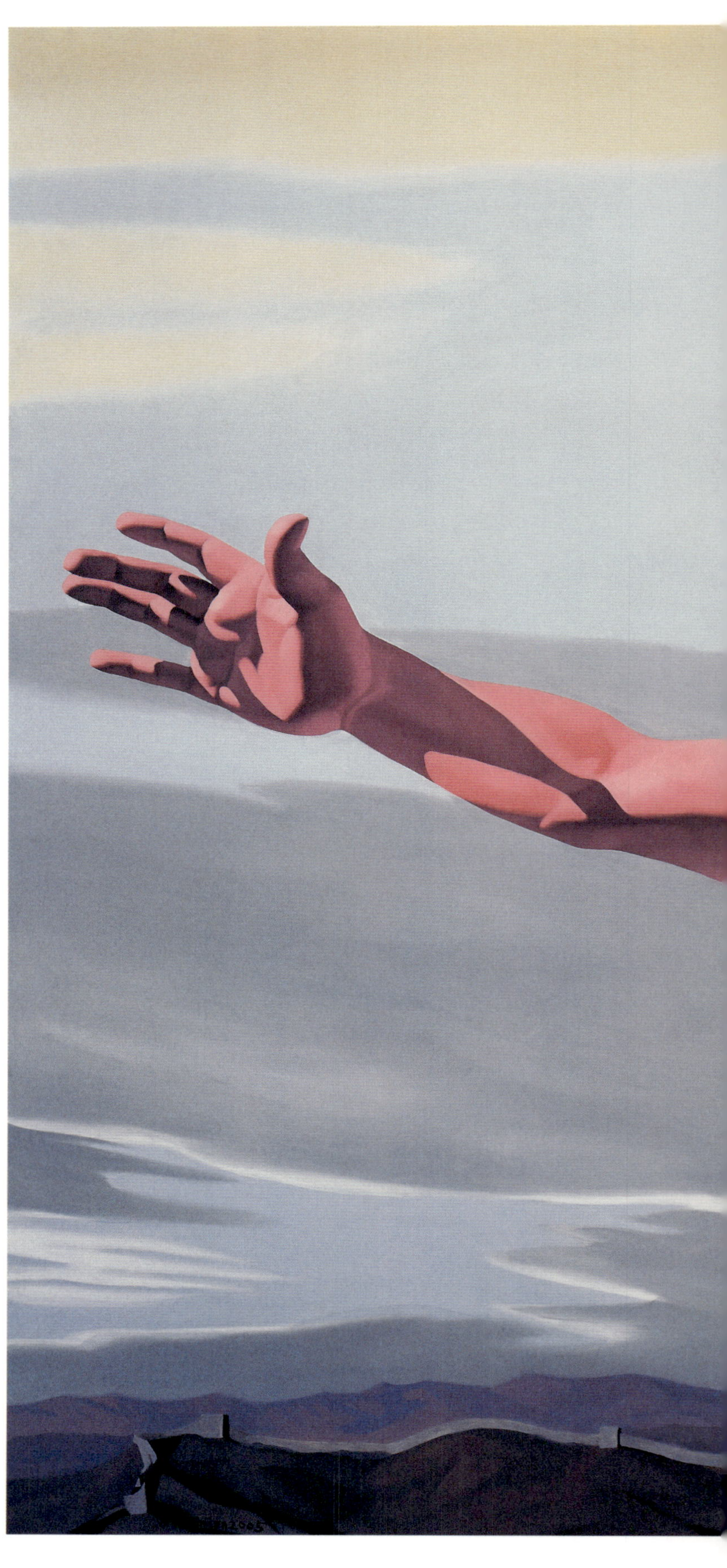

Hats Series – Within, Without the Great Wall *
帽子系列 — 長城内外 *
300 x 220cm *
2005 *
oil on canvas *
布上油畫

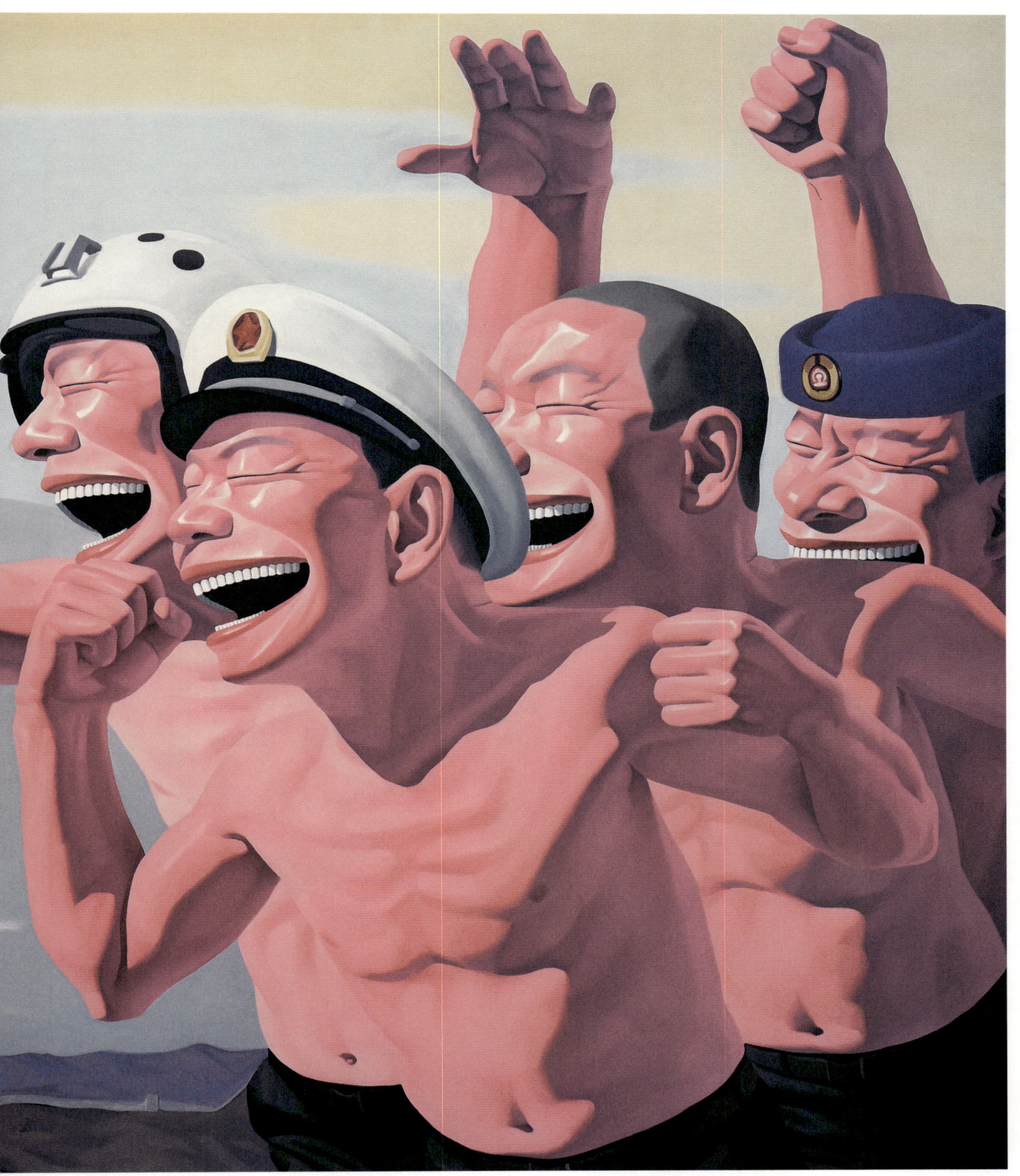

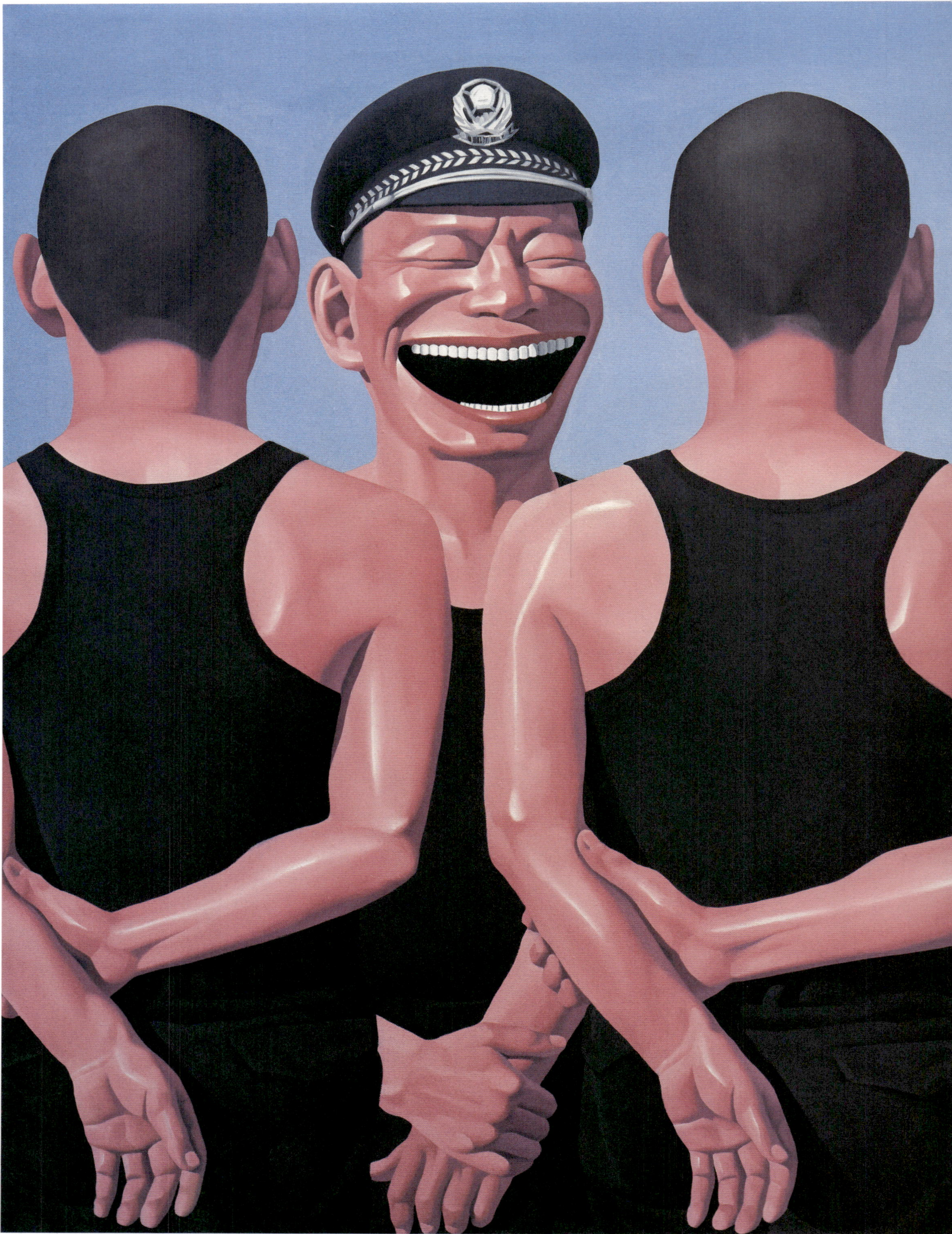

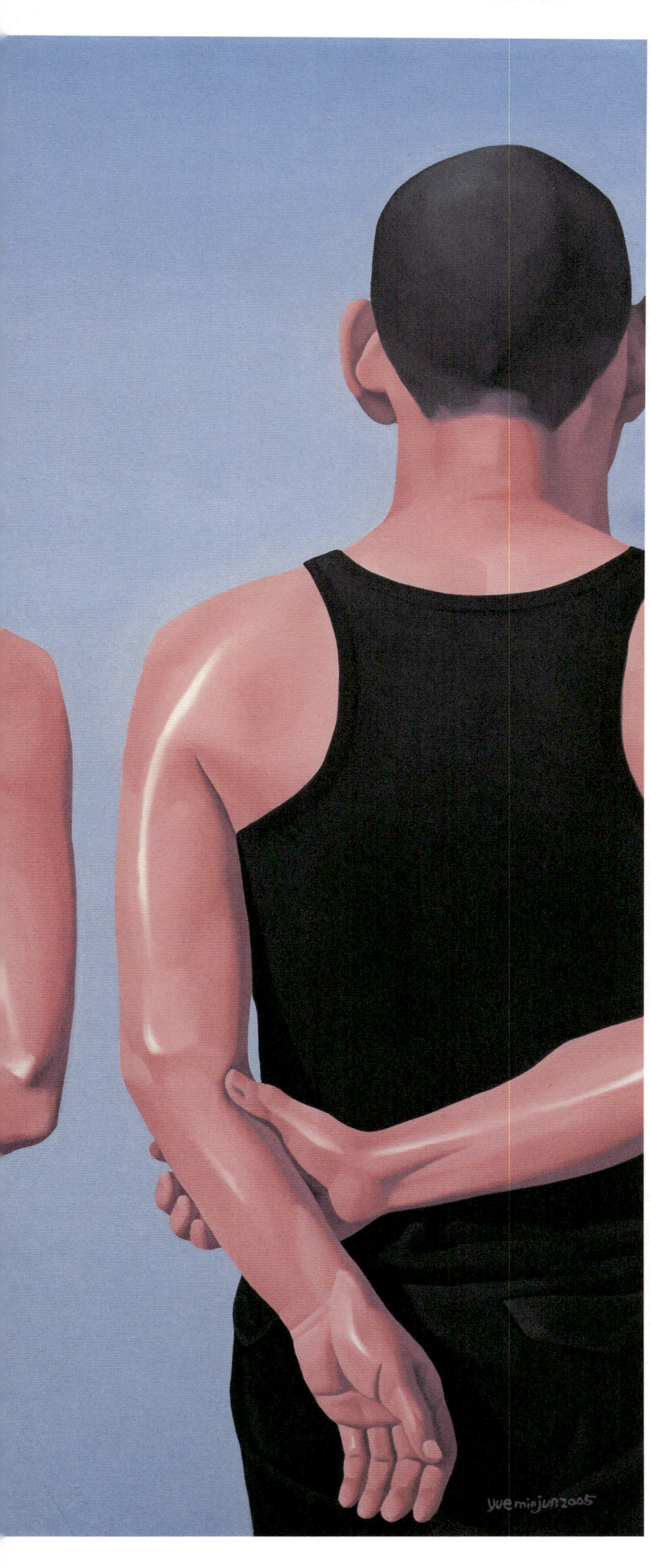

Hats Series – Untitled *
帽子系列 — 無題 *
140 x 170cm *
2005 *
oil on canvas *
布上油畫

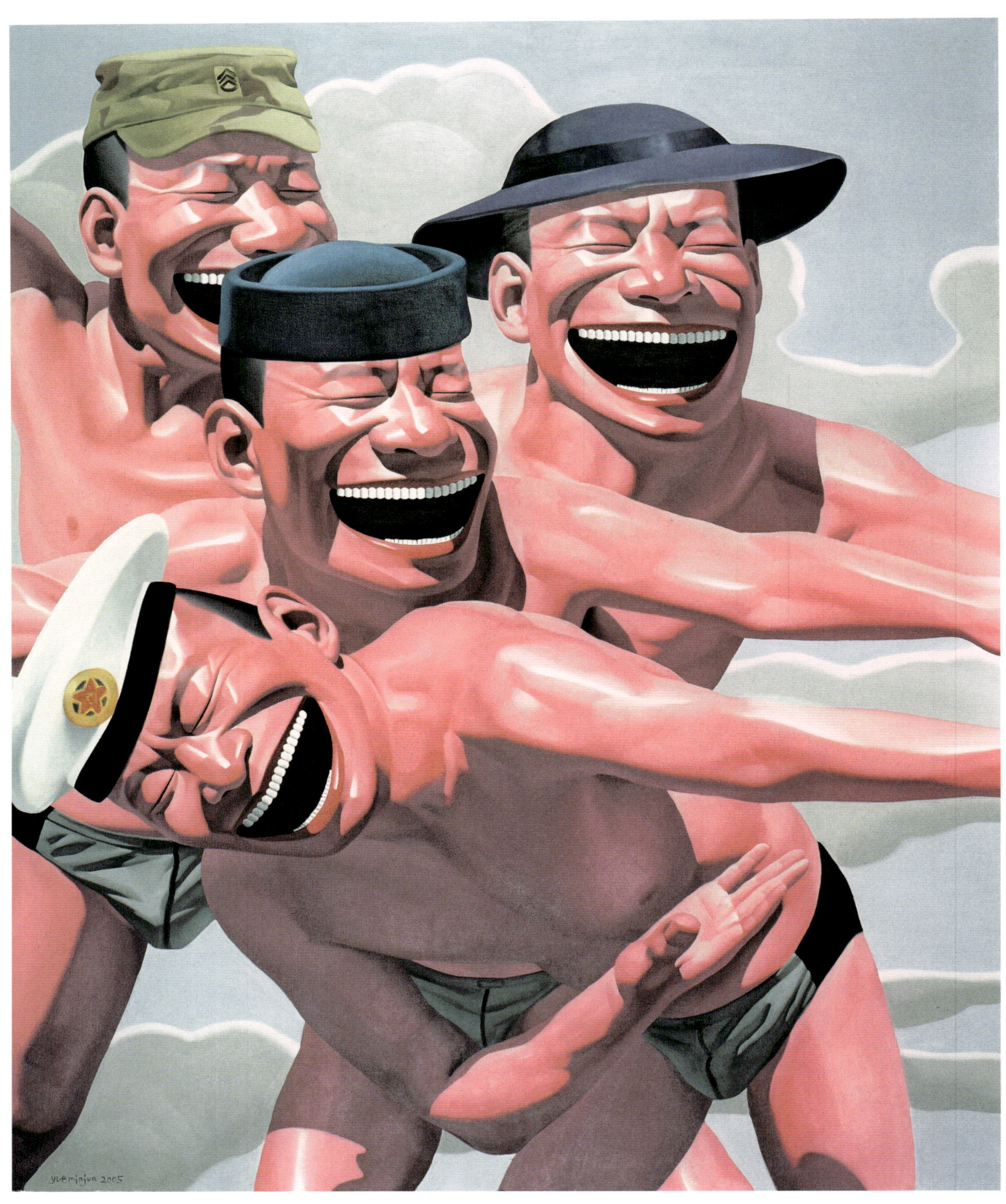

Hats Series – Welcome * 帽子系列 — 邀請 * 170 x 140cm * 2005 * oil on canvas * 布上油畫

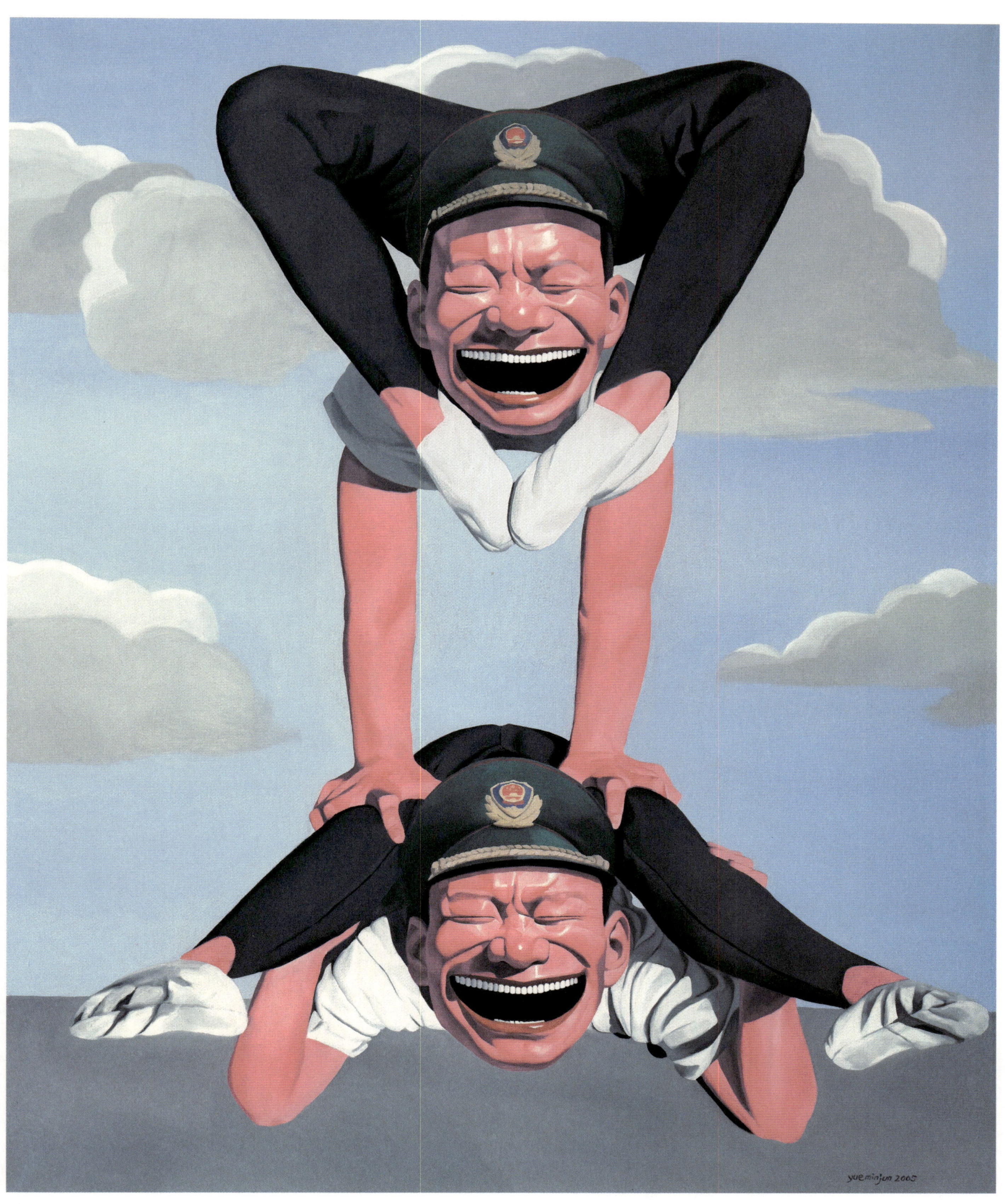

Hats Series – Acrobatics * 帽子系列 — 雜技 * 170 x 140cm * 2005 * oil on canvas * 布上油畫

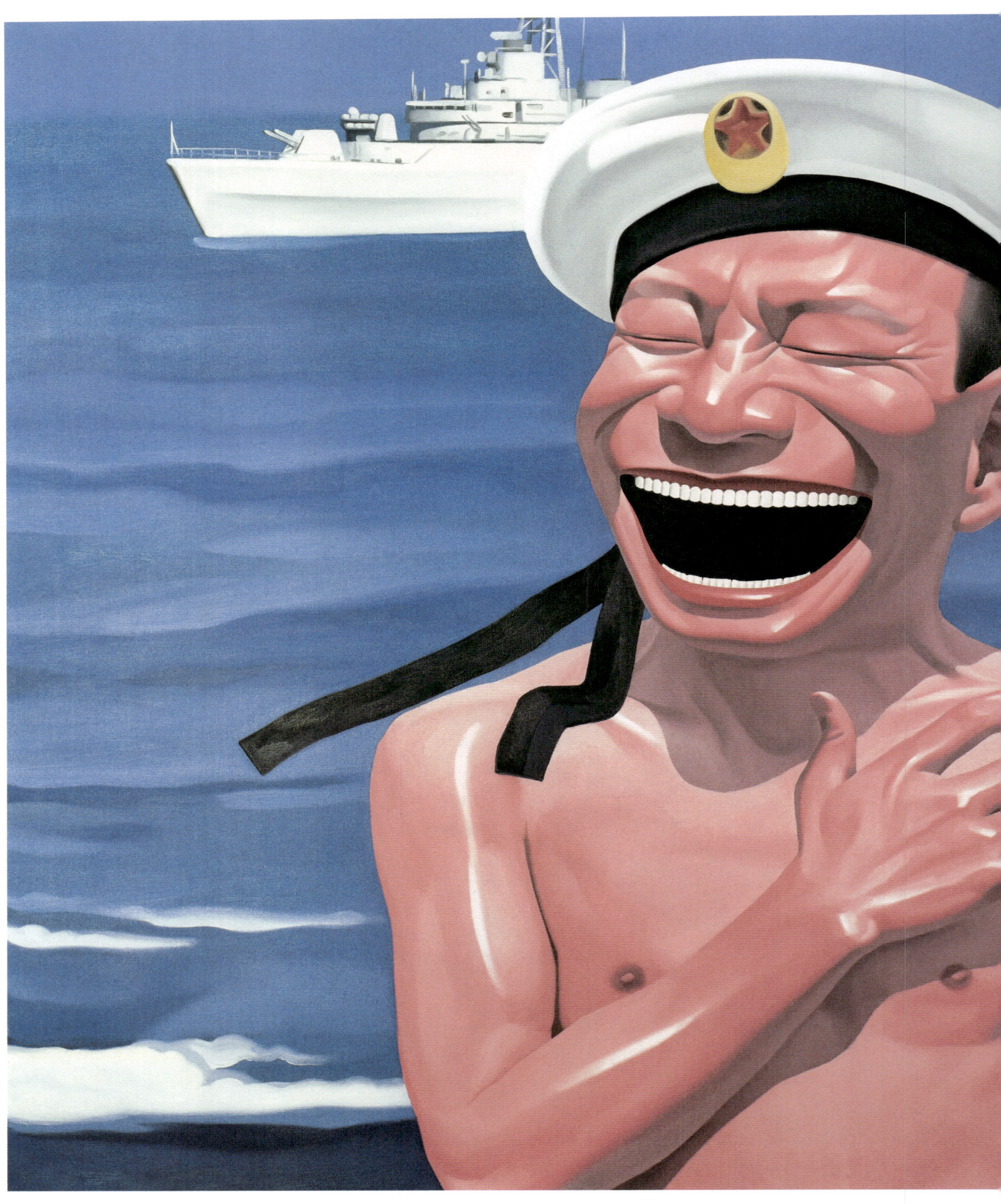

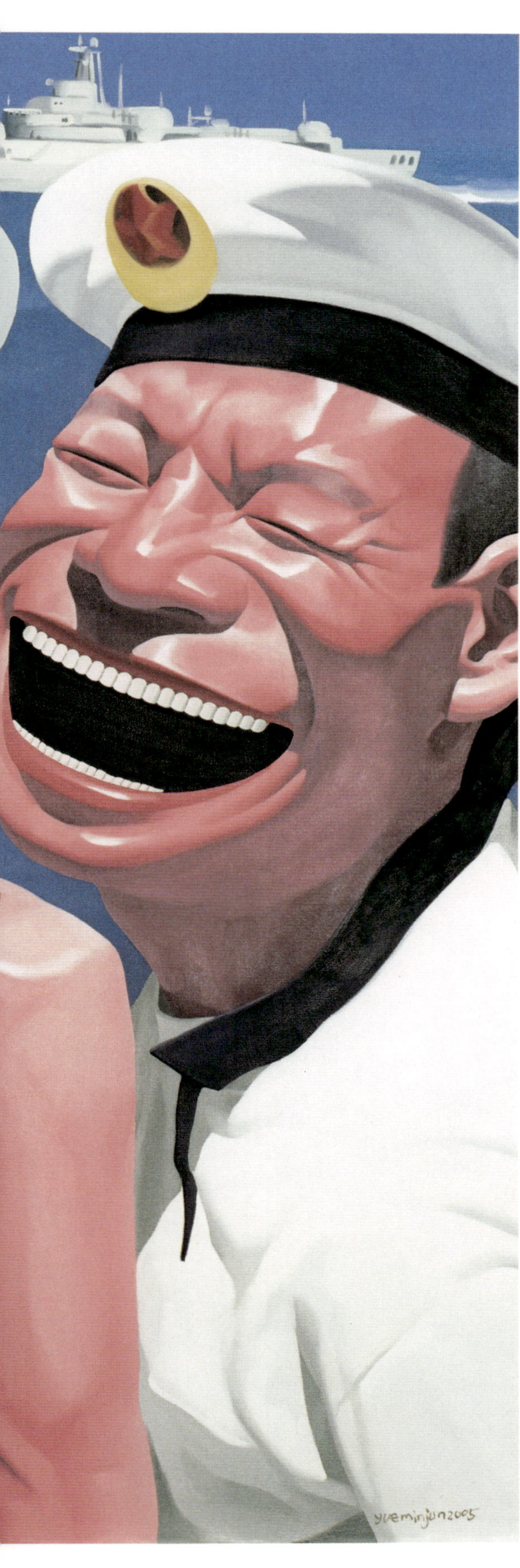

Hats Series – Coastal Areas *
帽子系列 — 祖國的海疆 *
170 x 140cm *
2005 *
oil on canvas *
布上油畫

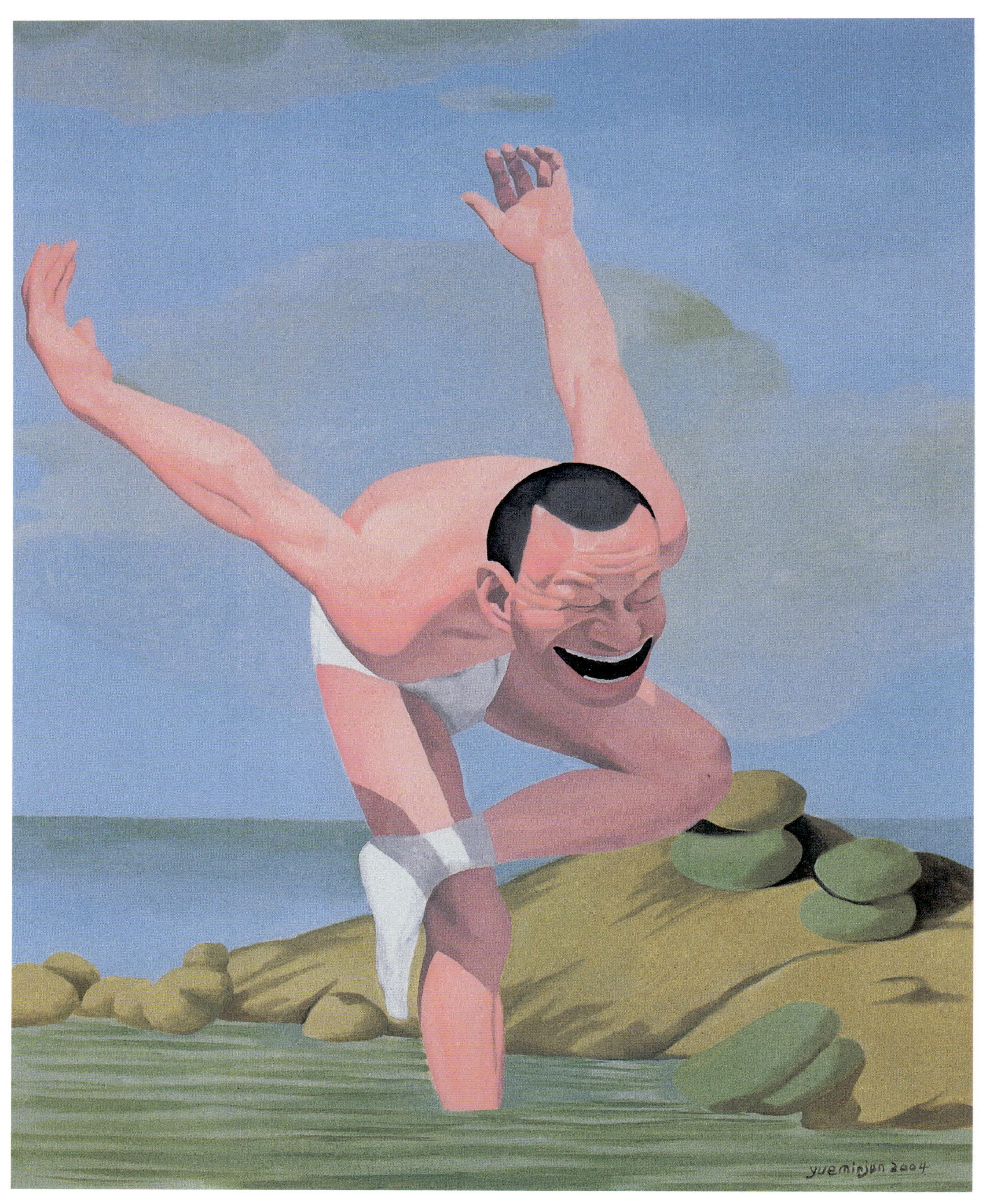

Free and At Leisure - 2 * 閑雲野鶴 – 2 * 100 x 80cm * 2004 * oil on canvas * 布上油畫

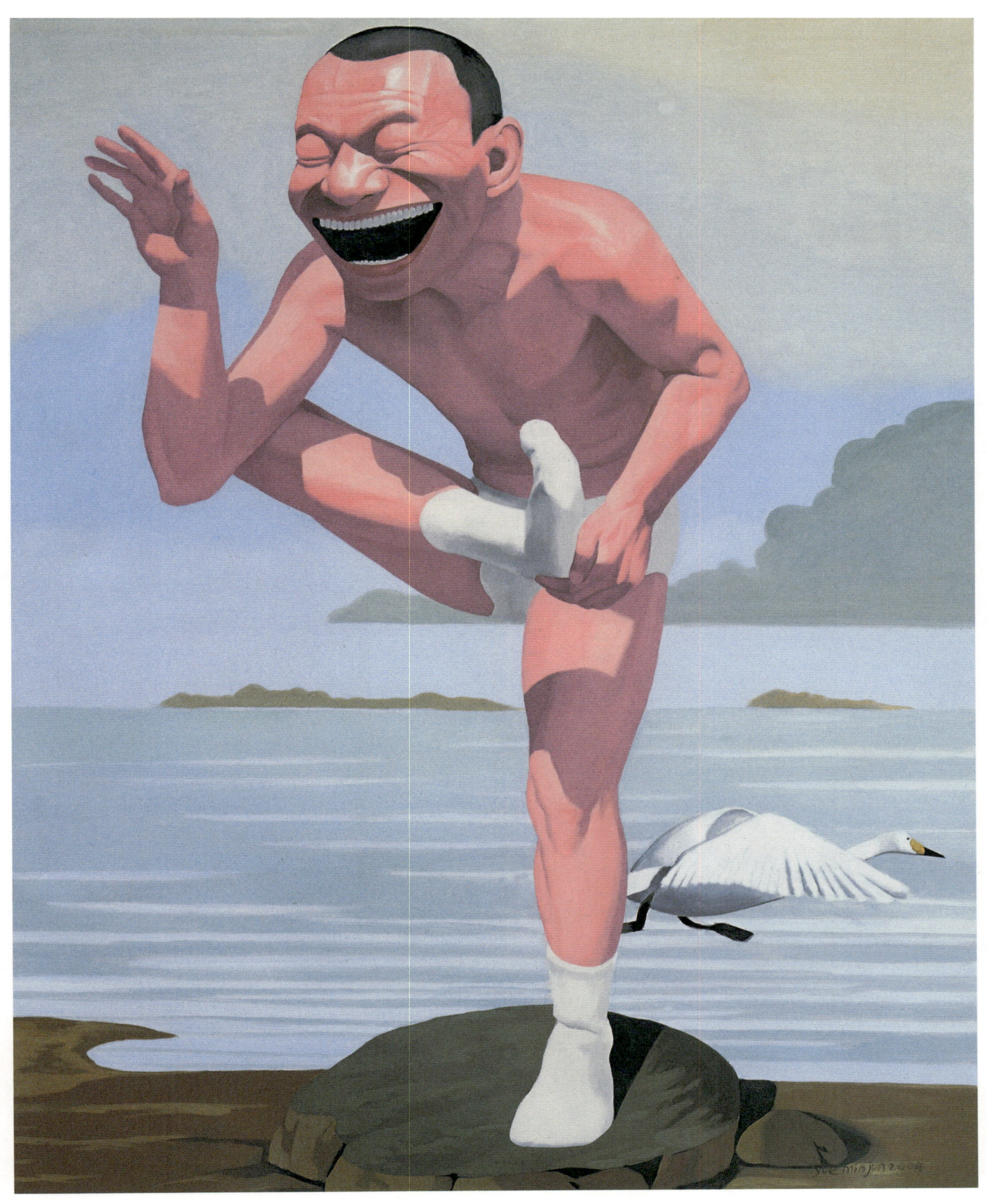

Free and At Leisure - 3 * 閑雲野鶴 – 3 * 100 x 80cm * 2004 * oil on canvas * 布上油畫

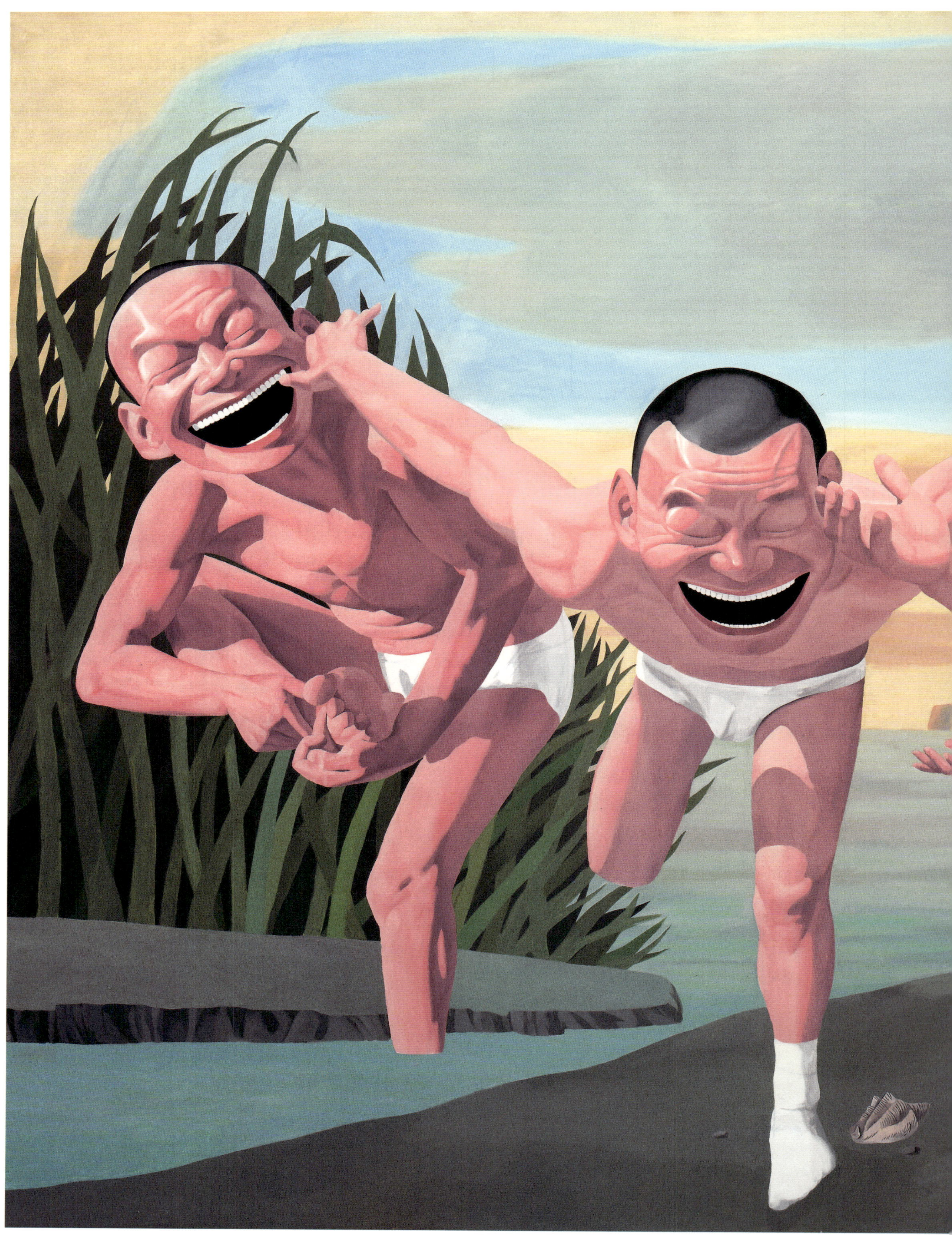

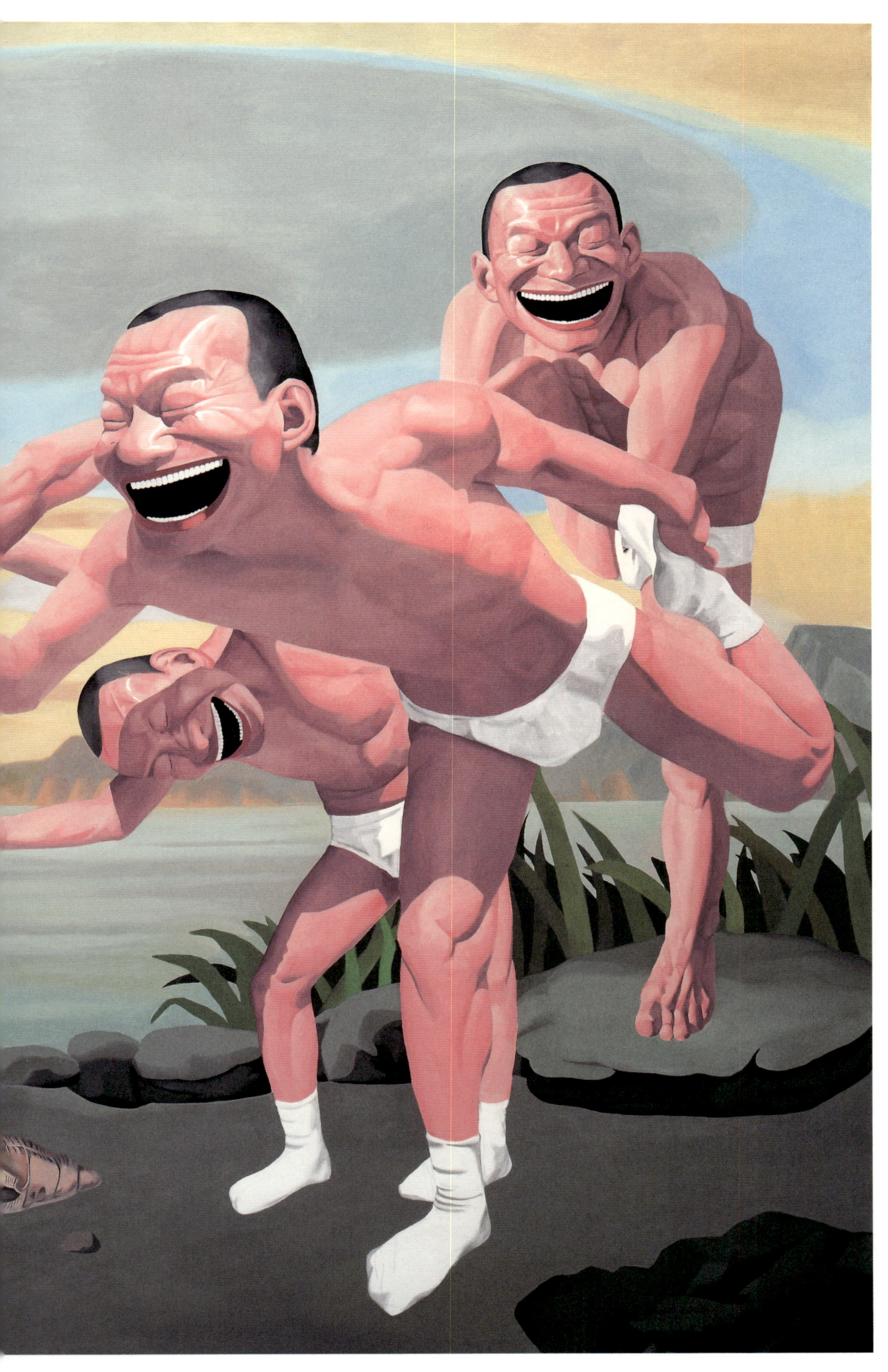

Free and At Leisure - 4 *
閑雲野鶴 – 4 *
400 x 280cm *
2004 *
oil on canvas *
布上油畫

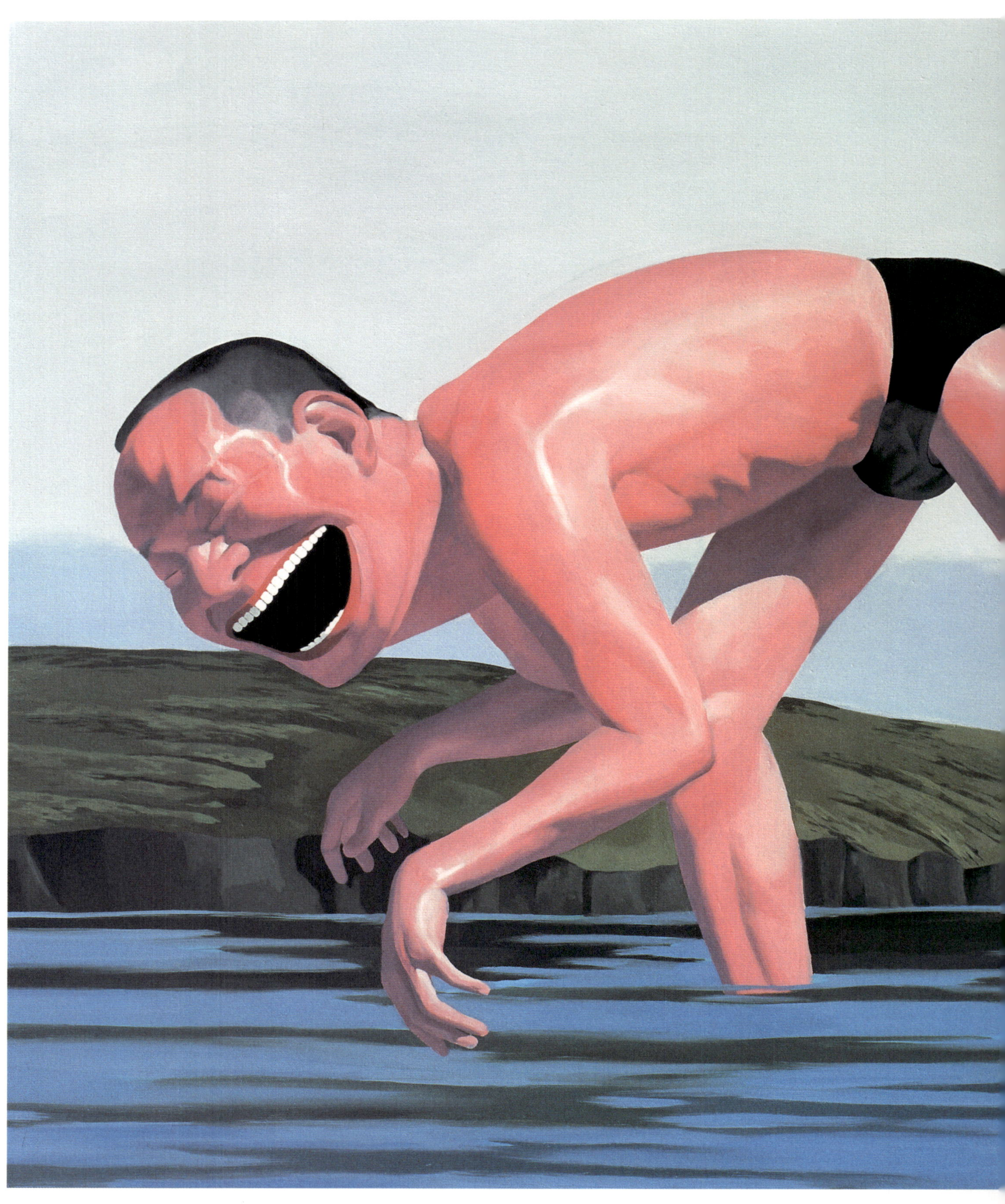

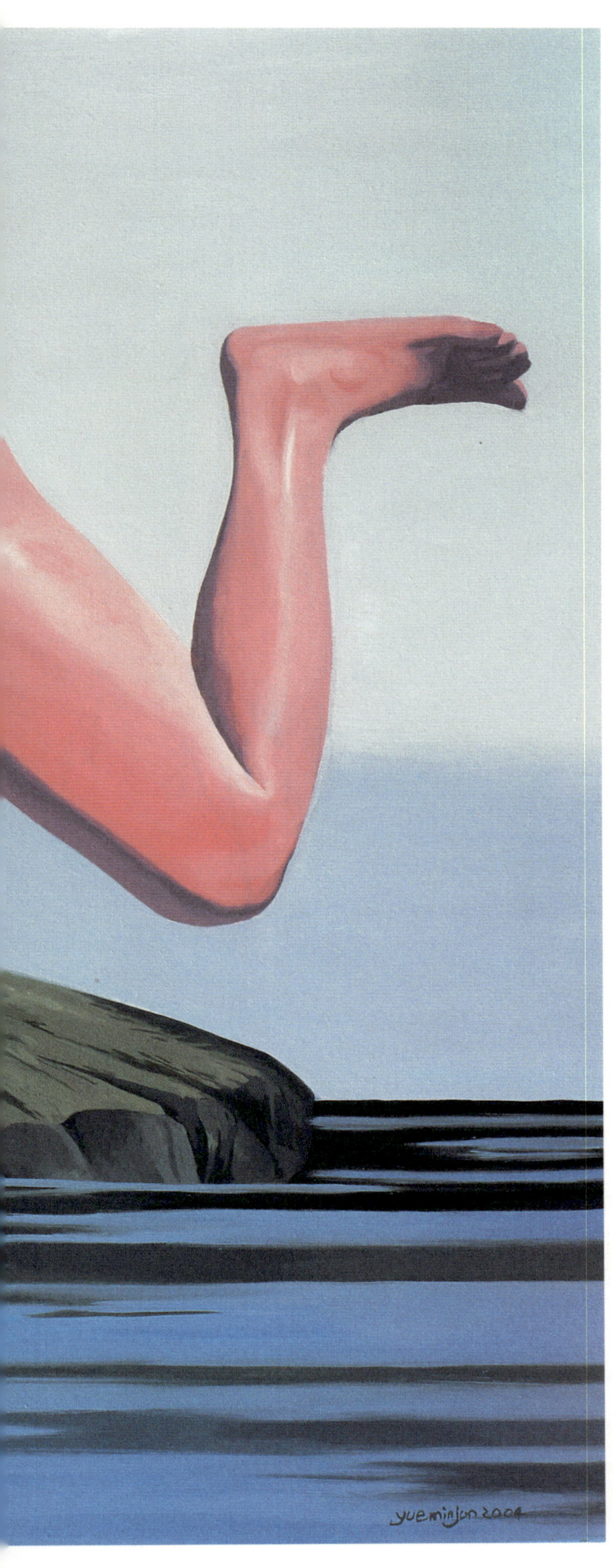

Free and At Leisure - 5 *
閑雲野鶴 – 5 *
140 x 108cm *
2004 *
oil on canvas *
布上油畫

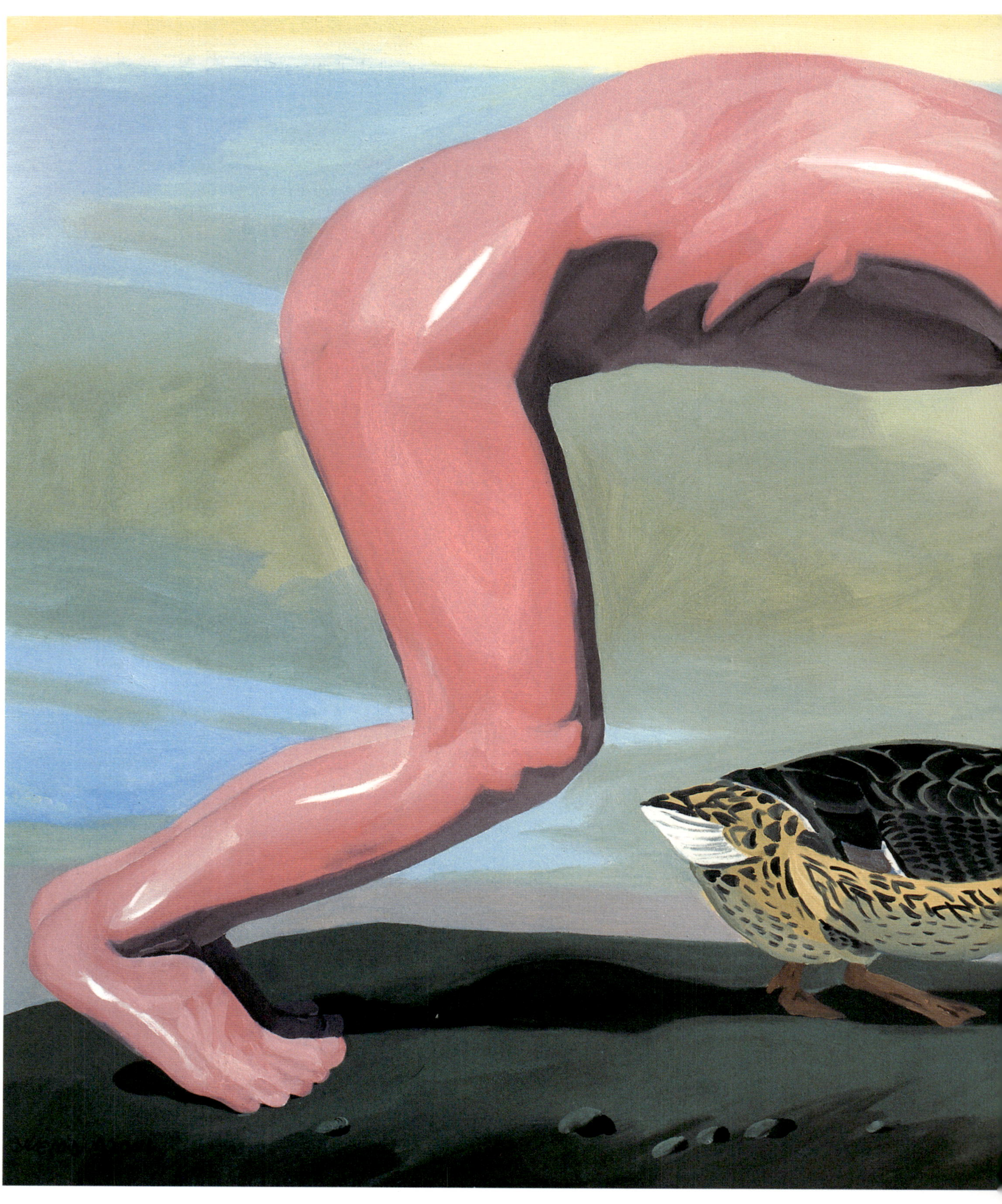

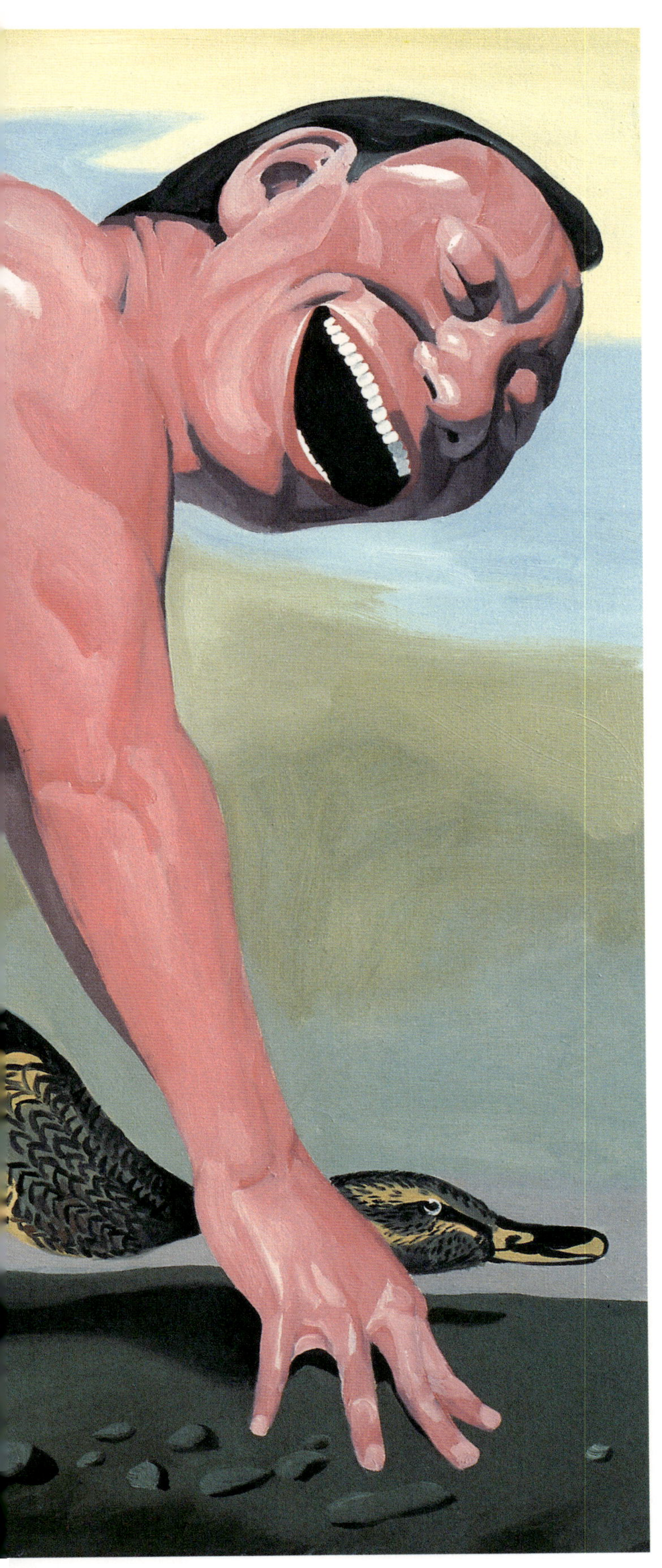

Free and At Leisure - 6 *
閑雲野鶴 – 6 *
140 x 108cm *
2004 *
oil on canvas *
布上油畫

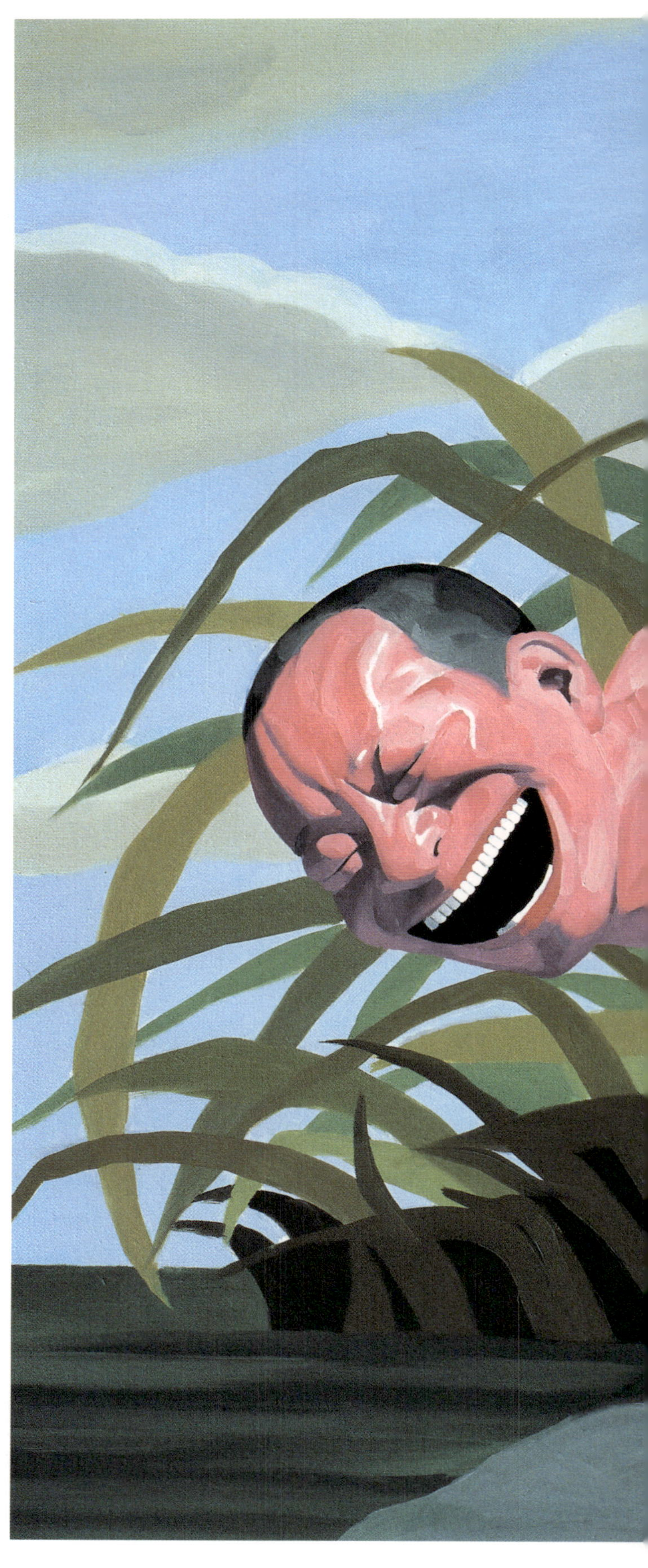

Free and At Leisure - 7 *
閑雲野鶴 – 7 *
140 x 108cm *
2004 *
oil on canvas *
布上油畫

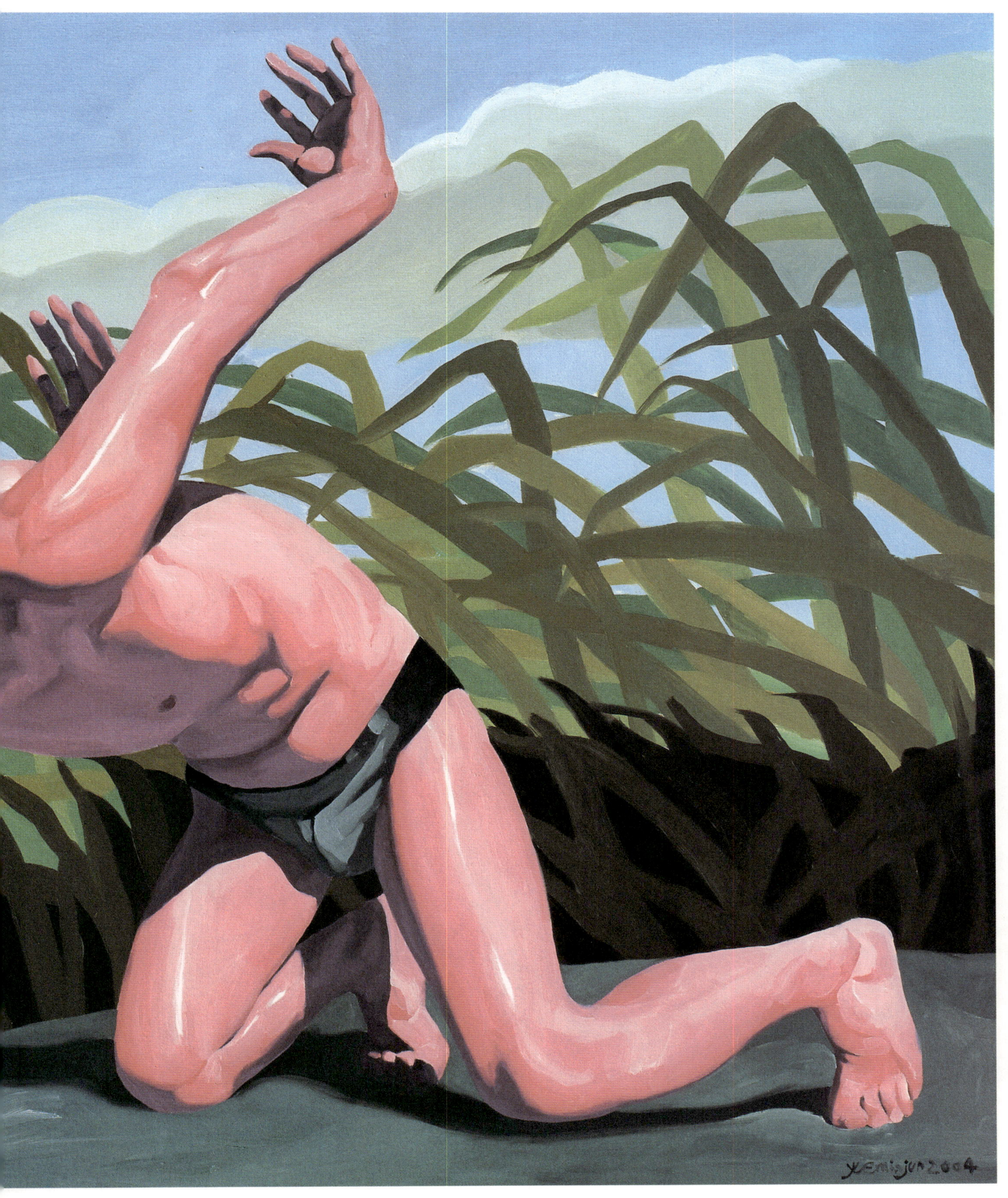

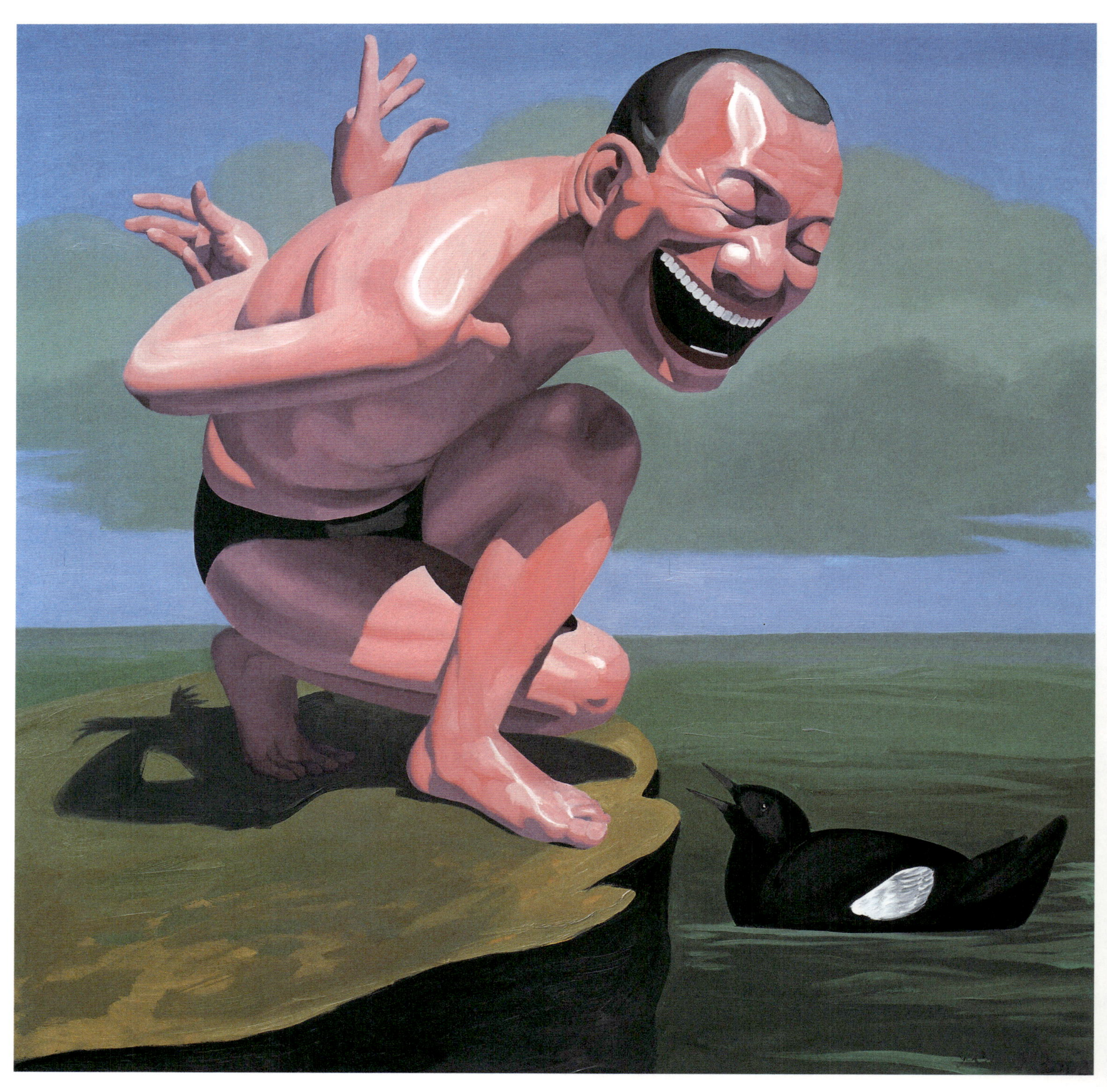

Free and At Leisure - 8 * 閑雲野鶴 – 8 * 140 x 140cm * 2003 * oil on canvas * 布上油畫

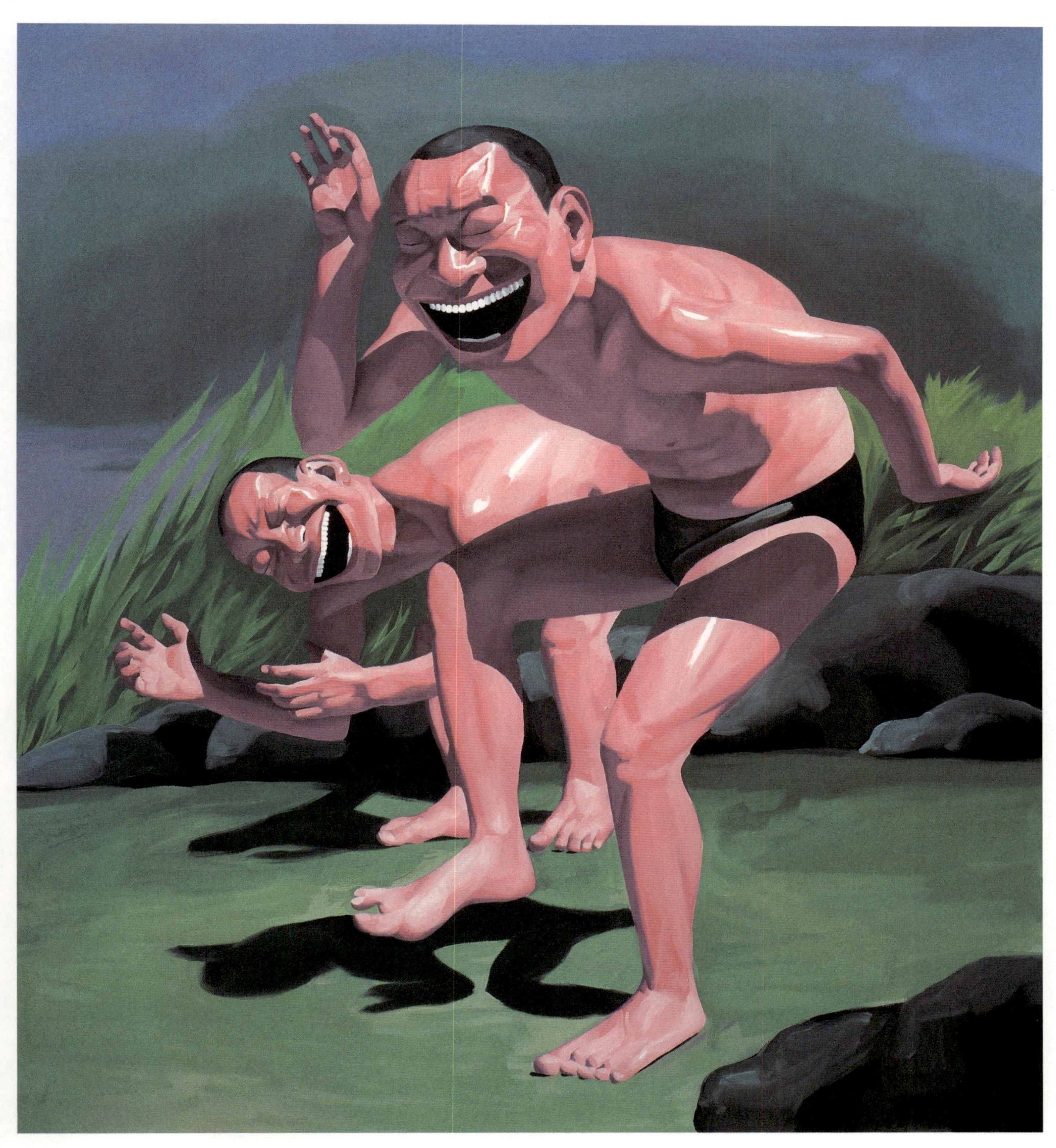

Free and At Leisure - 9 * 閑雲野鶴 – 9 * 140 x 126cm * 2004 * oil on canvas * 布上油畫

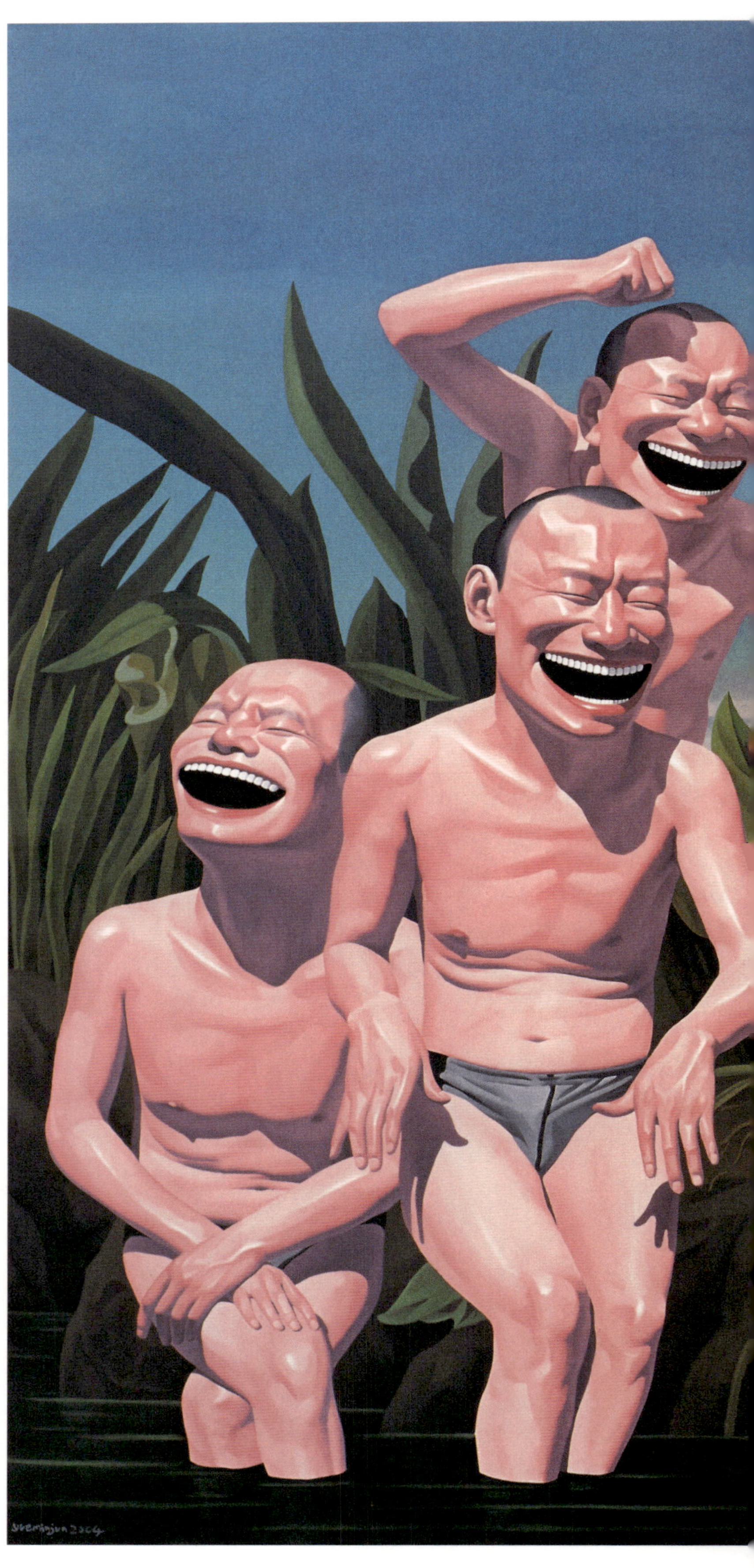

Free and At Leisure - 10 *
閑雲野鶴 – 10 *
300 x 220cm *
2004 *
oil on canvas *
布上油畫

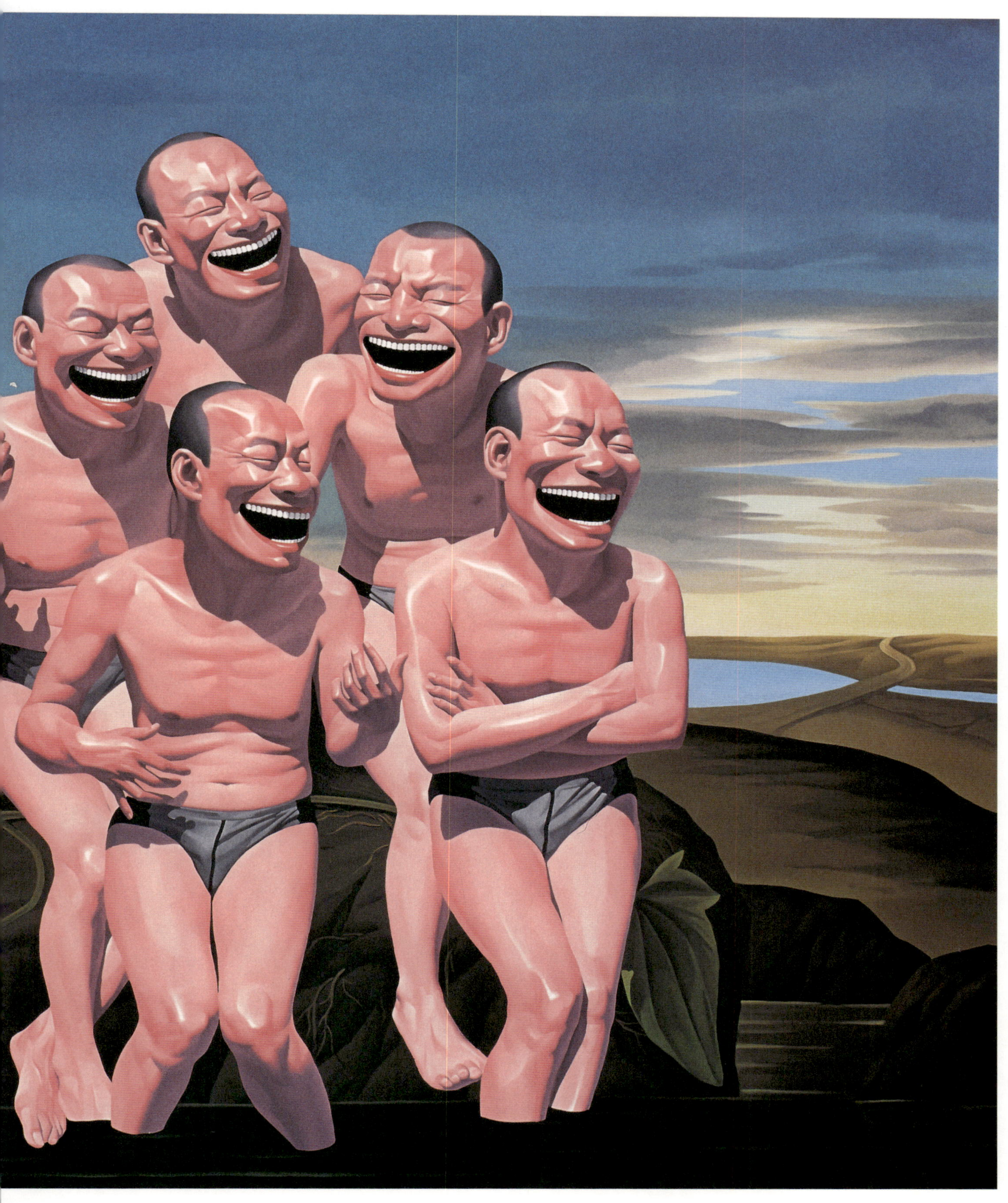

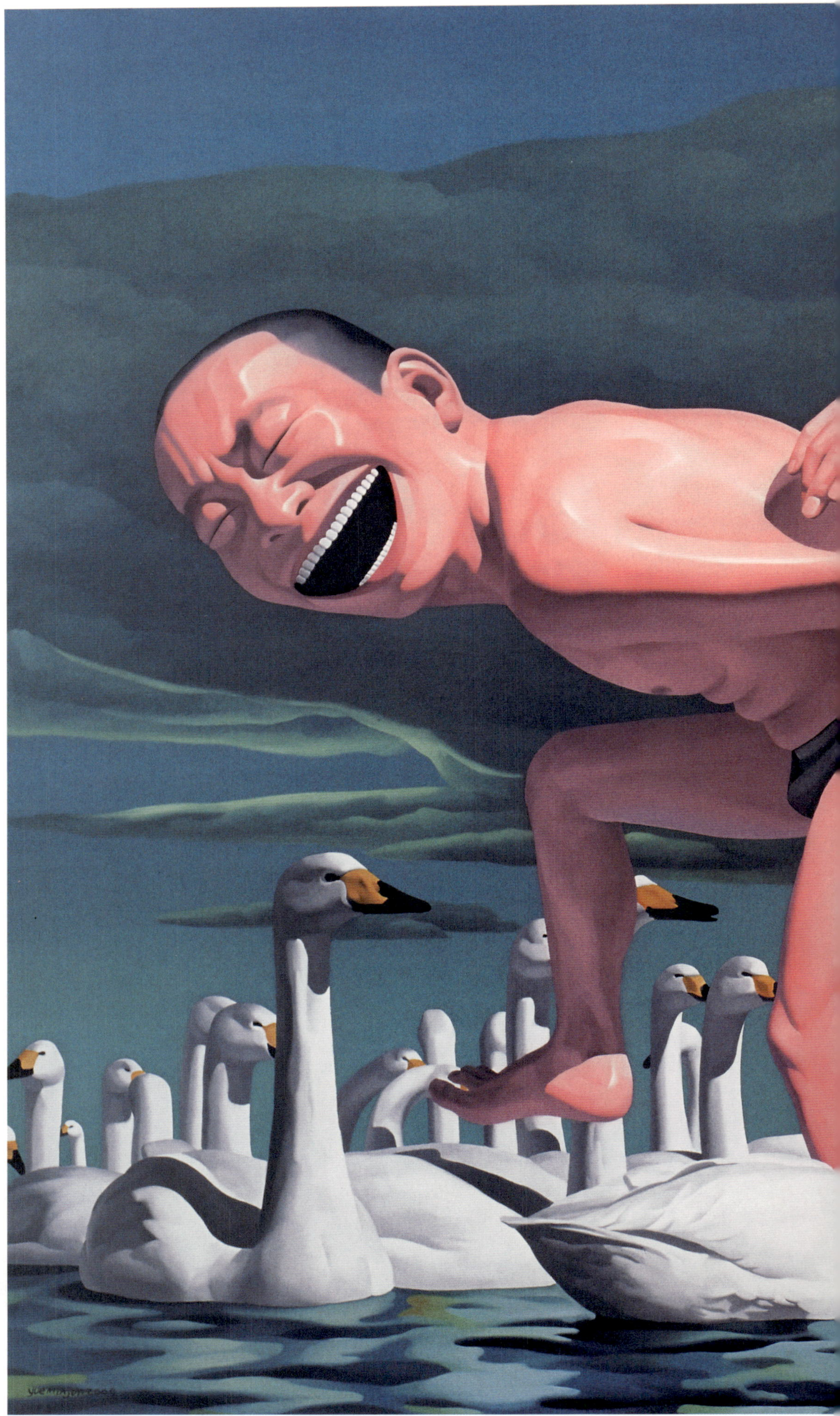

Free and At Leisure - 11 *
閑雲野鶴 – 11 *
300 x 220cm *
2004 *
oil on canvas *
布上油畫

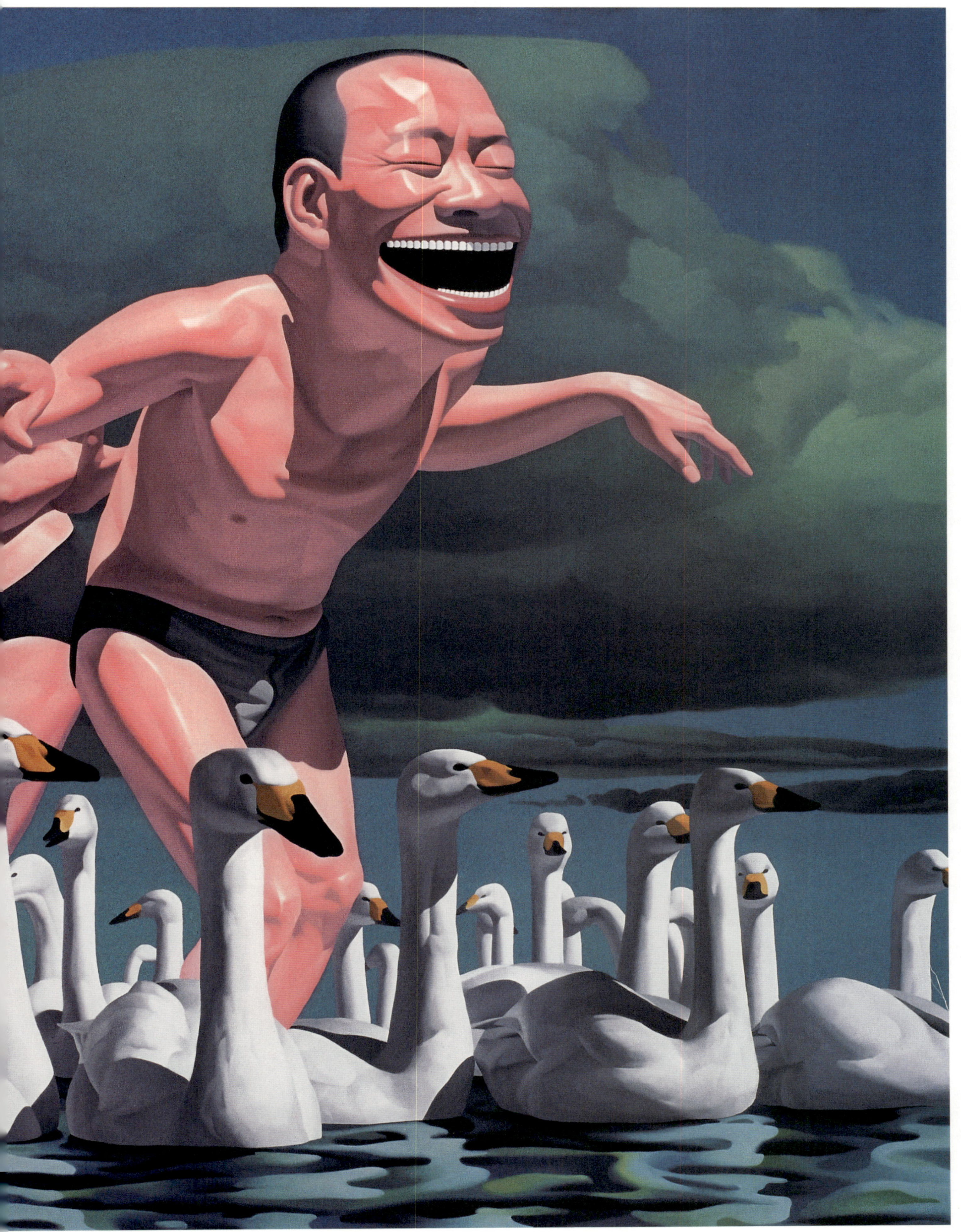

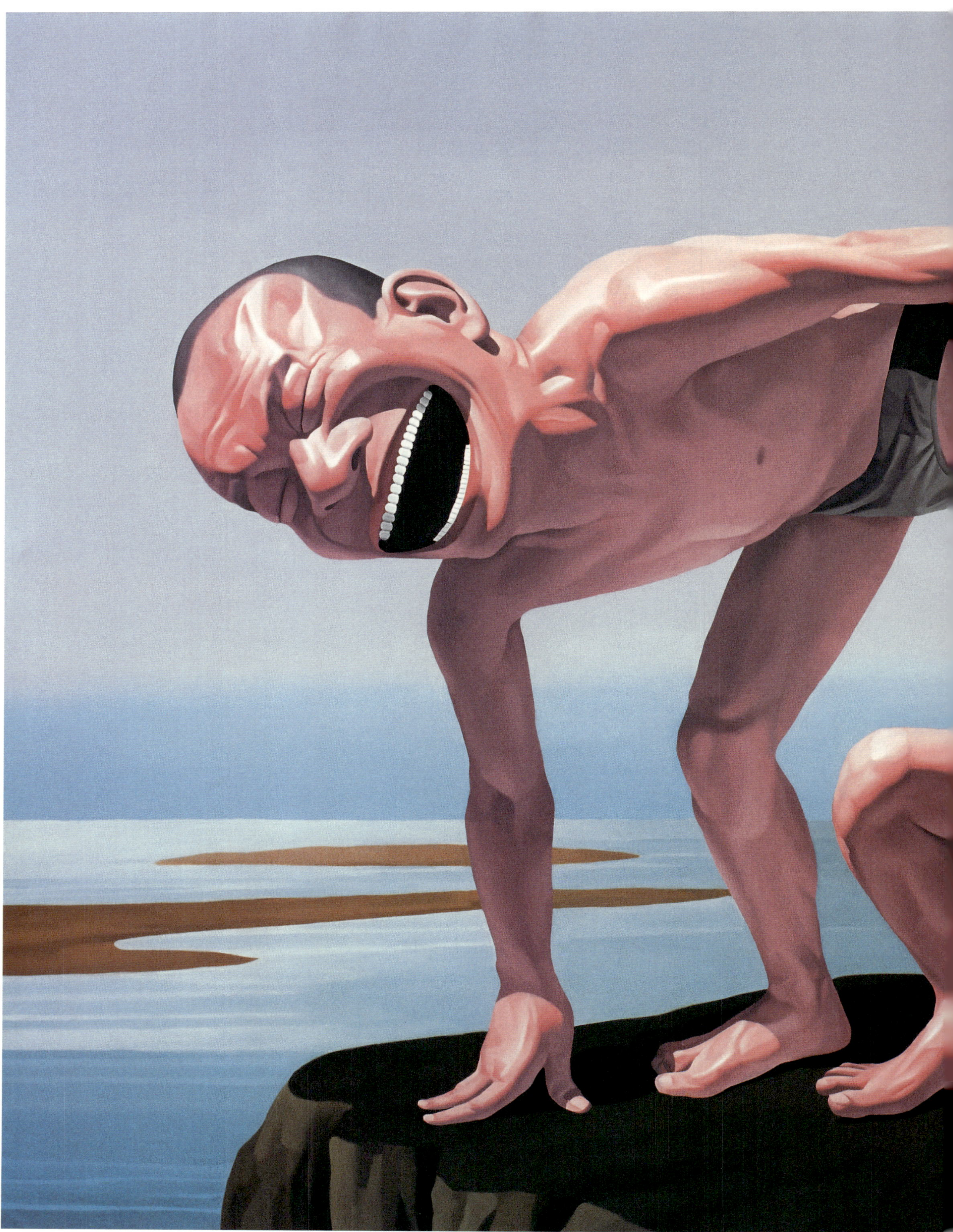

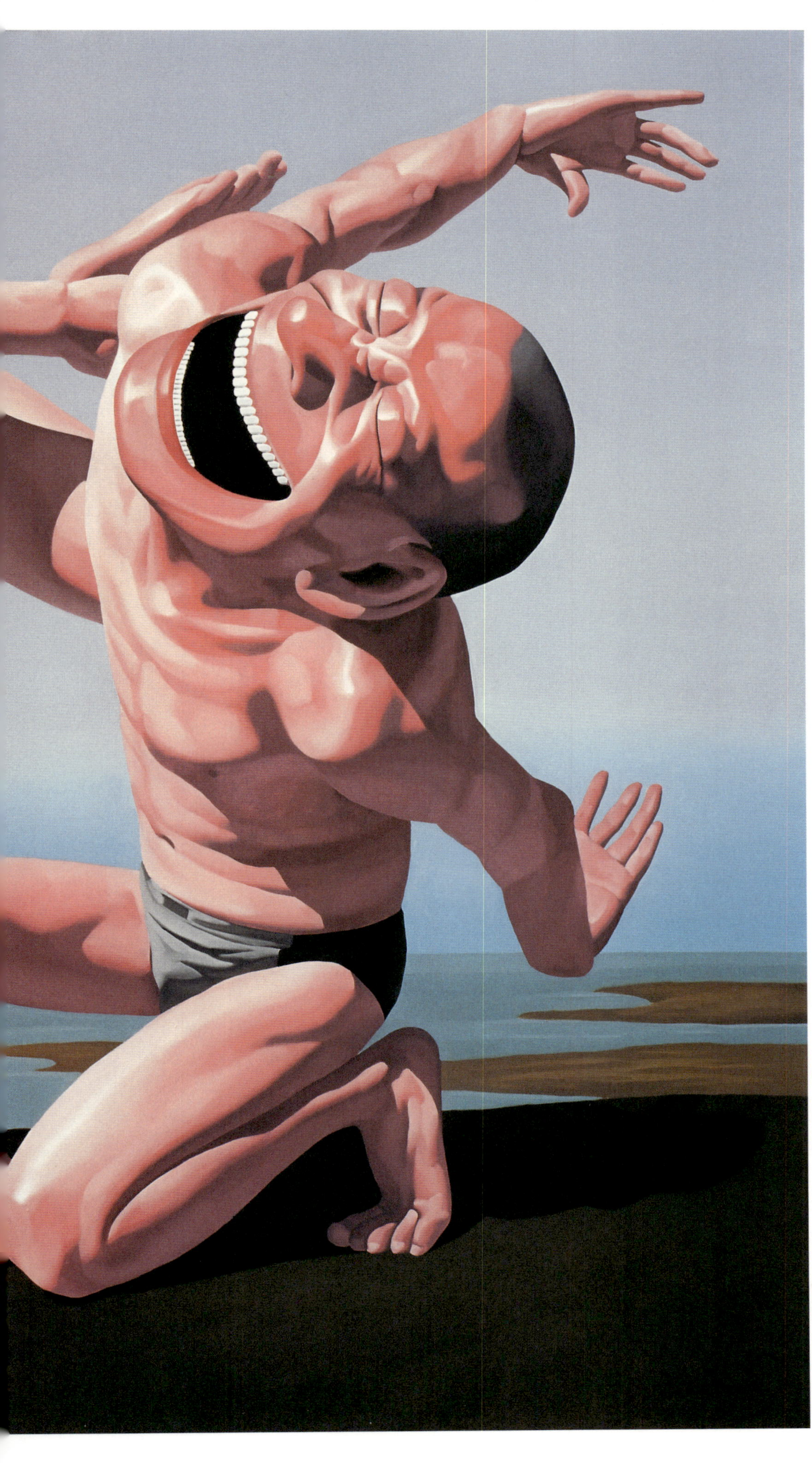

Free and At Leisure - 12 *
閑雲野鶴 – 12 *
300 x 220cm *
2004 *
oil on canvas *
布上油畫

(opposite)
Romanticism & Realism Study - 5 *
浪漫主義 + 現實主義研究 – 5 *
74 x 125 x 110cm *
2003 *
acrylic on fiberglass reinforced plastics *
玻璃鋼彩繪 *
5 - 1/4

(page 122 - 123)
Romanticism & Realism Study - 6 *
浪漫主義 + 現實主義研究 – 6 *
88 x 163 x 90cm *
2003 *
acrylic on fiberglass reinforced plastics *
玻璃鋼彩繪 *
6 - 1/4

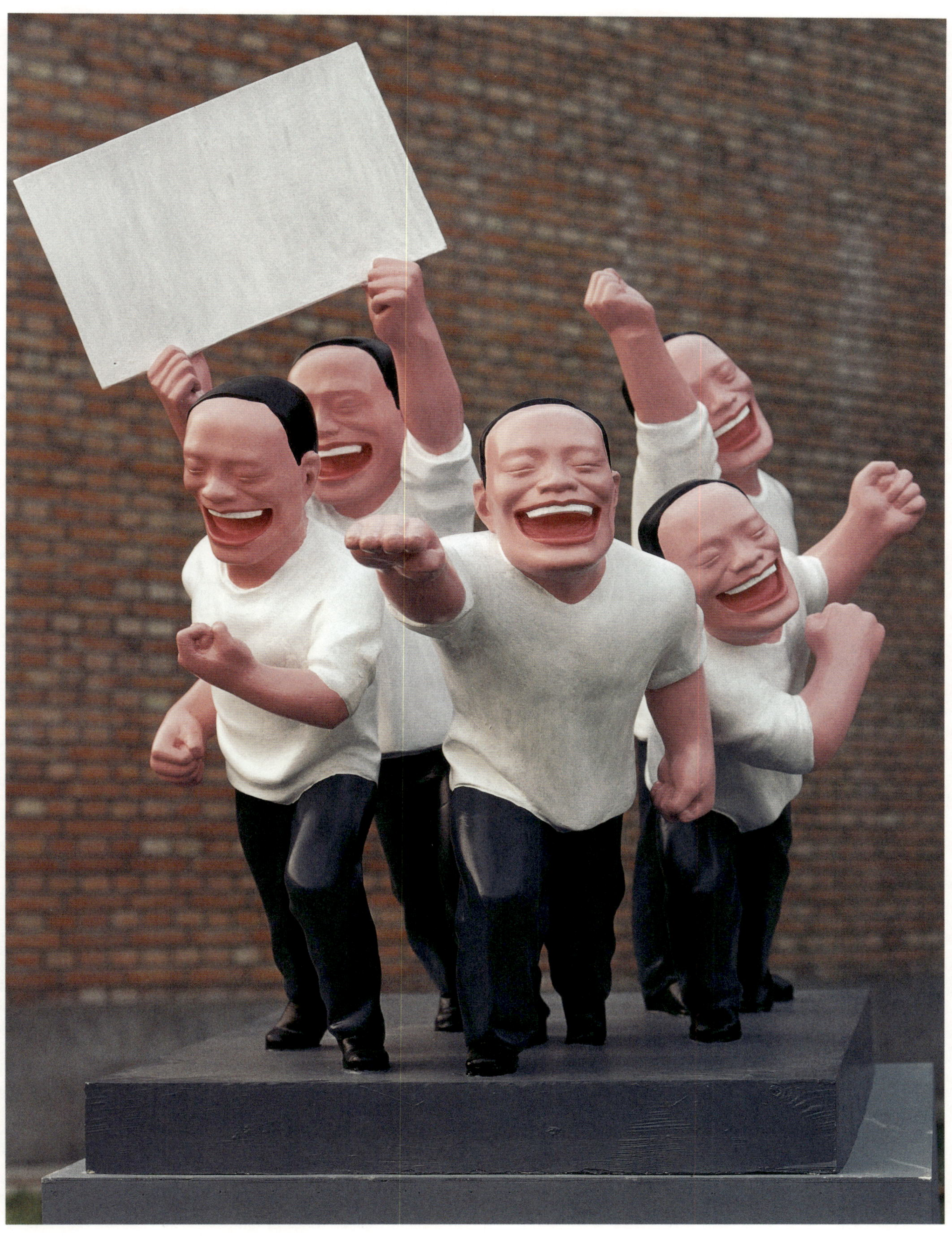

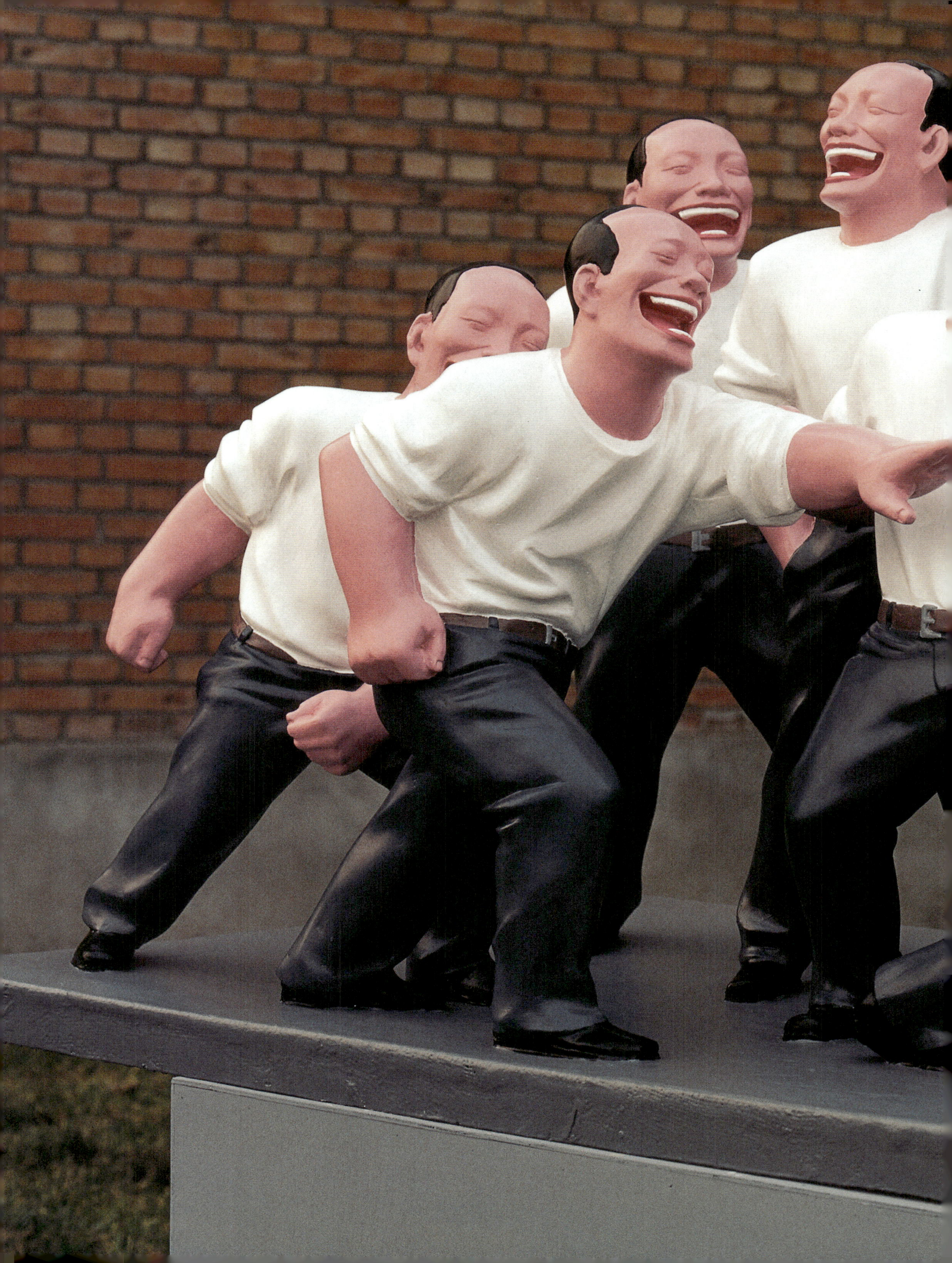

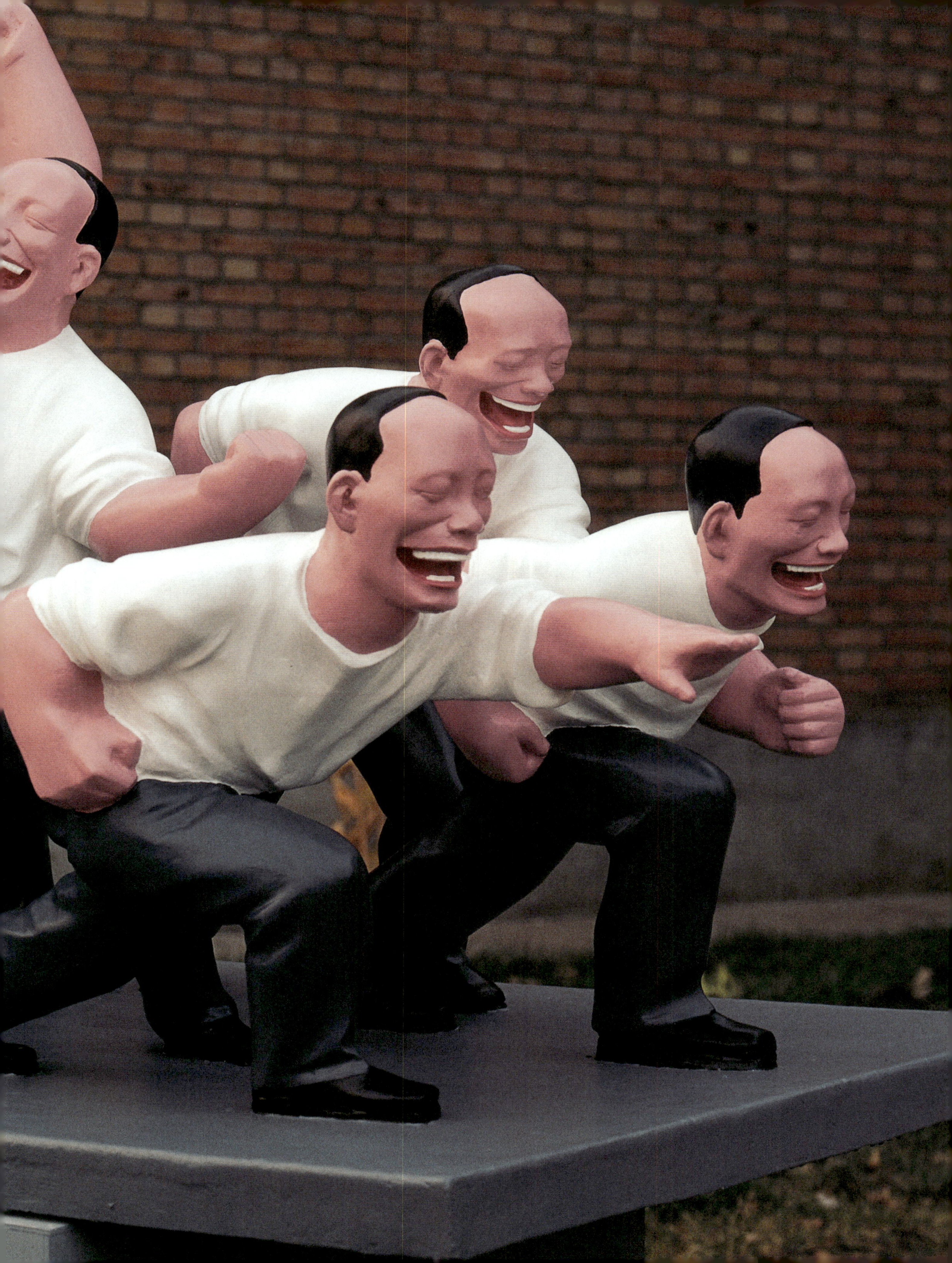

* * YUE MINJUN

1985 Studied in the Oil Painting Department of Hebei Normal University, China.

1962 Born in the town of Daqing in the province of Hei Long Jiang, China.

* * Art Experiences

2005 *Beautiful Cynicism*, Arario Beijing, China

Sky of Fate-Invited Exhibition of Chinese Paintings 2005, Shenzhen Art Museum, China

Plato and His Seven Spirits, BJ Century Overseas Chinese City, Shenzhen OCT Contemporary Art Terminal of He Xiangning Art Museum, China

Open 2005–International Exhibition of Sculptures and Installations, Lido, Venice, Italy

XIANFENG–Chinese Avant-garde Sculpture, Museum Beelden Aan Zee, Hague/Scheveningen, The Netherlands

Mahjong: Sigg Collection of Modern Chinese Art, Museum of Fine Arts, Bern, Switzerland

Dress Up in Art: Theme Exhibition on Traditional Chinese Operas, Today Art Museum, Beijing, China

No U-Turn: China Contemporary Art, TNUR Guand Museum of Art, Taiwan, China

Conceptual Art–Exhibition of Contemporary Paintings from China, Shenzhen Art Museum, Guangdong, China

2004 *Dreaming of the Dragon–Nation: Contemporary Art Exhibition from China*, Irish Museum of Modern Art, Dublin, Ireland

Shanghai Biennale 2004: Techniques of the Visible, China

Guangju Biennale 2004: A Grain of Dust, A Drop of Water, Korea

Art on the Beach: Sculptures, Enrico Navarra Gallery, Ramatuelle, France

20 Years of Hanart TZ Gallery, Hong Kong Art Center

China, the Body Everywhere?, Maseille Museum of Contemporary Art, France

2003 *From China with Art*, Indonesia National Gallery, Jakarta, Indonesia

The Rest of the World, Neuffer Am Park, Pirmasens, Germany

Newe Kunsthalle Mannheim 2, Kunsthalle Mannheim, Germany

CP Open Biennale 2003, Indonesia National Gallery, Jakarta, Indonesia

People and People: Chinese Modern and Contemporary Art Collections of GDMA

Guangdong Museum of Art(GDMA), Guangzhou, China

Living Conditions: Selections from the GDMA Collection of Contemporary Chinese Art, GDMA, Guangzhou, China

2002 *Chinese Contemporary Art Exhibition: Red Land, China*, Gwangju Art Museum, Korea

Korea and Chinese Painting-2002 New Expression, Seoul Culture & Art Center, Korea

Chinese Contemporary Art, Rekjavik Art Museum, Iceland

A Point in Time-Changsha, Beauty Art Museum, Changsha, China

The First Guangzhou Triennial, Guangdong Museum of Art, China

Inaugural Exhibition: Contemporary Terracotta Warriors, The Esplanade, Singapore

Golden Harvest-Chinese Contemporary Exhibition, Croatia National Art Museum, Croatia

2001 *Ornament and Abstraction*, Foundation Beyeler, Switzerland

Hotpot: Chinese Contemporary Art, Kunstnernes Hus, Oslo, Norway

Towards a New Image-Twenty Years of Contemporary Chinese Painting, National Art Museum, Beijing; Shanghai Art Museum, Shanghai; Sichuan Art Museum, Chendu; Guangdong Art Museum, Guangzhou, China

Song Zhuang, Stadtische Galerie im Buntentor Bremen & Kunstverein Ludwigshafen, Germany

2000 *Between...*, Chengdu Upriver Residence, Kunming Upriver Club, China

Portraits of Chinese Contemporaries, The Culture Centre of Francois Mitterrand, France

Our Friends, Bauhaus University Art Gallery, Weimar, Germany

1999 *Open Boundary: the 48th Venice Biennale*, Venice, Italy

Transparence, opacity?–14 Chinese Contemporary Artists, France, Italy

1999 Open Channels: The First Collecting Exhibition of Dongyu Museum of Fine Arts, Dongyu Museum, Shenyang, China

New Modernism for a New Millennium: Works by Contemporary Asian Artists from the Logan Collection, Linn Gallery, San Francisco, USA

1998 *The Grand Tour, Chinese Contemporary*, London, England

The First Exhibition of Upriver Gallery Collection, He Xiangning Art Gallery, Shenzhen, China

It's Me!–A Profile of Chinese Contemporary Art in the 90s, Forbidden City & Tai Miao, Beijing, China

Beijing Prediction: Contemporary Art of China, Beijing, China

1997 *"Quotation Marks": Chinese Contemporary Paintings*, Singapore Art Museum, Singapore

China Now, Tokyo, Japan; Basel, Switzerland

1996 *China!*, Bonn Art Museum, Germany; Kuenstlerhaus, Wien, Austria

Art to Swatch, take part in the Design of "1996 Artist Collection" of Swatch

1995 *Vision of China: Contemporary Chinese Painting by Chinese Masters*, Pacific City Club, Bangkok, Thailand

Contemporary Chinese Oil Painting Exhibition: From Realism to Post-Modernism, Theoremes Gallery, Brussels, Belgium

1994 *Faces Behind the Bamboo Curtain: Works of Yue Min Jun and Yang Shao Bin*, Schoeni Art Gallery, Hong Kong

1992 *Yuan Ming Yuan Artists Exhibition*, Yuan Ming Yuan, Beijing, China

1991 *Contemporary Modern Art Exhibition*, Beijing Friendship Guest House, China

1987 *"S" Art Exhibition*, Hebei Museum, China

* * Solo Exhibitions:

2006 *Reproduction Icons: Yue Minjun Works, 2004-2006*, He Xiangning Art Museum, Shenzhen, China

2005 *Post Auratic Self Portrayal of Yue Minjun*, CP Foundation, Jakarta, Indonesia

2004 *Yue Minjun: Sculptures & Paintings*, Schoeni Art Gallery, Hong Kong

2003 *Yue Minjun: Beijing Ironicals*, Prüss & Ochs Gallery, Berlin, Germany

Yue Minjun, Meile Gallery, Switzerland

2002 *Soaking In Silly Laughter: one of Art Singapore 2002*, Soobin Art Gallery, Singapore

Yue Minjun: Handling, One World Art Center, Beijing, China

2000 *Red Ocean–Yue Minjun*, Chinese Contemporary, London, England

*　*　岳敏君

1985 年　就讀于河北師範大學美術系

1962 年　生于黑龍江省,大慶市

*　*　藝術經歷

2005 年　《美麗的諷喻》阿拉利奥北京藝術空間，中國

《缘分的天空—— 2005 中國當代架上藝術（油畫）邀請展》深圳美術館，中國

《柏拉圖和它的七種精靈》北京世紀華僑城、深圳何香凝美術館，中國

《開放 2005 ——國際雕塑裝置展》威尼斯，意大利

《先鋒—— 中國前衛雕塑》海濱雕塑博物館，海牙，荷蘭

《麻將: 希客中國現代藝術收藏展》 伯爾尼美術博物館，瑞士

《畫妝: 中國戲曲主題藝術大展》 今日美術館，北京，中國

《明日, 不回眸——中國當代藝術》 國立臺北藝術大學關渡美術館，中國

《觀念藝術—— 中國當代繪畫作品展》 深圳美術館，廣東，中國

2004 年　《龍族之夢: 中國當代藝術展》愛爾蘭現代美術館，都柏林，愛爾蘭

《第五屆上海雙年展 2004: 影像生存》 上海美術館，中國

《第五屆光州雙年展 2004: 一塵一滴》 韓國

《沙丘雕塑》恩裏科・納瓦拉畫廊，法國

《漢雅軒 20 年慶聯展》香港藝術中心

《身體・中國》 馬賽當代藝術博物館，法國

2003 年　《來自中國的藝術》印尼國家美術館，雅加達，印尼

《世界的剩餘部分》 紐夫公園，珀瑪森斯，德國

《新的藝術展廳曼海姆》 曼海姆藝術展廳，德國

《印尼 2003 開放雙年展》 印尼國家美術館，雅加達，印尼

《人與人: 廣東美術館中國現當代美術藏品專題展（當代部分）》 廣東美術館，廣州，中國

《生存的向度: 廣東美術館藏中國當代藝術選展》 廣東美術館，廣州，中國

2002 年　《中國現代美術展: 紅色大陸，中華》光州市立美術館，韓國

《中韓當代藝術繪畫展: 2002 新表情》 漢城文化藝術中心，韓國

《中國當代藝術》 雷克亞未克藝術博物館，冰島

《時間的一個點: 在長沙》 美侖美術館，長沙，中國

《首屆廣州當代藝術三年展》 廣東美術館，中國

《澳海藝術中心開幕展: 當代兵馬俑》 澳海藝術中心，新加坡

《金色的收獲—— 中國當代藝術展》克羅地亞國家美術館，克羅地亞

2001 年　《裝飾與抽象》貝耶勒基金會博物館，瑞士

《煲—— 中國現代藝術大展》奧斯陸藝術家中心，挪威

《新形象—— 中國當代繪畫藝術二十年》中國美術館，上海美術館，廣東省美術館，四川省美術館，中國

《宋莊: 巡回藝術展》 布萊梅市本泰門市立美術館 & 路德維思港城市畫廊，德國

2000 年　《……之間……》成都上河美術館，昆明上河會館，中國

《當代中國肖像》法朗索瓦. 密特朗文化中心，法國

《我們的朋友》包豪斯大學美術館，魏瑪，德國

1999 年　《開放的邊界: 第 48 屆威尼斯雙年展》威尼斯，意大利

《透明不透明? ——十四位中國當代藝術家歐洲巡回展》法國, 意大利

《99 開啟通道: 東宇美術館首屆收藏展》東宇美術館, 沈陽, 中國

《新千年的新現代主義: 當代亞洲藝術洛根收藏展》利恩畫廊, 聖弗朗西斯科, 美國

1998 年 《光輝之旅: 中國當代藝術》倫敦, 英國

《上河美術館收藏展》何香凝美術館, 深圳, 中國

《是我! —— 九十年代藝術發展的一個側面》紫禁城 & 太廟, 北京, 中國

《"預言北京": 中國當代藝術報道》北京, 中國

1997 年 《"引號": 中國當代油畫展》新加坡美術館, 新加坡

《中國現在!》東京, 日本; 巴塞爾, 瑞士

1996 年 《中國!》波恩藝術博物館, 德國; 奧地利

《Swatch 多國籍文化預展》 參與瑞士 Swatch 藝術家系列的設計

1995 年 《中國視覺: 中國當代油畫展》大西洋城市俱樂部, 曼谷, 泰國

《中國當代油畫展: 從現實主義到後現代主義》特奧萊梅美術館, 布魯塞爾, 比利時

1994 年 《竹簾後的臉 —— 岳敏君、楊少斌畫展》少勵畫廊, 香港

1992 年 《圓明園畫家作品展》圓明園, 北京, 中國

1991 年 《新時期現代繪畫展》北京友誼賓館, 北京, 中國

1987 年 《S 造型藝術展》河北省展覽館, 石家莊, 中國

* * 個人展覽

2006 年 《復制的偶像: 岳敏君作品 2004-2006》何香凝美術館, 深圳, 中國

2005 年 《後奧若蒂克式自畫像 —— 岳敏君》CP 基金會, 雅加達, 印度尼西亞

2004 年 《岳敏君: 雕塑及油畫作品展》少勵畫廊, 香港

2003 年 《岳敏君作品展》麥勒畫廊, 瑞士

《岳敏君: 北京之反諷》Prüss & Ochs 畫廊, 柏林, 德國

2002 年 《沐浴在傻笑中》斯民藝苑, 新加坡

《岳敏君作品展 —— 處理》世方藝術中心, 北京, 中國

2000 年 《紅色的海洋 —— 岳敏君作品展》倫敦中國當代藝術畫廊, 英國

THE EXHIBITION AND CATALOGUE IS MADE POSSIBLE THROUGH THE GENEROSITY OF THE DONORS